Contents

Acknowledgments

I wish to thank:

The Institute for Rational-Emotive Therapy, New York for granting me permission (a) to reproduce: the Biographical Information Form © 1968; the Personality Data Form © 1968; the RET Self-help Form © 1984; and the pamphlet entitled 'How to Maintain and Enhance Your Rational-Emotive Therapy Gains' © 1984 and (b) to use extracts in original and modified form from my articles on Vivid RET first published in: *Rational Living*, 1983, *18*(1), 7–12; *Journal of Rational-Emotive Therapy*, 1983, *1*(1), 9–14 and *Journal of Rational-Emotive Therapy*, 1984, *2*(1), 27–31.

Guilford Press for granting me permission to use and modify material published in a chapter entitled 'Rational-emotive therapy' by Windy Dryden and Albert Ellis in K. S. Dobson (Ed.), *Handbook of Cognitive-Behavioral Therapies*. New York: Guilford Press, 1987.

Harper & Row for granting me permission to use and modify material published in a chapter entitled 'Rational-emotive therapy' by Windy Dryden and Albert Ellis in W. Dryden and W. L. Golden (Eds.), *Cognitive-Behavioural Approaches to Psychotherapy*. London: Harper & Row, 1986.

Plenum Press for granting me permission to reproduce material (page 7 line 18 — page 9 line 6) from a chapter entitled 'What is rational-emotive therapy (RET)' by Albert Ellis and Michael Bernard in A. Ellis and M. E. Bernard (Eds.), *Clinical Applications of Rational-Emotive Therapy*. New York: Plenum Press, 1985.

Progress in Clinical Science Series

Counselling Individuals:
The Rational–Emotive Approach

Windy Dryden Ph.D.
Department of Psychology
Goldsmiths' College (University of London)

Taylor & Francis
London   New York   Philadelphia
1987

UK   Taylor & Francis Ltd, 4 John St., London WC1N 2ET

USA   Taylor & Francis Inc., 242 Cherry St., Philadelphia, PA 19106–1906

British Library Cataloguing in Publication Data

Dryden, Windy
  Counselling individuals: the rational-emotive approach—
  (Progress in clinical science series).

  1. Rational-emotive psychotherapy
  I. Title.   II. Series
  616.89'14   RC489.R3
  ISBN 0-85066-666-X
  ISBN 0-85066-665-1 (pbk.)

Typeset in 11/13 Bembo by
Alresford Typesetting & Design, New Farm Road, Alresford, Hants.

Printed in Great Britain by Redwood Burn Ltd, Trowbridge, Wiltshire

Progress in Clinical Science Series

Foreword

This book is one of a series whose primary aim is to inform the professional practice of speech and language clinicians and their colleagues in the caring professions. The starting point for this series was a systematic review of those topics in human communication which are essential to the development of effective treatment programmes and the development of effective clinicians.

Whilst we have seen considerable advances in the scientific understanding of communication disorders in recent years much that is relevant to the practising clinician is either published in specialist scientific journals or exchanged on the conference floor. Bringing this theoretical and practical material together in book form seemed the first priority for a series of this kind. **Progress in Clinical Science** therefore aims to emphasize the scientific basis of modern clinical practice.

In addition we saw a need for texts capable of addressing broader issues in clinical practice. We wanted to provide a new resource for clinicians who wished to further their own social, interpersonal and scientific skills through further study. Topics here range from discussion of specific models of clinical intervention to the skills required for the scientific evaluation of the treatment enterprise.

Research into both the process and outcome of therapy programmes has revealed that individual therapist characteristics play a crucial role in the success or failure of treatment over a wide range of treatment approaches and client groups. Every therapist needs an injection of new stimulation in order to continue the process of evolution that characterizes effective clinical practice. We need to be self-critical and we need to introduce systems of peer review in order to ensure that the work we do on behalf of our clients is of the highest possible standard. This series emphasizes the need for efficacy research and the responsibility each individual clinician carries for the evaluation of their own clinical skills.

We are grateful for the help and support we have received from colleagues in many professional groups during the development of **Progress in Clinical Science**. It is our hope that the books in this series will cut across traditional disciplinary boundaries. The problems of theory construction, skill acquisition and treatment evaluation are common to every caring profession. We hope that **Progress in Clinical Science** will bring a fresh incentive for interdisciplinary collaboration at every level of professional development.

Harry Purser and Dave Rowley
Series Editors
Leicester Polytechnic, England
January 1987

Introduction

This book is primarily intended for those who work in a counselling role with individuals who are *not* severely psychologically disturbed. Here I adopt a pragmatic definition of counselling by which I mean 'a mode of helping designed to encourage people to overcome their emotional and behavioural problems and thence to lead satisfying lives'. Since counselling (as defined here) is deemed to be most suitable for clients who are *not* severely disturbed, it is likely to be a relatively shorter-term intervention than psychotherapy, which is more appropriate for clients with more severe psychological problems. Thus, this book is designed for counsellors, from a broad range of professional groups, whose clients are likely to have non-severe problems of anxiety, shame and embarrassment, depression, guilt, anger, hurt, jealousy and of self-discipline (e.g. procrastination).

The distinction I have made between counselling and psychotherapy raises issues which focus on the assessment of the severity of clients' psychological problems. Some counselling agencies ask all potential clients to attend for an 'intake' assessment interview to determine whether or not the 'applicant' is suitable for counselling (as defined here). In such cases, intake interviewers usually carry out detailed appraisals of: (a) the client's history of psychological disturbance, and (b) his or her current functioning. This assessment may indeed be carried out by counsellors themselves before offers of help are considered. If the present working definition of counselling is used as the criterion then clients most likely to benefit from this mode of helping are those who have emotional and behavioural problems in the neurotic range of disturbance; who do not have a long history of poor psychological functioning; and who can demonstrate evidence of having experienced good interpersonal relationships in their lives. This book then is designed specifically for use with this clientele.

This book is definitely not designed for use with clients whose problems are in the psychotic range of disturbance, although it should not be forgotten that such

1

individuals do have neurotic difficulties and counselling can be appropriate for such problems when the individuals are not actively psychotic.

This leaves clients who have severe personality problems, a long history of poor psychological functioning and impaired interpersonal relationships — the so-called 'personality disorders'. While this book can be used to inform therapeutic work with such individuals, it has not been written with this clientele in mind, and thus needs to be supplemented by such books as Albert Ellis' (1985) *Overcoming resistance: Rational-emotive therapy with difficult clients*.

Not all counsellors carry out a detailed assessment-based intake interview before offering assistance to people seeking their help. Such helpers tend to assume that they can help a client unless evidence exists to the contrary, at which point they would seek to refer the client concerned to a more appropriate helping agent. For such counsellors I reiterate the above remarks concerning this book's proposed usage.

This book is best used as a supplement to training courses in rational-emotive counselling and should not be regarded as a training resource in its own right. The book is divided into two parts. Part One is devoted to outlining rational-emotive theory. Here I discuss: (a) some of the major theoretical concepts that underpin rational-emotive counselling; (b) the role of cognition and action in rational-emotive theory; (c) the rational-emotive view of psychological disturbance and health; and (d) the determinants of the major dysfunctional emotions and behaviours for which clients seek counselling help. Part Two is devoted to the practice of rational-emotive counselling. Here I discuss: (a) the indications and contra-indications for individual counselling and the counsellor-client relationship, (b) inducting clients into rational-emotive counselling and assessing their major problems; (c) promoting intellectual insight into rational concepts; (d) promoting emotional insight into rational concepts; (e) overcoming obstacles to client change; and (f) the distinctive features of rational-emotive counselling as compared with other approaches to cognitive-behavioural counselling.

Rational-emotive counselling is one of the major approaches to counselling based on cognitive-behavioural principles. While rational-emotive practitioners primarily use methods derived from rational-emotive counselling, they also use methods derived from these other approaches to cognitive-behavioural counselling (see Dryden and Golden, 1986). The present book outlines the major strategies and techniques that are most closely associated with rational-emotive counselling and does not seek to cover other cognitive-behavioural methods. In the final chapter I suggest several references that deal with these other methods.

PART ONE: THEORY

1. The Basic Theory of Rational-Emotive Counselling

Overview

In this opening chapter, I trace the historical development of rational-emotive counselling and outline some of its predominant philosophical and psychological influences. Then I cover the following major theoretical concepts of rational-emotive counselling: rationality, hedonism and enlightened self-interest versus selfishness. I point out that rational-emotive counselling has a decided humanistic emphasis and also highlights the role of activity in human happiness. I continue by outlining the rational-emotive view that humans have two biologically-based tendencies(i.e., relevant to their psychological problems): a tendency to think irrationally, and a tendency to work towards changing such thinking. This leads on to a discussion of the two fundamental human disturbances put forward by rational-emotive theory: ego disturbance and discomfort disturbance. I conclude the chapter by stating briefly the rational-emotive position on *thought*, *emotion* and *action*, emphasizing the interactional view it takes of these three processes.

The Historical Development of Rational-Emotive Counselling and Psychotherapy

Albert Ellis founded rational-emotive therapy (RET) in 1955 when he was a New York clinical psychologist, having begun his career in the helping professions in the early 1940s. As a result of research he was doing at that time for a massive work to be entitled *The Case for Sexual Liberty*, he gained a local reputation for being an authority on sexual and marital relationships. He was consulted by his friends on their sexual and relationship problems and discovered that he could be successful in helping them with these problems in a short period of time. He decided to pursue

3

formal training in clinical psychology after discovering that there were no formal training possibilities then offered in sex and marital counselling. After getting a PhD degree in clinical psychology, he chose to be trained in psychoanalysis, believing, then, that it was the deepest and most effective form of psychotherapy available. He decided on this course of action because his experiences as an informal sex-marital counsellor had taught him that disturbed relationships were really a product of disturbed persons, 'and that if people were truly to be helped to live happily with each other they first had better be shown how they could live peacefully with themselves' (Ellis, 1962, p. 3).

Ellis initially enjoyed working as a psychoanalyst partly because it allowed him to express both his helping and problem solving interests. However, he became increasingly dissatisfied with psychoanalysis as an *effective* and *efficient* form of treatment. In the early 1950s, Ellis began to experiment with different forms of therapy, including psychoanalytically-orientated psychotherapy and eclectic-analytic therapy. But although he became more effective with his clients, he remained dissatisfied about the efficiency of these methods. During this period of experimentation, he returned to his life-long hobby of reading philosophy to help him with his search for an effective and efficient form of therapy. One of the major influences on his thought at that time was the work of the Greek and Roman Stoic philosophers (e.g. Epictetus and Marcus Aurelius). They emphasized the primacy of philosophic causation of psychological disturbances — a viewpoint which was not popular in America in the 1950s — and de-emphasized the part played by psychoanalytic psychodynamic factors. In essence the Stoic viewpoint, which stated that people are disturbed not by things but by their view of things, became the foundation of RET in particular, and this perspective (following Ellis' pioneering formulations) remains at the heart of present-day cognitive-behavioural approaches to psychotherapy.

Major philosophical influences

Apart from Stoicism, present-day RET owes a philosophical debt to a number of other sources that have influenced its development. Immanuel Kant's writings on the power (and limitations) of cognition and ideation strongly impressed Ellis (Ellis, 1981 a) and the work of Spinoza and Schopenhauer was also important in this respect. Philosophers of science, such as Popper (1959, 1963), Reichenbach (1953), and Russell (1965), were influential in helping Ellis see that all humans develop hypotheses about the nature of the world. Moreover, these philosophers stressed the importance of testing out the validity of such hypotheses rather than assuming that they are necessarily correct; the practice of RET is synonymous, in many respects, with the logico-empirical methods of science (Ellis, 1962, 1979 a).

RET also stresses the flexibility and antidogmatism of the scientific method and holds that rigid absolutism is the very core of human disturbance (Ellis 1983 a).

Although the philosophy of RET is at variance with devout religiosity there is one respect in which Christian philosophy has been most influential. RET's theory of human value (which will be discussed later) is similar to the Christian viewpoint of condemning the sin, but forgiving the sinner (Ellis, 1983 a; Hauck, 1972; Powell, 1976). Due to its stand on self-acceptance and its bias against all forms of human rating, RET allies itself with the philosophy of ethical humanism (Russell, 1930, 1965) which opposes the deification and devilification of humans. Since RET considers that humans are at the centre of their universe (but not of *the* Universe) and have the power of choice (but not of unlimited choice) with regard to their emotional realm, it has its roots in the existential philosophies of Heidegger (1949) and Tillich (1977). Indeed, RET has a pronounced humanistic-existential outlook (Ellis, 1973).

Ellis was influenced, particularly in the 1960s, by the work of the general semanticists, (e.g. Korzybski, 1933). These theorists outlined the powerful effect that language has on thought and the fact that our emotional processes are heavily dependent on the way we, as humans, structure our thought by the language we employ.

Major psychological influences

In developing RET, Ellis was similarly influenced by the work of a number of psychologists. He received a training analysis from an analyst of the Karen Horney school and Horney's (1950) concept of the 'tyranny of the shoulds' was certainly an early influence on his emphasis on the primacy of absolute, dogmatic evaluative thought in the development and maintenance of much psychological disturbance. The work of Adler was important to the development of RET in several respects.

'Adler (1927) was the first great therapist to really emphasize inferiority feelings — while RET similarly stresses self-rating and the ego anxiety to which it leads. Like Adler and his Individual Psychology, RET also emphasizes people's goals, purposes, values and meanings. RET also follows Adler in regard to the use of active-directive teaching, the stress placed on social interest, the use of a holistic and humanistic outlook, and the employment of a highly cognitive-persuasive form of psychological treatment' (Ellis, 1981 b).

Although RET was originally termed 'Rational Psychotherapy', it has always advocated the use of behavioural methods as well as cognitive and emotive techniques in the practice of counselling and therapy. Indeed, Ellis utilized some of the methods advocated by several of the earliest pioneers in behaviour therapy (Dunlap, 1932; Jones, 1924; Watson and Rayner, 1920), first in overcoming his own early fears of speaking in public and of approaching women, and second in the active-directive form of sex therapy which he practised in the early 1950s. This behavioural active-directive emphasis remains prominent in present-day rational-emotive counselling and psychotherapy.

In its thirty years existence, RET has been practised in various therapeutic modalities (individual, group, marital and family), by many kinds of helping professionals (e.g. psychologists, psychiatrists, social workers) with a variety of client populations (e.g. adults, children, the elderly) suffering from a wide range of psychological disorders. Apart from their use in counselling and psychotherapy, rational-emotive principles have been applied in educational, industrial, and commercial settings. A very recent development has been the application of RET to public education in the form of 9-hour intensive workshops. In this respect, it is playing a significant role in the field of preventative psychology. RET is practised throughout the world and there are RET 'Institutes' in the United States, Italy, West Germany, Holland, Australia, England and Mexico. It is thus a well-established form of cognitive-behavioural therapy.

Major Theoretical Concepts

Rational-emotive counselling is based on a set of assumptions which stress the complexity and fluidity of human beings. Given this fundamental view of human nature the RET approach to counselling rests on the following theoretical concepts.

Rationality

In my experience, when counsellors are first introduced to rational-emotive counselling, they often become preoccupied with the term 'rational'. Their initial reaction to this term is usually negative because they think, erroneously, that it means 'unemotional' and conclude, again wrongly, that RET counsellors seek to help their clients by encouraging them to become unemotional. 'Rationality' *does* play a central role in rational-emotive theory but it has a very specific meaning within this theory.

To understand the specific RET meaning of 'rationality' it is first important to realize that within rational-emotive theory humans are seen as having two basic goals — to stay alive and to be happy. While there are shared methods of pursuing the former basic goal (e.g. seeking adequate shelter from the elements, maintaining a proper diet, etc.) there are a myriad of different ways of pursuing the latter. Humans are remarkably idiosyncratic in what they find personally meaningful or fulfilling.

Given the above considerations, the term 'rational' means: *that which helps people to achieve their basic goals and purposes.* Furthermore, in rational-emotive theory, people are seen as having primary (but not exclusive) control over their major psychological processes (i.e. thoughts, emotions and actions). Given that we use these processes in the pursuit of our basic goals, it follows that our thoughts, feelings and actions are deemed to be 'rational' when they help us in the pursuit of these goals. Conversely, the term 'irrational' in rational-emotive theory means: *that which prevents people from achieving their basic goals and purposes.* Much RET counselling is spent helping clients to identify and change their 'irrational' (or self-defeating) thoughts, emotions and actions, given that such processes impede goal achievement.

There are no absolute criteria of 'rationality' in rational-emotive theory. These criteria need to be seen as *relative to* the goals and purposes that the individual deems to be important. RET counsellors endeavour to help their clients remove the obstacles to goal attainment that clients themselves construct, and do not seek to impose an absolute standard of 'rationality' as some people, new to RET counselling, incorrectly think.

Hedonism

We have seen how rational-emotive theory considers that humans are basically hedonistic — in the sense that they seek to stay alive and to achieve a reasonable degree of happiness. Again, counsellors new to rational-emotive counselling wrongly consider that the rational-emotive concept of hedonism implies urging clients to pursue a life based on the 'pleasures of the flesh', rather than encouraging them to pursue their personally meaningful goals. Thus, a person whose goal is to raise money for starving children in Ethiopia, and involves herself in activities directed towards this end, is acting 'hedonistically' in the sense that it is meaningful for her and that she is happy doing so. Her hedonistic decision — based on the principle of social interest (Adler, 1964) — is a far cry from the 'pleasures of the flesh' connotation of hedonism.

Rational-emotive theory makes an important distinction between short-term and long-term hedonism. For example, it is important for me to write this book. It represents a personally-meaningful project I have set for myself, i.e. to encourage counsellors to offer what I have found to be an effective, brief method of psychological counselling. As such, writing this book is an example of long-term hedonism, since it will take time for me to complete, and a longer time for it to have an effect on the counselling community. I also enjoy watching television which, as it is immediately available to me, constitutes an example of short-term hedonism. Pursuing my short-term interests to the extent that it significantly interferes with my long-term hedonistic project is irrational according to the definition of 'rationality' provided above, since the book is more personally meaningful to me than is watching television. Pursuing my long-term hedonistic interests to the exclusion of my more immediately available interests may also be irrational in the sense that I might become stale; a condition that would probably affect my creativity. Therefore counselling individuals involves not only encouraging them to become aware of their short- and long-term goals, but also helping them to achieve a healthy balance between the two. What represents a healthy balance for a given individual is ultimately best judged by that person, and not by his or her counsellor.

Enlightened self-interest versus selfishness

At this point, the reader may consider that rational-emotive theory advocates selfishness. This is not so, if by selfishness is meant the exclusive pursuit of one's own goals while cynically disregarding the goals of others. Rather, rational-emotive theory recommends that people act according to the principle of enlightened self-interest, which is deemed to be the healthy alternative to selfishness. By enlightened self-interest is meant putting oneself first most of the time, while putting others (particularly significant others) a close second. It thus includes an important dimension of what Adler (1964) calls 'social interest'. It is recognized that decisions concerning whose interests to serve at a given moment — self or others — are complex and depend on (a) the context, (b) the importance of one's own goals versus the importance that others attribute to their goals, and (c) the likely consequences of making such decisions.

Enlightened self-interest means that from a long-term perspective I will give priority to pursuing my most important goals with respect to their goals, since as Ellis (1979 a) notes, it is likely that other people will do the same. Thus, if I do not give priority to my own goals it is unlikely that others will put my interests before theirs. In this respect, Ellis (1979 a) notes that 'those people who spend their lives sacrificing themselves for others tend to get less than their share of happiness' (p. 55). However, if a given client genuinely considers that one of his basic goals is to put the interests of others before his own, and can provide good evidence that this stance will bring him happiness, then good RET counsellors will respect this decision and will not try to dissuade the client from pursuing this goal.

In summary, it can be seen from the above that in counselling individuals RET counsellors strive to help their clients to be mindful of the balance between their own short- and long-term goals, and the balance between their own interests and the interests of others who live in their social world.

Humanistic emphasis

Rational-emotive counselling does not pretend to be 'purely' objective, scientific, or technique-centred but takes a definite *humanistic-existential approach* to human problems and their basic solutions. It primarily deals with disturbed human evaluations, emotions and behaviours. It is highly rational and scientific, but uses rationality and science in the service of humans in an attempt to enable them to live and be happy. It is hedonistic, but, as has been shown, espouses long-range instead of short-range hedonism; so that people may achieve the pleasure of the moment and those of the future and may arrive at maximum freedom *and* discipline. It hypothesizes that nothing superhuman probably exists and that devout belief in superhuman agencies tends to foster dependency and increase emotional disturbance. It assumes that no humans, whatever their antisocial or obnoxious behaviour, are damnable nor subhuman. It particularly emphasizes the importance of *will* and *choice* in human affairs, even though it accepts the likelihood that some human behaviour is partially determined by biological, social, and other forces (Bandura, 1986; Ellis, 1976). In addition rational-emotive theory emphasizes the important role played by activity in human happiness. It acknowledges that humans have a better chance of being happy when they *actively* strive towards their goals, and that they are less likely to be successful in this regard if they are passive or half-hearted in their endeavours (Dryden, 1984 a). It also stresses the important role played by activity in the change process. Clients who translate their counselling-derived insights into action in their daily lives usually achieve better results from counselling than clients who do not take such action.

Two basic biologically-based tendencies

Unlike most other theories of counselling which stress the impact of significant life events on the development of psychological disturbance, rational-emotive theory hypothesizes that the biological tendency of humans to think irrationally has a notable impact on such disturbance. Its view that irrational thinking is heavily determined by biological factors (always interacting with influential environmental conditions) rests on the seeming ease with which humans think crookedly, and the prevalence of such thinking even among people who have been rationally raised (Ellis, 1976). While Ellis has acknowledged that there are social influences operating here, he has also noted '. . . even if everybody had had the most rational upbringing, virtually all humans would often irrationally escalate their individual and social preferences into absolutistic demands on (a) themselves, (b) other people, and (c) the universe around them' (Ellis, 1984 a, p. 20).

The following ten points constitute evidence in favour of the rational-emotive hypothesis of the biological basis of human irrationality:

Virtually all humans including intelligent and competent people show evidence of major human irrationalities.

Virtually all the disturbance-creating irrationalities (absolutist 'shoulds' and 'musts') that are found in our society are also found in just about all social and cultural groups that have been studied historically and anthropologically.

Many of the irrational behaviours that we engage in, such as procrastination and lack of self-discipline, go counter to the teachings of parents, peers, and the mass media.

Humans — even intelligent and competent people — often adopt other irrationalities after giving up former ones.

People who vigorously oppose various kinds of irrational behaviours often fall prey to these very irrationalities. Atheists and agnostics exhibit zealous and absolutist philosophies and even highly religious individuals act immorally.

Insight into irrational thought and behaviours helps only partially to change them. For example, people can acknowledge that drinking alcohol in large quantities is harmful, yet this knowledge does not necessarily help them abstain from heavy drinking.

Humans often return to irrational habits and behavioural patterns even though they have often worked hard to overcome them.

People often find it easier to learn self-defeating than self-enhancing behaviours. Thus, people very easily overeat but have great trouble following a sensible diet.

Psychotherapists who presumably should be good role models of rationality often act irrationally in their personal and professional lives.

People frequently delude themselves into believing that certain bad experiences (e.g. divorce, stress, and other misfortunes) will not happen to them.

However, rational-emotive theory holds that humans have a second basic biological tendency, namely, to exercise the power of human choice and to work towards changing their irrational thinking. Thus, they have the ability to see that they make themselves disturbed by the irrational views they bring to situations, the ability to see that they can change their thinking and, most importantly, the ability to actively and continually work towards changing this thinking by the application of cognitive, emotive, and behavioural methods. While rational-emotive theory asserts that humans have a strong biological tendency to think irrationally (as well as rationally), it holds that they are by no means slaves to this tendency and can transcend (although not fully) its effects. In the final analysis the rational-emotive image of the person is quite an optimistic one (Ellis, 1973; Ellis and Bernard, 1985).

Two fundamental human disturbances

According to rational-emotive theory humans can make absolute demands on self, other people, and the world. However, if these demands are more closely investigated they can be seen to fall into two major categories of psychological disturbance: *ego disturbance* and *discomfort disturbance* (Ellis, 1979 b, 1980 a).

In ego disturbance, a person makes demands on self, others and the world and if these demands are not met in the past, present or future, the person becomes disturbed by damning 'self'. As I have shown (Dryden, 1984 a), self-damnation involves the process of giving my 'self' a global negative rating, and 'devil-ifying' my 'self' as being bad or less worthy. The rational and healthy alternative to self-damnation is self-acceptance which involves *both* refusing to give one's 'self' a single rating (because it is an impossible task, due to one's complexity and fluidity; and because it normally interferes with attaining one's basic goals and purposes) *and* acknowledging one's fallibility.

In discomfort disturbance, the person again makes demands on self, others and the world which are related to dogmatic commands that comfort and comfortable life conditions must exist. When these demands are not met in the past, present, or future then the person becomes disturbed. Tolerating discomfort in order to aid goal attainment and long range happiness is the healthy and rational alternative to demands for immediate gratification.

Thus, as will be shown later, self-acceptance and a high level of frustration tolerance are two of the main cornerstones of the rational-emotive image of the psychologically healthy being (Ellis, 1979 a).

Psychological interactionism: Thoughts, emotions and actions

As discussed earlier in this chapter, RET counsellors are interested in helping their clients to stay alive and to pursue happiness. During the counselling process this involves the counsellor and client working as a team to identify and change aspects of the client's functioning which are irrational. Both client and counsellor seek to answer the question: 'How is the client stopping herself from pursuing her personally defined meaningful goals?' As counsellor and client investigate the factors concerned, the search normally involves close scrutiny of the *thoughts* that the client has about herself, others and the world in relation to the goal at hand; the relevant *emotions* she has about herself, others and the world; and her *actions* in the area of concern.

It is important to stress here that rational-emotive theory states that a person's thoughts, emotions and actions cannot be treated separately from one another. Rather they are seen as overlapping or interacting processes — an example of what psychologists call 'psychological interactionism'. For instance, let us take the case of one of my clients, Helen, who has just moved to London. She wants to go out and make friends but does not do so because she is 'scared of meeting new people'. Her feelings of anxiety encourage her to brood on 'horrific' thoughts and images of rejection and loneliness and help to influence her tendency to withdraw from people. So she stays within the 'safe' but lonely confines of her bed-sitting room. Her thoughts (predictions of rejection and consequent attitude of self-loathing) help to create her anxiety and help to reinforce her inactivity — 'Why go out and expose myself to those outside risks?' Finally, her inactivity seems to encourage her negative thoughts about herself — 'I'm no good for being so gutless!' — and gives her ample opportunity for anxious brooding, even though withdrawal protects her from the greater anxiety of meeting new people.

The place of cognition

Despite the above interactionist view, it is true, however, that RET is most noted in the field of counselling and psychotherapy for the special place it accords cognition (or thinking) in human psychological processes. In particular, as we shall see, rational-emotive counselling emphasizes the role that evaluative thought plays in psychological health and disturbance. One of rational-emotive theory's unique contributions to the field of counselling lies in the distinction it makes between rational beliefs (evaluative cognitions that help people to achieve their basic goals and purposes) and irrational beliefs (evaluative cognitions that prevent people from achieving these goals). I will elaborate upon this distinction in the following chapter; however, I would like the reader to keep in mind throughout the book that although rational-emotive counselling does accord a special place to cognition in human functioning, it nevertheless agrees with the interactionist position reviewed above.

2. Cognition and Action in Rational-Emotive Theory

Overview

In this chapter I consider in detail the different types of cognitions that are relevant to counselling, namely: beliefs, inferences, decisions, self-instructions, and problem-solving cognitions. I point out that while rational-emotive theory emphasizes that these cognitions interact and overlap, it also accords a central role to *beliefs* in psychological functioning. I also note that cognitions may occur in the form of words and images. Finally, I consider the role of action in rational-emotive theory. In this respect, I note the purposive nature of actions, introduce the concepts of 'action tendencies' and 'response options' and comment on the issue of behavioural competence.

Although rational-emotive theory has become most well-known for its contribution to our understanding of one type of cognition (i.e. beliefs), RET counsellors also focus on other types of cognitions in the course of their practical work with clients. In the following section I distinguish among these different cognitions and although for purposes of clarity I consider them separately, I wish to stress that in reality they interact and overlap.

Types of Cognitions
Beliefs

One of the rational-emotive theory's unique contributions to the field of counselling lies in its distinction between rational beliefs and irrational beliefs.

Rational beliefs. In rational-emotive theory, rational beliefs are *evaluative cognitions* of personal significance which are preferential (i.e. non-absolute) in nature. They are expressed in the form of 'desires', 'preferences', 'wishes', 'wants', and 'likes', (and they can, of course, also take a negative form, e.g. 'I don't want x to happen').

Positive (non-absolute) *evaluative conclusions* result when people either get what they want or don't get what they don't want (e.g. 'it is good that . . .'). Similarly, negative (non-absolute) *evaluative conclusions* result when people either don't get what they want or do get what they don't want (e.g. 'it is bad that . . .').

Positive emotions of pleasure and satisfaction are experienced when people get what they want, while positive feelings of relief tend to occur when people don't get what they don't want. Similarly, negative emotions of displeasure and dissatisfaction (e.g. sadness, concern, regret, annoyance, disappointment) are experienced when people either don't get what they want, or do get what they don't want. These negative emotions (the strength of which is closely related to the importance of the person's rational belief) are regarded in rational-emotive theory, as *appropriate* responses to negative events, and do not significantly interfere with a person's pursuit of established or new goals and purposes. This is one good reason why the term 'rational' in rational-emotive counselling should not be equated with 'unemotional'.

In summary, rational beliefs are 'rational' in two respects: first, they are non-absolute (or relative) in nature; and second, they tend not to impede the attainment of a person's basic goals and purposes.

Irrational beliefs. In rational-emotive theory, irrational beliefs are *evaluative cognitions* of personal significance which are absolute (or dogmatic) in nature. They are expressed in the form of 'musts', 'shoulds', 'oughts', 'have to's', 'got to's', etc. (and they can, of course, occur in the form of 'must not's', 'should not's', etc.).

Positive (absolute) *evaluative conclusions* result when people get what they believe they must have, or don't get what they believe they must not get (e.g. 'it is absolutely wonderful that . . .'). Similarly, negative (absolute) *evaluative conclusions* result when people either don't get what they believe they must have, or do get what they believe they must not get (e.g. 'it is terrible that . . .').

Positively-toned emotions of mania are experienced when people either get what they believe they must have or don't get what they must not get. Similarly, negative emotions of depression, anxiety, guilt, anger, etc. are experienced when people either don't get what they believe they must have, or do get what they believe they must not get. These negative emotions are regarded in rational-emotive theory, as *inappropriate responses* to negative events, and do tend to interfere significantly with a person's ability to adjust when their existing goals cannot be achieved, and with that person's pursuit of new goals and purposes.

In summary, irrational beliefs are 'irrational' in two respects: first, they are absolute (or dogmatic) in nature; and second, they tend to impede the attainment of a person's basic goals and purposes.

Rational-emotive theory makes four additional important points about beliefs:

People often *escalate* their rational beliefs into irrational beliefs. For example, a person may begin by believing: 'I want very much to do well in my examination' and then escalate this non-absolute belief into an absolute one thus: 'Since I want to get a good mark in my examination, therefore I absolutely have to do so'. It is important to note that this escalation process often occurs implicitly and in counselling individuals it is helpful to check whether escalation has occurred whenever clients report rational beliefs. When clients stick rigorously to their rational beliefs (i.e. do not escalate their non-absolute beliefs into irrational beliefs) statements like '. . . but I don't have to', '. . . but there is no reason why I must' etc. are present, again often implicitly e.g. 'I want very much to do well in in my examination, (but I don't *have* to do so)'.

Rational beliefs seem to underlie rational or functional actions (which facilitate the attainment of one's basic goals and purposes), whereas irrational beliefs tend to underpin irrational or dysfunctional actions such as withdrawal, procrastination, alcoholism, and substance abuse (which impede goal achievement) (Ellis, 1982 a).

Beliefs (both rational and irrational) can be either general or specific. Taking the example of irrational beliefs: 'I must succeed at all important tasks' is an example of a general irrational belief, while: 'I must succeed at this particular task' is an example of a specific one. As Wessler and Wessler (1980) note, a specific belief may represent a special case of a general belief.

As I have noted elsewhere (Dryden, 1986), it is important to distinguish between a word and its meaning. This principle should be borne in mind when considering beliefs in rational-emotive counselling. For example, take the word 'should'. The word 'should' *can* represent the presence of an irrational belief (e.g. 'You should not cheat me' — this really means here 'You *absolutely* should not cheat me'). However, the word 'should' has other meanings in the English language. For example, in a previous sentence, while referring to the important distinction between words and meanings, I wrote: 'This principle should be borne in mind when considering beliefs in RET counselling'. I hope as readers of this book, you can see that I am not dogmatically insisting that you bear this point in mind, rather I am advising or recommending you to do so. Thus, not all 'shoulds', 'musts', etc. indicate the presence of irrational beliefs.

Inferences

Inferences (or interpretations) are cognitions that go beyond the information that is immediately available to a person. In order to fully understand what inferences are it is first necessary to introduce another type of cognition called a *description* (Wessler and Wessler, 1980).

Descriptions are cognitions which report the nature of any stimulus that a person has awareness of. They do not add anything that cannot be directly observed. For example, imagine that I am standing facing a window with my hands in my pockets so that you can only see my back. If I ask you to describe my behaviour you might say: 'You are standing facing the window with your hands in your pockets'. This constitutes a description because you have not gone beyond the information that is immediately available to you. However, were you to say: 'You are looking out of the window', then that would not be a description in that you would be going beyond the data at hand; since my eyes are, in fact, closed. You would be making an *inference* about what you observe.

So inferences go beyond the data at hand. They are, in fact, hypotheses (or hunches) about the nature of reality. Since inferences are best viewed as hypotheses they need to be tested against the available data. This point is important since clients often make the error of confusing their 'hypotheses' with 'facts'. Inferences, of course, can be accurate as well as inaccurate, e.g., in the above example I *may* have been looking out of the window. Sometimes it is impossible to test the validity of one's inferences. Again, take the example where I am facing the window with my eyes closed. Imagine that you have made the inference that I am looking out of the window. In order to test the validity of your inference you would need to determine whether, in fact, I have my eyes open. Thus, you would have to approach me and look at my eyes. Just before you look at my eyes, however, I may have them open but decide to close them just before you look at them. Thus your previous inference would have been correct, but in the process of testing it, the situation changes and it *seems* as if your inference has been invalidated.

While making inferences people are influenced by interpersonal and physical contexts. Thus, it is reasonable to expect that when a person has his hands in his pockets and is facing a window, then he is looking out of the window. Psychologists often say that a person's inference (e.g. 'You are looking out of the window') represents the 'best bet' that can be made given the context and the available information (c.f. Gregory, 1966). In RET counselling (as in other forms of cognitive-behavioural counselling, c.f. Dryden and Golden, 1986), we often find that clients make the 'worst bet' in forming hypotheses about themselves, other people, and the world, in that their inferences can be viewed as distorted (particularly in a negative direction).

Inferences are non-evaluative. Inferences are best seen as *non-evaluative* in nature in order to differentiate them from beliefs which are *evaluative* cognitions (as has been noted in the section on beliefs). This distinction can often appear blurred as some inferences seem to have an evaluative component. For example, in a recent counselling session one of my female clients predicted that other people would laugh at her during a class presentation. Her inference, 'Other people will laugh at me', seems to imply a negative evaluation. However, we do not know just from her stated inference whether her evaluation is an absolute negative one ('It would be terrible if they laugh at me'); a non-absolute negative one ('It would be unfortunate if . . .'); an absolute positive one ('It would be absolutely marvellous if . . .'); a non-absolute positive one ('It would be good if . . .'); or a neutral one ('I don't care if . . .'). Thus inferences, *per se*, do not tell us what a person's beliefs (or evaluative cognitions) might be. As we shall see later in the book the best way of identifying a person's evaluations is to examine carefully whether his/her emotions are inappropriate/self-defeating i.e. irrational (e.g. depression, anxiety or guilt etc.) or appropriate/self-promoting i.e. rational (e.g. sadness, concern or regret). Thus, inferences, no matter how distorted, are rarely reliable guides to a person's emotions because they do not contain *explicit* reference to evaluative cognitions. Thus in rational-emotive theory: **emotions are based largely on evaluative thinking rather than on inferential thinking**.

Inferences can be grouped into various categories and I will briefly review those that are most relevant to counselling.

Causal attributions. This category of inferences represents a person's attempts to account for the 'causes' of one's own or another's emotions and actions. Causal attributions can be internal to the 'author' of the experience ('He didn't turn up on time because he didn't care enough'; 'I cry easily because I'm too sensitive'); external to the 'author' of the experience ('He didn't turn up on time because he was delayed by the traffic'; 'I cry easily because my parents didn't love me as a child'), or a combination of internal and external factors ('He didn't turn up on time because someone called on him at the last moment and he was too unassertive to excuse himself'; 'I cry easily because my family members play on my over-sensitivity').

One of the initial major tasks of rational-emotive counsellors is to help clients shift from making causal attributions about emotional and behavioural disturbance which are *exclusively* external in nature (e.g. 'I'm depressed because my lover has left me') to making causal attributions which are *largely* (but not exclusively) internal in nature (e.g. 'I'm depressed about my lover leaving me because that event has encouraged me to conclude that I am worthless'). It should be noted from the previous sentence that RET counsellors guard against encouraging clients from making causal attributions about psychological disturbance that are exclusively internal in nature. They do so because, according to RET theory, external events do *contribute* to (but do not '*cause*') such disturbance.

Predictions. Predictions vary along the important dimension of probability of occurrence. In general, high probability events tend to have greater influence on people's responses than low probability events. However, some clients will not, for example, take steps towards a valued goal if there exists the slightest chance that their efforts may prove unsuccessful. This is a very good sign that they are making dire evaluations (irrational beliefs) about the slight chance that they may fail ('It would be terrible if I were to fail').

In counselling, clients' predictions typically relate to others' responses to self (e.g. 'If I ask that woman to dance, then she will reject me'); changes in the physical environment (e.g. 'If I don't check one last time that I have turned off the oven, then it will explode during the night') or to one's own future reactions (e.g. 'If I go into that crowded supermarket, then I will faint'). While most clients' predictions refer to events that would be evaluated negatively, some positively evaluated predictions feature in clients' problems (e.g. the compulsive gambler who predicts that he will win a fortune this time if he bets a week's wages on the favourite in the 3.30 race at Ascot).

Motives. Frequently, people try to infer why they and others act as they do, and discussions concerning these motives often occur in the counselling process. For example, in a recent counselling session, a young depressed student who regarded herself as unloveable inferred that the reason why a fellow student was being nice to her was that the other person wanted to borrow her notes. Testing such hypotheses, particularly those that relate to the motives of others, is fraught with difficulties. When I suggested to my client that she could check this by asking the student concerned she replied: 'She would only deny wanting to borrow my notes and she would be lying'.

Rational-emotive theory makes these additional important points about inferences:

> As has been noted about beliefs, inferences can be either general or specific. Wessler and Wessler (1980) have argued that general inferences (e.g. 'All women will eventually leave me') tend to be more enduring than specific inferences ('Sarah will eventually leave me'). The latter may be specific examples of the former.

> Clients may have particular inferential styles (i.e. consistent and recurring ways of forming inferences). Thus, some clients may consistently make causal attributions which are internal in nature. This may be particularly so with regard to their own behaviour. Thus one of my clients views 'intelligence' as accounting for much of the variance in people's behaviour. He minimizes consistently the impact of environmental factors on behaviour. Clients who display an internal attributional style tend to use a small number of 'filters' in viewing the world. Clients often reveal

the following typical filters through which they tend to view the world: 'caring', 'sanity', 'strength', 'intelligence', etc.

Inferences are often 'chained' together (Moore, 1983). The following represents a typical example of an inference chain that a client may reveal in counselling: 'If I speak up in class then I will say something stupid — If that happens then everybody will laugh at me — If that happens then I will blush severely — If I blush then people will play on that in the future — If they do that it will prove that they think I'm stupid'. As we shall see in chapter 6, it is frequently helpful in counselling individuals to find the most relevant inference in the chain i.e. the one which the client evaluates. This is often, but not always, the last reported inference in the chain.

Decisions

Wessler and Hankin-Wessler (1986) have stressed that decisions (or decisional cognitions) play an important role in the perpetuation of psychological disturbance and in determining whether or not people make changes in their lives. People can decide whether to inspect their distorted inferences and irrational beliefs and choose whether or not to change them. People can also decide to tolerate or avoid their own painful emotions and decide to change their behaviour or to continue to act in a dysfunctional manner. A very common form of decision that is often expressed by clients is 'I can't . . .'. It is important to realise that this statement may provide clues that the person is making negative inferences and holding irrational beliefs about events and his or her response options. In rational-emotive counselling it is often important to deal with these cognitions before tackling decisions.

It is helpful to distinguish between short- and long-term goals when discussing clients' decisions. A common focus in rational-emotive counselling is to encourage clients to tolerate uncomfortable emotions while they pursue their valued goals. While a client may, for example, desire the long-term goal of gaining increasing social confidence, he or she may also have the short-term goal of avoiding discomfort. In order to gain the benefit of the former, the person has to *decide* to tolerate the latter. In my experience as a rational-emotive counsellor, it is not only important to help clients to challenge and change their negative inferences and irrational beliefs about the experience of discomfort, but also to help them to see the reasons why deciding to tolerate discomfort are so important in the change process.

Finally, as Greenwald (1973) has shown, it is important for clients to realise that the process of making decisions to change is not a singular event. Decisions to change cognitions or behaviours have often frequently to be re-affirmed if clients are to derive lasting benefits from counselling.

Self-instructions

One of the assumptions of rational-emotive counselling is that people have both an experiencing and an observing part of themselves. Thus, a person 'detaches' her 'observing self' from her 'experiencing self' when identifying and deciding whether or not to change the cognitions that underpin psychological disturbance. The 'observing self' can also give instructions to the 'experiencing self'. These are known as *self-instructions*. Here the work of Meichenbaum (1977, 1985) is particularly helpful. Meichenbaum has shown that people can help themselves by instructing themselves to tolerate and to cope with certain negative emotions, to act in productive ways, and to provide themselves with praise for doing well.

Coping with negative emotions. Imagine a person who is scared of having a panic attack. A counsellor might encourage this person to use the following self-instructions to cope with her anxious feelings: 'When anxiety comes, just pause; keep focusing on the present; label my anxiety on a 0–10 scale and watch it change; don't try to eliminate anxiety totally, just keep it manageable; take slow controlled breaths', etc.

Facilitating productive action. For a client who gets overwhelmed when confronted with many tasks, the counsellor might suggest the following self-instructions: 'Look at what I have to do; get my tasks into order of priority; focus on one thing at a time'.

Self-rewarding. When clients have succeeded in coping with their negative emotions and/or acting in a productive manner, they can instruct themselves in the following ways that are deemed to be self-rewarding: 'I handled my feelings pretty well; I did well that time, that's good; I'm really making progress on this'. When clients fail to cope with their negative emotions and/or act productively, they often get discouraged. To counteract this tendency counsellors need to help them to develop constructive self-instructions concerning their 'failures'. For example, they can use the following: 'OK I had a panic attack. Look for what went wrong; I didn't manage it this time. Look for what can be learned from this experience'.

Clients can also use self-instructions to direct themselves to identify and challenge their distorted inferences and irrational beliefs. For example, a person might say 'OK I'm anxious; look for and challenge my demands; seek out and correct my negative thoughts'.

Problem-solving cognitions

The ability to solve problems related to psychological disturbance has been broken down into several cognitively-based skills (c.f. Platt, Prout and Metzger, 1986). People who do bring a problem-solving 'set' to their difficulties appear to use specific cognitions that are usually implicit or covert in nature. Very often clients lack these cognitions and have to be taught to use them during counselling. The following cognitively-based skills are often associated with effective personal and interpersonal problem-solving.

Problem-defining. Clients often fail to solve personal and interpersonal problems because of the very way they define them (e.g. 'My anxiety proves that I'm a nervous type and nothing can be done about it'). Helping clients to overcome problems involves encouraging them to re-define problems in a way which encourages problem-solving (e.g. 'My anxiety is based on irrational beliefs that can be changed'). Re-defining also involves the skill of *alternative thinking*, the capacity to generate and apply alternatives to personal and interpersonal problems (e.g. 'What other ways are there to view the situation?').

Consequential thinking. This involves the capacity to consider the consequences of one's actions. Impulsive clients, for example, often do not consider what impact their actions might have on themselves and other people and can be trained to use outcome-oriented cognitions to good effect (e.g. 'What is likely to happen if I do this?').

Means-ends thinking. While clients are developing alternative solutions to problems, they often need to consider the sequencing of planned remedial steps leading to their goals (e.g. 'What steps do I have to take before I can do 'x?', 'What should I preferably do first?'). In addition, clients often need to anticipate obstacles and plan to overcome them if they are to achieve their ends (e.g. 'If 'Y' happens, what can I do to overcome it?').

Perspective taking. This involves the ability to stand back and look at a situation from someone else's point of view, and the ability to put oneself into the position of others. This latter ability is particularly helpful when a client would judge others less harshly than she considers others would judge her. Clients often fail to solve their problems because they only judge themselves, other people and situations from one fixed, and often distorted, perspective. Teaching clients perspective-taking involves encouraging them to employ cognitions like: 'What would other people think if they were in my position?'; 'If other people did what I've just done would I judge them as I think they are judging me?'.

Cognitive interactionism and the centrality of beliefs

Although the types of cognitions reviewed in this chapter have been discussed separately, in reality they overlap and interact with one another. However, rational-emotive theory places beliefs (or evaluative cognitions) at the heart of this process of interacting cognitions. Thus, according to RET theory, people's beliefs have a greater influencing effect on their other cognitions (i.e. inferences, decisions, self-instructions and problem-solving thinking), than these cognitions have on their beliefs. This hypothesis, however, awaits empirical enquiry.

I have often conducted an informal experiment to demonstrate the important influence that beliefs have on inferences. First, I divide people into two groups. I ask group 1 (the 'irrational belief' group) to imagine that they believe: 'I must not see a spider and it would be terrible if I did', and group 2 (the 'rational belief' group) to imagine that they believe: 'I prefer not to see a spider and if I did it would be undesirable, but not terrible'. I then tell both groups to assume that there is a spider in the room in which they are gathered and ask them, while adhering to their assigned belief: to rate how large the spider is; to determine whether it is moving towards them, away from them, or standing still; and to consider whether or not there are any other spiders in the room, and if so, how many (i.e. inferences of size, movement, and number). The results of this informal experiment are normally as follows: the 'irrational belief' group members consistently rate the spider as larger, report that it is moving towards them more often, and consider that there are a greater number of spiders than estimated by members of the 'rational belief' group. This shows that beliefs do colour the kinds of inferences people make (in this case, about spiders).

Then I take two further groups of people who have not participated in the original experiment. I give group 3 the inferences of the 'irrational belief' group (i.e. group 1) and group 4 the inferences of the 'rational belief' group (i.e. group 2) and ask both groups to judge whether they would hold irrational or rational beliefs if they had just made these inferences about spiders. The results of this second experiment are far less clear-cut, showing that inferences, as such, are not good guides to the kinds of beliefs people hold about stimuli (in this case, spiders).

Words and images

RET counsellors share the view of other cognitive psychotherapists that cognitions can take the form of either words or images. However, given the central role accorded to beliefs in determining emotions in rational-emotive theory, it is not the words and images themselves which have direct impact on emotions, but the evaluative meaning implicit in them. For example, I used to be very anxious when travelling on the London underground system at a time when I had mental images where I threw myself in front of a train. My anxiety could not be attributed to the images, *per se*, because I still occasionally have these images, but without anxiety. Rather, my anxiety was largely determined by my irrational belief about the image ('It is terrible to have such images that I really should not have). My present feelings are those of discomfort rather than anxiety whenever I have the image because I now rationally believe 'I don't like having this image, but there is no reason why

I must not have it'. In addition, as discussed in the previous section, my beliefs also coloured my inferences, i.e. when my belief about the image was irrational I estimated that the likelihood that I would actually throw myself in front of a train was much greater than when my belief about the image was rational.

The Role of Action in Rational-Emotive Theory

Rational-emotive theory holds that people have the greatest chance of fulfilling themselves when they actively pursue their basic goals and purposes. Happiness is maximized when people actively absorb themselves in vocational and avocational pursuits, and when they engage in appropriate recreational activity (Ellis, 1979 a). Conversely, when people are inactive they tend to sabotage their chances for happiness. Thus, action plays an important role in rational-emotive theory.

Actions and beliefs

As has already been noted, people's actions are largely (but not exclusively) determined by their beliefs about themselves, others, and present and future situations. Productive (or rational) actions tend to stem from rational beliefs while unproductive (or irrational) actions tend to stem from irrational beliefs.

Actions can be purposive

RET counsellors tend to agree with their Adlerian colleagues that actions can be purposive i.e. they seek to achieve something, e.g. the cessation of an emotional state (anxiety) or a response from the physical and interpersonal environment. An example of the latter might be a man who acts in a withdrawn and sulking manner when his wife refuses to have sex with him. While he probably does hold the irrational belief 'It's terrible when I don't get what I want. Poor me!', his behaviour can also be seen as purposive in that his action is designed, albeit implicitly, to elicit a response from his wife — in this case remorse, and later, sex. It is important to note in this context that other people respond to our actions and behavioural expressions of emotion rather than to the emotions themselves.

Action tendencies and response options

When people experience emotions they also have a tendency to act in a certain number of ways, depending upon the emotion that is experienced. Action tendencies are purposive; if actualized, they serve to help the person achieve a particular goal. In the emotional disorders such goals tend to be productive in the short-term, but unproductive in the long term. Action tendencies can be seen as *general* categories of behaviour rather than as *specific* responses (withdrawal rather than walking out of church).

As an illustration consider a person who is experiencing anxiety and has a pronounced tendency to withdraw from a threat. This action tendency, if actualized, tends to help the person to avoid discomfort, but it is unproductive in the long-term as it tends to discourage the person from dealing constructively with the threat. Whether or not people actually respond according to an action tendency depends largely upon what alternative ways of responding exist, and the inferences and evaluations the person makes of these response options (response options are *specific* ways of responding that are available to the person in a given situation).

Imagine a woman who is anxious about going to church. Given her anxiety, she chooses from among her response options to sit near the exit so that she can leave easily if she gets anxious (action tendency = to withdraw). If she were to sit in the middle of a row near the front of the church, far from the exit, and become anxious in these circumstances, she might not choose the response option of leaving the church even though she still has the tendency to withdraw. This is because she infers that, were she to do so, other people might notice her and consider her to be 'strange', a prospect which she would evaluate in an absolute and negative manner (irrational belief = 'It would be terrible if other churchgoers were to think that I am strange'). Given that she has now excluded leaving the church as a viable response option she is now left to experience her anxiety with no constructive ways of dealing with it. She is now caught in a dilemma since she believes both that 'It is terrible to be anxious in church', and 'It would be terrible to be noticed and considered strange'. It is little wonder that this woman did have a panic attack at her own wedding.

Among a person's response options are specific responses which serve to actualize given action tendencies and specific responses which run counter to given action tendencies. An important feature of rational-emotive counselling is encouraging clients to act against their habitual self-defeating action tendencies — a strategy which aims to help them to tolerate discomfort and thence begin to cope better with the problematic situation.

Behavioural competence

Rational-emotive theory recognizes that people execute behaviours at varying levels of skill and RET counsellors try, when appropriate, to help their clients to become more skillful at executing acts that already exist in their behavioural repertoire, and to acquire behavioural responses that are absent from their repertoire (e.g. relaxation skills and assertive skills).

In addition, RET counsellors pay attention to the inferences and evaluations clients make about their level of competence. For example, at the inferential level, people can either underestimate or overestimate their level of skill, or give an improved level of skill a particular interpretative meaning (e.g. 'If I become more assertive then I will lose my sensitivity towards people'). At the evaluative level people may rate *themselves* for having a certain level of skill (e.g. 'I'm not very socially skilled; that proves I'm no good' = irrational belief), or evaluate the effort that it may take to become more skillful ('It will take a lot of practice to learn more productive study skills; I wish it were easier but that doesn't mean that I can't tolerate the effort' = rational belief).

In conclusion, while it can be seen from this section that rational-emotive theory accords action an important role in human functioning, it can also be seen that cognitions are deemed to play an influential part even in the realm of human action. However the emphasis throughout this book will be on changing beliefs.

3. Psychological Disturbance and Health

Overview

In this chapter I consider psychological disturbance and health from a rational-emotive perspective. After outlining the rational-emotive view on the nature of psychological disturbance and health, I focus on how humans acquire and perpetuate their own psychological disturbance. I conclude the chapter by considering the rational-emotive theory of therapeutic change.

The Nature of Psychological Disturbance and Health
Psychological disturbance

Irrational beliefs and their derivatives. Rational-emotive theory posits that at the heart of psychological disturbance, lies the tendency of humans to make devout, absolutist evaluations (i.e. irrational beliefs) of the inferred in their lives. As has been shown, these evaluations are couched in the form of dogmatic 'musts', 'shoulds', 'have to's', 'got to's', and 'oughts'. These absolutist cognitions represent a philosophy of religiosity which, according to rational-emotive theory, is the central feature of human emotional and behavioural disturbance (c.f. Ellis, 1983 a). As has been shown, these beliefs are deemed to be irrational in that they usually (but not invariably) impede and obstruct people in the pursuit of their basic goals and purposes. Absolute musts do not invariably lead to psychological disturbance because it is possible for a person to devoutly believe 'I must succeed at all important projects', have confidence that he or she will be successful in these respects, and actually succeed in them and thereby not experience psychological disturbance. However, the person remains vulnerable because there is always the possibility that he or she may fail in the future. So while on probabilistic grounds

RET theory argues that an absolutist philosophy will frequently lead to psychological disturbance it does not claim that this is absolutely so. Thus, even with respect to its view of the nature of human disturbance rational-emotive theory adopts an anti-absolutist position.

Rational-emotive theory goes on to posit that if humans adhere to an absolutist and devout philosophy they will strongly tend to make a number of core irrational conclusions which are deemed to be derivatives of their 'musts'. These major derivatives are viewed as irrational because they too tend to sabotage a person's basic goals and purposes.

The first major derivative is known as *awfulizing*. This occurs when an inferred event is rated as being more than 100 per cent bad — a truly exaggerated and magical conclusion which stems from the belief: 'This must not be as bad as it is'.

The second major derivative is known as *I-can't-stand-it-itis*. This means believing that one cannot experience virtually any happiness at all, under any conditions, if an event which 'must' not happen actually occurs, or threatens to occur.

The third major derivative, known as *damnation* represents a tendency for people to rate themselves and other people as 'sub-human' or 'undeserving' if they or other people do something that they 'must' not do, or fail to do something which they 'must' do. 'Damnation' can also be applied to the world or life conditions which are rated as being 'rotten' for failing to give the person what he or she 'must' have.

While RET holds that 'awfulizing', 'I-can't-stand-it-itis' and 'damnation' are secondary irrational processes, in that they stem from the philosophy of 'musts', these processes can sometimes be primary (Ellis, 1984 a). Indeed, Wessler (1984) has argued that they are more likely to be primary and that 'musts' are derived from them. However, the philosophy of 'musts', on the one hand, and those of 'awfulizing', 'I-can't-stand-it-itis' on the other, are, in all probability, interdependent processes and often seem to be different sides of the same 'cognitive coin'.

Other forms of distorted thinking stemming from irrational beliefs. Rational-emotive theory notes that humans also make numerous kinds of illogicalities when they are disturbed (Ellis, 1985 b). In this respect it agrees with cognitive therapists (Beck *et al.*, 1979; Burns, 1980) that such cognitive distortions are a feature of psychological disturbance. However, rational-emotive theory holds that such distortions almost always stem from the 'musts', although this hypothesis has yet to be empirically tested. Some of the most frequent distortions are:

> *All-or-none thinking:* 'If I fail at any important task, as I *must* not, I'm a *total* failure and *completely* unlovable!'.

Jumping to conclusions and negative non-sequiturs: 'Since they have seen me dismally fail, as I *should* not have done, they will view me as an incompetent worm'.

Fortune telling: 'Because they are laughing at me for failing, they know that I *should* have succeeded, and they will despise me forever'.

Focusing on the negative: 'Because I *can't stand* things going wrong, as they *must* not, I can't see any good that is happening in my life'.

Disqualifying the positive: 'When they compliment me on the good things I have done, they are only being kind to me and forgetting the foolish things that I *should* not have done'.

Allness and neverness: 'Because conditions of living *ought* to be good and actually are so bad and so intolerable, they'll *always* be this way and I'll never have any happiness'.

Minimization: 'My good shots in this game were lucky and unimportant. But my bad shots, which I *should* never have made, were as bad as could be and were totally unforgiveable'.

Emotional reasoning: 'Because I have performed so poorly, as I *should* not have done, I feel like a total idiot, and my strong feeling proves that I *am* no damned good!'.

Labelling and overgeneralization: 'Because I *must* not fail at important work and have done so, I am a complete loser and failure!'.

Personalizing: 'Since I am acting far worse than I *should* act and they are laughing, I am sure they are only laughing at me; and that is *awful!*'.

Phoneyism: 'When I don't do as well as I *ought* to do and they still praise and accept me, I am a real phoney and will soon fall on my face and show them how despicable I am!'.

Perfectionism: 'I realize that I did fairly well, but I *should* have done perfectly well on a task like this, and am therefore really an incompetent!'.

Although RET counsellors at times discover all the illogicalities just listed — and a number of others that are less frequently found with clients — they particularly focus on the unconditional shoulds, oughts, and musts that seem to constitute the philosophic core of irrational beliefs that lead to emotional disturbance. For they hold that if they do not get to and help clients surrender these core beliefs, the clients will most probably keep holding them and create new irrational derivatives from them.

RET counsellors also particularly look for 'awfulizing', for 'I-can't-stand-it-itis', and for 'damnation'; and they show clients how these almost invariably stem from their 'musts' and can be surrendered if they give up their absolutist demands on themselves, on other people, and on the universe. At the same time, rational-emotive counsellors usually encourage their clients to have strong and persistent desires, wishes, and preferences, and to avoid feelings of detachment, withdrawal and lack of involvement.

More importantly, RET holds that unrealistic and illogical beliefs do not in themselves create emotional disturbance. Why? Because it is quite possible for people to unrealistically believe, 'Because I frequently fail, I always do' and it is possible for them also to believe illogically, 'Because I have frequently failed, I always will'. But they can, in both these instances, rationally conclude, 'Too bad. Even though I always fail, there is no reason why I must succeed. I would prefer to but I never have to do well. So I'll manage to be as happy as I can be even with my constant failure'. They would then rarely be emotionally disturbed.

To reiterate, the essence of human emotional disturbance, according to rational-emotive theory, consists of the absolutist *musts* and *must nots* that people think *about* their failure, *about* their rejections, *about* their poor treatment by others, and *about* life's frustrations and losses. Rational-emotive counselling therefore differs from other forms of cognitive-behavioural counselling — such as those inspired by Beck (1976), Bandura (1969, 1977), Goldfried and Davison (1976), Janis (1983), Lazarus (1981), Mahoney (1977), Maultsby (1984), and Meichenbaum (1977) — in that it particularly stresses therapists looking for clients' dogmatic, unconditional *musts*, differentiating them from their preferences, and teaching them how to surrender the former and retain the latter (Ellis, 1984 a).

Psychological health

If the philosophy of religiosity is at the core of much psychological disturbance then what philosophy is characteristic of psychological health? Rational-emotive theory argues that a philosophy of relativism or 'desiring' is a central feature of psychologically healthy humans. This philosophy acknowledges that humans have a large variety of desires, wishes, wants, preferences, etc., but if they refuse to escalate these non-absolute values into grandiose dogmas and demands they will not become psychologically disturbed. They will, however, experience appropriate negative emotions (e.g. sadness, regret, disappointment, annoyance) whenever their desires are not fulfilled. These emotions are considered to have constructive motivational properties in that they both help people to remove obstacles to goal attainment and aid them to make constructive adjustments when their desires cannot be met. This point will be developed further in chapter four.

Three major derivatives of the philosophy of desiring are postulated by rational-emotive theory. They are deemed to be rational in that they tend to help people reach their goals, or formulate new goals if their old ones cannot be realized.

The first major derivative is known as *rating* or *evaluating badness*. Here, if a person does not get what she wants she acknowledges that this is bad. However, because she does not believe 'I have to get what I want' she contains her evaluation along a 0–100 per cent continuum of 'badness' and does not therefore rate this situation as 'awful' — a magical rating which is placed on a nonsensical 101 per cent– ∞ (infinity) continuum. In general, when the person adheres to the desiring philosophy, the stronger her desire the greater her rating of badness will be when she does not get what she wants.

The second major derivative is known as *tolerance* and is the rational alternative to 'I-can't-stand-it-itis'. Here the person acknowledges that an undesirable event has happened (or may happen); believes that the event should occur empirically if it does (i.e. does not demand that what exists must not exist); rates the event along the badness continuum; attempts to change the undesired event, or accepts the 'grim' reality if it cannot be modified; and actively pursues other goals even though the situation cannot be altered.

The third major derivative known as *acceptance* is the rational alternative to 'damnation'. Here the person accepts herself and others as fallible human beings who do not have to act other than they do and as too complex and fluid to be given any legitimate or global rating. In addition, life conditions are accepted as they exist. People who have the philosophy of acceptance fully acknowledge that the world is highly complex and exists according to laws which are often outside their personal control. It is important to emphasize here that acceptance does not imply resignation. A rational philosophy of acceptance means that the person acknowledges that whatever exists empirically should exist, but does not have to exist in any absolute sense forever. This prompts the person to make active attempts to change reality. The person who is resigned to a situation usually does not attempt to modify it.

Criteria of psychological health. Rational-emotive theory puts forward 13 criteria of psychological health (Ellis and Bernard, 1985). These are:

1   *Self-interest:* As has already been noted, emotionally healthy people tend to be first or primarily interested in themselves and to put their own interests at least a little above the interests of others. They sacrifice themselves to some degree for those for whom they care — but not overwhelmingly or completely.

2   *Social interest:* Social interest is usually rational and self-helping because most people choose to live and enjoy themselves in a social group or community; and if they do not act morally, protect the rights of others, and abet social survival, it is unlikely that they will

create the kind of a world in which they themselves can live comfortably and happily.

3 *Self-direction:* Healthy people tend to assume responsibility for their own lives while simultaneously preferring to cooperate with others. They do not need or demand considerable support or succour from others.

4 *High frustration tolerance:* Rational individuals give both themselves and others the right to be wrong. Even when they intensely dislike their own and others' behaviour, they refrain from damning themselves or others, as persons, for unacceptable or obnoxious behaviour. People who are not plagued with debilitating emotional distress tend to go along with St. Francis and Reinhold Niebuhr by changing obnoxious conditions they can change, accepting those they cannot, and having the wisdom to know the difference between the two.

5 *Flexibility:* Healthy and mature individuals tend to be flexible in their thinking, open to change, and unbigoted and pluralistic in their view of other people. They do not make rigid, invariant rules for themselves and others.

6 *Acceptance of uncertainty:* Healthy men and women tend to acknowledge and accept the idea that we seem to live in a world of probability and chance, where absolute certainties do not, and probably never will, exist. They realize that it is often fascinating and exciting, and definitely not horrible, to live in this kind of probabilistic and uncertain world. They enjoy a good degree of order but do not demand to know exactly what the future will bring, or what will happen to them.

7 *Commitment to creative pursuits:* Most people tend to be healthier and happier when they are vitally absorbed in something outside themselves and preferably have at least one powerful creative interest, as well as some major human involvement, that they consider so important that they structure a good part of their daily existence around it.

8 *Scientific thinking:* Nondisturbed individuals tend to be more objective, rational, and scientific than more disturbed ones. They are able to feel deeply and act concertedly, but they tend to regulate their emotions and actions by reflecting on them and evaluating their consequences in terms of the extent to which they lead to the attainment of short- and long-term goals.

9 *Self-acceptance:* Healthy people are usually glad to be alive and accept themselves just because they are alive and have some capacity to

enjoy themselves. They refuse to measure their intrinsic worth by their extrinsic achievements, or by what others think of them. They frankly choose to accept themselves unconditionally; and they try to completely avoid rating their totality or their being. They attempt to enjoy rather than to prove themselves.

10   *Risk taking:* Emotionally healthy people tend to take a fair amount of risk and to try to do what they want to do, even when there is a good chance that they may fail. They tend to be adventurous, but not foolhardy.

11   *Long-range hedonism:* As was noted earlier, well adjusted people tend to seek both the pleasures of the moment and those of the future, and do not often court future pain for present gain. They are hedonistic, that is, happiness-seeking and pain-avoidant, but they assume that they will probably live for quite a few years and that they had there-fore better think of both today and tomorrow, and not become obsessed with immediate gratification.

12   *Non-utopianism:* Healthy people accept the fact that utopias are probably unachievable and that they are never likely to get every-thing they want or avoid all pain. They refuse to strive unrealistic-ally for total joy, happiness, or perfection, or for lack of anxiety, depression, self-downing, and hostility.

13   *Self-responsibility for own emotional disturbance:* Healthy individuals tend to accept a great deal of responsibility for their own disturbance, rather than defensively blame others or social conditions for their self-defeating thoughts, feelings, and behaviours.

Acquisition and Perpetuation of Psychological Disturbance
Acquisition of psychological disturbance

Rational-emotive theory does not put forward an elaborate view concerning the acquisition of psychological disturbance. This partly follows from the rational-emotive hypothesis that humans have a distinct *biological* tendency to think and act irrationally (Ellis, 1976), but it also reflects the viewpoint that theories of acquisition do not necessarily suggest therapeutic interventions. While rational-emotive theory holds that humans' tendencies towards irrational thinking are bio-logically rooted, it also acknowledges that environmental variables do contribute to psychological disturbance and thus encourage people to make their biologi-cally-based demands (Ellis, 1976). Ellis (1984 b) said 'parents and culture usually teach children *which* superstitions, taboos and prejudices to abide by, but they do

not originate their basic tendency to superstitiousness, ritualism and bigotry'
(p. 209).

Rational-emotive theory also posits that humans vary in their disturbability.
Some people emerge relatively unscathed psychologically from being raised by uncaring or overprotective parents, while others emerge emotionally damaged from
more 'healthy' childrearing regimes (Werner and Smith, 1982). In this respect,
rational-emotive theory claims that 'individuals with serious aberrations are more
innately predisposed to have rigid and crooked thinking than those with less aberrations, and that consequently they are likely to make less advances' (Ellis, 1984 b,
p. 223). Here Ellis is talking about severity of emotional and behavioural disorders.
Thus, the rational-emotive theory of acquisition can be summed up in the view
that as humans we are not made disturbed simply by our experiences; rather we
bring our ability to disturb ourselves to our experiences.

Perpetuation of psychological disturbance

While rational-emotive theory does not posit an elaborate view to explain the
acquisition of psychological disturbance, it does deal more extensively with how
such disturbance is perpetuated.

The three RET insights. First, people tend to maintain their psychological
problems by their own 'naive' theories concerning the nature of these problems
and to what they can be attributed. They lack what RET calls *RET Insight No.
One*: that psychological disturbance is primarily determined by the absolutist
irrational beliefs that people hold about negative life events. Rather they consider
that their disturbances are 'caused' by these situations. Since people make incorrect
hypotheses about the major determinants of their problems, they consequently
attempt to change the events rather than their irrational beliefs. Second, people
may have Insight No. One but lack *RET Insight No. Two*: that people remain
disturbed by re-indoctrinating themselves *in the present* with their irrational beliefs.
While they may see that their problems are determined by their beliefs they may
distract themselves and thus perpetuate their problems by searching for the
historical antecedents of these beliefs, instead of directing themselves to change
them as currently held. Third, people may have Insights Nos. One or Two but
still sustain their disturbance because they lack *RET Insight No. Three*: only if
people diligently work and practise in the present as well as in the future to think,
feel and act against their irrational beliefs are they likely to change them, and make
themselves significantly less disturbed. People who have all three insights clearly
see that they had better persistently and strongly challenge their beliefs cognitively, emotively and behaviourally to break the perpetuation of disturbance

cycle. Merely acknowledging that a belief is irrational is usually insufficient to effect change (Ellis, 1979 c).

The philosophy of low frustration tolerance (LFT). Rational-emotive theory contends that the major reason why people perpetuate their psychological problems is because they adhere to a philosophy of low frustration tolerance (LFT) (Ellis, 1979 b, 1980 a). Such people believe that they must be comfortable, and thus do not work to effect change because such work inevitably involves experiencing discomfort. They are short-range hedonists in that they are motivated to avoid short-term discomfort even though accepting and working against their temporary uncomfortable feelings would probably help them to reach their long-range goals. Such people evaluate cognitive and behavioural therapeutic tasks as 'too painful', and even more painful than the psychological disturbance to which they have achieved some measure of habituation. They prefer to remain with their 'comfortable' discomfort rather than face the 'change-related' discomfort which they believe they must not experience. Maultsby (1975) has argued that people often back away from change because they are afraid that they will not feel right about it. He calls this the 'neurotic fear of feeling a phoney' and actively shows clients that these feelings of 'unnaturalness' are in fact the natural concomitants of re-learning. Another prevalent form of LFT is 'anxiety about anxiety'. Here, individuals believe that they must not be anxious, and thus do not expose themselves to anxiety-provoking situations because they might become anxious if they did so — an experience they would evaluate as 'awful'. As such, they perpetuate their problems and restrict their lives to avoid experiencing anxiety.

Disturbances about disturbances. 'Anxiety about anxiety' constitutes an example of the clinical fact that people often make themselves disturbed about their disturbances. Having created secondary (and sometimes tertiary) disturbances about their original disturbance, they become pre-occupied with these 'problems' about problems' and thus find it difficult to get back to solving the original problem. Humans are often very inventive in this respect. They can make themselves depressed about their depression, guilty about being angry, as well as anxious about their anxiety, and so on. Consequently, people often need to tackle their disturbances about their disturbances before they can successfully solve their original problems (Ellis, 1979 b, 1980 a).

Defences. Rational-emotive theory endorses the Freudian view of human defensiveness in explaining how people perpetuate their psychological problems (Freud, 1937). Thus, people maintain their problems by employing various defence mechanisms (e.g. rationalization, avoidance) which are designed to help deny the existence of these problems, or to minimize their severity. The rational-emotive view is that these defences are used to ward off self-damnation tendencies and that under such circumstances, if these people were to honestly take responsibility for their problems, they would severely denigrate themselves for having them. In addition, these defence mechanisms are also employed to ward off discomfort anxiety; again, if such people admitted their problems they would rate them as 'too hard to bear' or 'too difficult to overcome'.

Payoffs. Rational-emotive theory notes that people sometimes experience a form of perceived payoff for their psychological problems other than avoidance of discomfort (Ellis, 1979 a). The existence of these payoffs serves to perpetuate these problems. Thus, a woman who claims to want to overcome her procrastination may avoid tackling the problem because she is afraid that should she become successful she might then be criticized by others as being 'too masculine', a situation she would evaluate as 'awful'. Her procrastination serves to protect her, she believes, from this 'terrible' state of affairs. It is important to note that rational-emotive theory considers that people are affected by payoffs because they make inferences and evaluations about the consequences, or likely consequences, of their behaviour. They are not influenced directly by these consequences.

Self-fulfilling prophecies. Finally, the well documented 'self-fulfilling prophecy' phenomenon helps to explain why people perpetuate their psychological problems (Jones, 1977; Wachtel, 1977). Here, people act according to their evaluations and consequent predictions, and thus often elicit from themselves or from others responses which they then interpret in a manner which confirms their initial hypotheses. Thus, a socially anxious man may believe that other people would not want to get to know 'a worthless individual such as I truly am'. He then attends a social function and acts as if he were worthless, avoiding eye contact and keeping away from others. Unsurprisingly, such social behaviour does not invite approaches from others — a lack of response which he interprets and evaluates thus: 'You see, I was right. Other people don't want to know me. I really am no good'.

In conclusion, rational-emotive theory holds that people 'naturally tend to perpetuate their problems and have a strong innate tendency to cling to self-defeating, habitual patterns and thereby resist basic change. Helping clients change then poses quite a challenge for RET practitioners' (Dryden, 1984 a, p. 244).

The Rational-Emotive Theory of Therapeutic Change

The rational-emotive view of the person is basically an optimistic one. Although it posits that humans have a distinct biological tendency to think irrationally, it also holds that they have the capacity to choose to work towards changing this irrational thinking and its self-defeating effects.

There are various levels of change. Rational-emotive theory holds that the most profound and longlasting changes that humans can effect are ones that involve philosophic restructuring of irrational beliefs. Change at this level can be specific or general. Specific philosophic change means that individuals change their irrational absolutist demands (musts, shoulds) about given situations to rational relative preferences. General philosophic change involves people adopting a non-devout attitude towards life events in general.

To effect a philosophic change at either the specific or general level, people had better:

First, realize that they create, to a large degree, their own psychological disturbances and that while environmental conditions can contribute to their problems, they are in general of secondary consideration in the change process.

Fully recognize that they do have the ability to significantly change these disturbances.

Understand that emotional and behavioural disturbances stem largely from irrational, absolutist dogmatic beliefs.

Detect their irrational beliefs and discriminate them from their rational alternatives.

Dispute these irrational beliefs using the logico-empirical methods of science.

Work towards the internalization of their new rational beliefs by employing cognitive, emotive and behavioural methods of change.

Continue this process of challenging irrational beliefs and using multi-modal methods of change for the rest of their lives.

When people effect a philosophic change by modifying their irrational beliefs to rational beliefs, they often are able to spontaneously correct their distorted inferences of reality (overgeneralizations, faulty attributions, etc.). However, they often had better challenge these distorted inferences more directly, as Ellis has always emphasized (e.g., Ellis, 1962), and as Beck (Beck *et al.*, 1979) has also stressed.

While rational-emotive theory argues that irrational beliefs are the breeding ground for the development and maintenance of inferential distortions, it is possible for people to effect inferentially-based changes without making a profound philosophic change. Thus, they may regard their inferences as hunches about reality rather than facts, may generate alternative hypotheses and may seek evidence and/or carry out experiments which test out each hypothesis. They may then accept the hypothesis which represents the 'best bet' of those available (Gregory, 1966).

Consider a man who thinks that his co-workers view him as a fool. To test this hypothesis he might first specify their negative reactions to him. These constitute the data from which he quickly draws the conclusion: 'They think I'm a fool'. He might then realize that what he has interpreted to be negative responses to him might not be negative. If they seem to be negative, he might then carry out an experiment to test out the meaning he attributes to their responses. Thus, he might enlist the help of a colleague whom he trusts to carry out a 'secret ballot' of others' opinions of him. Or, he could test his hunch more explicitly by directly asking them for their view of him. As a result of these strategies this person may conclude that his co-workers find some of his actions foolish, rather than considering him to be a complete fool. His mood may lift because his inference of the situation has changed, but he may still believe: 'If others think I'm a fool that would be awful and prove that I really am worthless'. Thus, he has made an inferential change, but not a philosophic one. If this person were to attempt to make a philosophic change he would first assume that his inference was true, then address himself to his beliefs about this inference and hence challenge these if they were discovered to be irrational. Thus he might conclude, 'Even if I act foolishly that makes me a person with foolish behaviour, not a foolish person. And even if they deem me a total idiot, this is simply their view with which I can choose to disagree'. Rational-emotive counsellors hypothesize that people are more likely to make a profound philosophic change if they first assume that their inferences are true and then challenge their irrational beliefs, rather than if they first correct their inferential distortions and then challenge their underlying irrational beliefs. However, this hypothesis awaits full empirical enquiry.

People can also make direct changes in the situation. Thus, in the example quoted above, the man could leave his job or distract himself from the reactions of his colleagues by taking on extra work and devoting himself to this. Or he might carry out relaxation exercises whenever he comes in contact with his co-workers and thus distract himself once again from their perceived reactions. Additionally, the man might have a word with his supervisor who might then instruct the other workers to change their behaviour toward the man.

When this model is used to consider behavioural change, it is apparent that a person can change his or her behaviour to effect inferential and/or philosophic change. Thus, again using the above example, a man whose co-workers view him as a fool might change his own behaviour towards them and thus elicit a different set of responses from them which would lead him to reinterpret his previous inference, (behaviour change to effect inferential change). However, if it could be determined that they did indeed consider him to be a fool then the man could actively seek them out and show himself that he could stand the situation and that just because they think him a fool doesn't make him one, i.e. he learns to accept himself in the face of their views while exposing himself to their negative reactions (behaviour change to effect philosophic change).

While rational-emotive counsellors prefer to help their clients make profound philosophic changes in their beliefs they do not dogmatically insist that their clients make such changes. If it becomes apparent that clients are not able at any given time to change their irrational beliefs, then RET counsellors would endeavour to help them either to change the situation directly by avoiding the troublesome situation, or by behaving differently, or to change their distorted inferences about the situation. This book focuses on rational-emotive methods of changing beliefs rather than inferences. For methods devoted to changing inferences, I recommend that the reader consult Beck *et al.* (1979) and Beck and Emery (1985).

In the next chapter, I build upon these theoretical underpinnings and consider a cognitively-based analysis of the most common forms of psychological disturbance for which clients seek counselling.

4.   Understanding Clients' Problems

Overview

In this chapter, I present a cognitively-based analysis of: (a) the major emotional and behavioural problems for which people seek counselling help and (b) their rational alternatives. I deal with anxiety and concern, shame/embarrassment and regret, depression and sadness, guilt and remorse, anger and annoyance, hurt and disappointment, irrational and rational jealousy, and problems of self-discipline. I conclude the chapter by considering briefly a number of additional issues, namely: a mixture of emotions; 'false' emotions; and strength versus rationality of emotions.

It is important for the reader to understand at the outset of this chapter that rational-emotive theory uses 'feeling' words in a precise way; a major purpose of this chapter is to show how RET defines such feelings by clarifying their cognitive correlates. Since clients often use the same words in different ways from their rational-emotive counsellors (e.g. what a client means by anxiety may be different from its meaning in rational-emotive theory), the latter seek to adopt a shared meaning framework with their clients concerning emotions. This often involves teaching clients the rational-emotive language of emotions but can also involve using the clients' own feeling language but in a way that helps them to differentiate between the rational and irrational versions of these emotions (e.g. rational anxiety versus irrational anxiety).

Anxiety
Inferences

Typically in anxiety, a person makes inferences that there exists a threat to her personal domain by which is meant those objects — tangible and intangible — in which a person has an involvement (Beck, 1976). The threat refers generally to a future event, or to future implications of a current event.

Beliefs

RET theory states that anxiety results when a person believes: 'This threat must not occur and it would be terrible if it did' (irrational belief).

Action tendencies and response options

When a person is anxious, her major action tendencies are to avoid or to withdraw from the inferred threat in order to obtain short-term relief from anxiety. As will be shown, the person is more likely to avoid or withdraw from the threat when she cannot respond constructively to it. In addition to keeping away from, or physically withdrawing from a threat, people often engage in various forms of behaviour which serve the purpose of obtaining short-term relief from anxiety, but which also have long-term destructive effects on the person's growth.

Thus clients who present with anxiety often also report problems of self-discipline, e.g. procrastination, alcohol and drug abuse, etc. (specific responses which actualize the action tendency to avoid or to withdraw). Another action tendency associated with anxiety can be described as attempting to 'ward off' the threat. This may, for example, involve the use of obsessive and/or compulsive patterns of behaviour and thought. Such tactics serve to perpetuate anxiety and the dysfunctional cognitions upon which the anxiety is based. Seeking reassurance is another response that some individuals tend to make when they are anxious. Here a person looks to other people for guarantees that threats to their personal domain will not happen. When reassurance is given, the person gains short-term relief from anxiety, but once again, the dysfunctional cognitions that underpin the anxious experience are perpetuated. Finally, some people who experience anxiety have an action tendency which encourages them to expose themselves to *more* dangerous instances of the threat. This is known as 'counterphobic behaviour'.

Typically in anxiety, the person considers that she could not deal with the threat if it occurred. She may judge that there are no viable responses that she can make in the situation; she does not have the sufficient competence to execute such responses; or the responses which she could make would not nullify the threat. Because the person judges that she cannot deal effectively with the threat, she tends to assume that she will be overwhelmed by it.

Other issues

Ellis (1979 b, 1980 a) has distinguished between two types of anxiety. One occurs when the person has irrational beliefs about threats to her self worth (ego anxiety), and the other occurs when she has such beliefs about threats to her level of personal comfort (discomfort anxiety). These two types of anxiety often interact leading to the spiralling effect of mounting anxiety or panic. A feature of this spiralling effect is that the person tends to experience very unpleasant bodily sensations which are, as recent research has found, exacerbated by a process called 'overbreathing' (an increase in the rate and depth of respiratory ventilation which occurs particularly when the individual is under stress; Clark, *et al.*, 1985). Thus, while helping people to overcome anxiety, rational-emotive counsellors not only have to help them to change their inferences and beliefs about the threat but also may usefully help those vulnerable to 'overbreathing' to utilize effective controlled breathing techniques when they experience anxiety.

Concern: The rational alternative to anxiety

In rational-emotive theory, concern is the rational alternative to anxiety. In concern, a person again makes an inference that there exists a threat to her personal domain, but her belief about this is rational: 'I don't want this threat to occur, but there is no reason why it must not happen. If it occurs, it is undesirable but not terrible'.

When a person is concerned but not anxious about an inferred threat to her personal domain, she tends to consider that she can deal with the threat, i.e. she can execute successfully assertive and/or coping options from her response repertoire. She is thus able to actualize her action tendency to confront and deal successfully with the threat, and not avoid or withdraw from it, as in anxiety.

Shame and Embarrassment
Inferences

In shame, a person tends to infer that (a) she has revealed a personal weakness (or acted stupidly) in public, and (b) others will notice this display and will evaluate her negatively. In embarrassment, the same types of inferences are made as in shame, with the exception that the personal weakness is regarded by the person as less serious than in shame (e.g. spilling coffee versus stammering).

Beliefs

Both shame and embarrassment tend to result when the person agrees with the negative evaluations that she infers others have made of her, e.g. 'They're right, I am worthless for revealing my weakness'. Such conclusions tend to stem from such irrational beliefs as: 'I must not reveal my weaknesses in public', and 'I must not be disapproved by others'. Thus self-devaluation is a core cognitive process in both shame and embarrassment.

Action tendencies and response options

When a person is feeling ashamed or embarrassed, her major action tendency is to remove herself from the 'social spotlight', or the gaze of others, e.g. through avoiding eye contact or through physical withdrawal from the social situation. When the person remains in the situation she feels awkward ('I don't know what to do with myself') yet still feels as if she wants to withdraw ('I want the ground to open up and swallow me'). Remaining in the situation, the person may paradoxically display further signs that may draw attention to herself, e.g. through blushing or becoming agitated.

However, as Duck (1986) has shown other people may come to the person's rescue, particularly when her social 'gaffe' is not too serious, e.g. by disclosing that similar incidents have happened to them, or by reassuring the person that no harm has been done. Yet, when the person is in a self-devaluing frame of mind and considers that others are unsympathetic to her, she may not be able to use such cues to restore the social equilibrium, and may indeed draw further attention to herself by failing to take advantage of such help.

Regret: The rational alternative to shame/embarrassment

In rational-emotive theory, regret is the rational alternative to shame and embarrassment. In regret, a person again makes an inference that she has revealed a personal weakness or acted stupidly in public and that others will notice this and may evaluate her negatively, but her belief about this is rational: 'I don't like the fact that I've acted in this way and the fact that others may think badly of me, but there's no reason why I must not have committed this shameful or embarrassing act, and there's no reason why people must not think badly of me. It's a pity that this has happened, but not terrible, and I choose to accept myself as a fallible human being for acting in this way'.

When a person experiences regret, but not shame or embarrassment, about revealing a personal weakness in public, she tends to consider that she can choose to focus on the humour implicit in the event, if it exists, or to apologize without desperation for inconveniencing others, if this is relevant. She is also able to utilize the attempts of others to help her to restore the social equilibrium. She is thus able to actualize her action tendency to continue to participate actively in social interaction.

Depression
Inferences

According to the rational-emotive model, depression tends to occur when a person makes inferences that she has experienced a significant loss to her personal domain (Beck, 1976). The loss might be the death of a significant other, the loss of a love relationship, the loss of a limb, the loss of personal functioning, or the loss associated with failure to achieve a valued goal.

Beliefs

However, while inferences of loss tend to be present when the person is psychologically depressed, according to rational-emotive theory, they do not by themselves account for the person's depression. Rather, the person has to hold irrational beliefs about the loss, e.g. when a man believes: 'I absolutely should not have experienced this loss' he then tends to conclude that the loss 'is terrible and unbearable', and the loss means either that 'I am no good' or that 'the world and other people are no good for allowing the loss to occur'. Such irrational beliefs tend to underpin the fact that depressed persons are often hopeless about the future.

Action tendencies and response options

When a person is depressed, her major action tendency is to withdraw from experiences that were previously reinforcing to her, or from other people who were previously valued. The person tends to withdraw 'into herself' and to become immobilized. Another behavioural pattern that often accompanies less severe psychological depression is related to problems of self-discipline. Thus, for example, a person may start drinking when depressed, or may get involved in other self-defeating activities in order to escape from the pain of depression, e.g. promiscuous sexual relationships and drug taking.

Typically in depression, the person considers that she is unable to execute appropriate responses to the loss ('helplessness'), or that nothing she could do will improve the situation ('hopelessness').

Other issues

As in anxiety, depression can be related to losses in self worth (ego depression) or losses in personal comfort (discomfort depression). Again, both types of depression often interact and people can experience ego depression about their discomfort depression and vice versa (Teasdale, 1985).

Hauck (1971) has discussed two types of depression that are prominently featured in rational–emotive theory (his third type will be discussed in the section on 'hurt'). First, Hauck argues, as shown above, that depression can occur because the person has a negative view of self. Thus, a client may become depressed because she concludes: 'I am unworthy (or less worthy) because I did not achieve a valued goal as I should have done'. This is depression based on self-devaluation or ego depression. Second, depression may be related to 'other pity' which, in my opinion, occurs less frequently in clinical practice than ego depression. Here the person focuses on the misfortunes or losses of others and believes: 'Such misfortunes or losses should not have occurred. It is terrible that the world allows such things to happen'.

Sadness: The rational alternative to depression

In rational–emotive theory, sadness is the rational alternative to depression. In sadness, the person again makes an inference that she has experienced a significant loss to her personal domain, but her belief about this is rational: 'I didn't want this loss to occur, but there is no reason why it should not have happened. It is bad that it has occurred but not terrible'. In this respect healthy grief is seen in rational–emotive theory as profound sadness.

When a person is sad but not depressed about a loss to her personal domain, she tends to consider that she can engage in constructive actions from her response repertoire. She is able to actualize her action tendency to express her feelings about her loss and to talk about it with significant others and not withdraw into herself, as in depression.

Guilt
Inferences

Typically, in guilt a person infers that she has broken her personal code of moral values either by doing something that she considers to be 'bad' (the 'sin' of commission), or not doing something she considers to be 'good' (the 'sin' of omission).

Beliefs

Rational-emotive theory states that guilt results when a person believes: 'I absolutely should not have done what I did, or should have done what I did not. I am a damnable individual for doing so, or not doing so, and should be punished'.

Action tendencies and response options

When a person is feeling guilty, her major action tendencies involve: (a) 'undoing' — this process which aims to 'right the wrong' is often unproductive e.g. attempting to repair 'broken relationships' by desperately begging forgiveness from others (often accompanied by statements of self-loathing); (b) self-punishment, where the person may harm herself in a physical way, or involve herself in activities that may lead her into harm because she believes that she deserves punishment; (c) attempting to anaesthetise herself from the pain of guilt, usually in a self-defeating manner by taking drugs or alcohol; or (d) avoiding responsibility, by making defensive excuses whereby the person claims that she did not do wrong, or blames others for her actions.

Typically in guilt, since the person is in a self-condemnatory frame of mind, she is likely to choose options from her response repertoire which tend to make it more likely that she will 'sin' in future. For example, a common pattern in eating disorders involves the person resolving to diet, establishing a strict dieting regime, breaking this regime, condemning herself, and eating to take away the pain of guilt.

If the person experiencing guilt considers that she has wronged another, she is likely to make unrealistic promises to the other to the effect that 'I will never do that again', without attempting to understand the factors which led her to act that way. She thus finds it difficult to learn from her errors, and thus tends not to be able to keep such promises. Thus, people who experience guilt are often so preoccupied with 'purging' their badness, or with self-punishment, that they tend not to look for explanations for their behaviour other than those that involve internal attributions of badness.

Remorse: The rational alternative to guilt

In rational-emotive theory, remorse, or sorrow, is the rational alternative to guilt. In remorse, a person again infers that she has violated her personal code of moral values, but her belief about this is rational: 'I don't like what I did, or didn't do, but there's no reason why I must not have done it. I'm a fallible human being who did the wrong thing and therefore not damnable'.

When a person feels remorse, but not guilt, about breaking her personal code of moral values, she tends to take responsibility for her actions without damning her 'self' and tries to understand why she acted or failed to act as she did. If others are involved the person may choose to communicate to them the reasons for her actions, and apologize, without desperation to them for 'causing' them pain. She is thus able to repair 'broken' relationships in a rational manner, i.e. while accepting self and others, and to make reparation where appropriate.

Other issues

It is important to distinguish between 'feeling' guilt (i.e. condemning self for acting badly) and acknowledging that one is guilty of doing something wrong — better termed 'accepting responsibility for one's actions'. When a rational-emotive counsellor asks whether the client wishes to overcome her feelings of guilt, the client often thinks that she is being asked to consider that she hasn't broken her moral code rather than to consider the option of accepting herself as a fallible human being for transgressing this code (the latter strategy represents the counsellor's actual intent).

As noted above, clients often consider that having guilty feelings will prevent them from breaking their moral code in the future. However, often the reverse is true. Since guilt involves the belief 'I am bad', a self-fulfilling prophecy often comes into play since a person who considers herself 'bad' will tend to act 'badly' in the future.

Anger

The term anger has several meanings in the counselling literature. Rational-emotive theory differentiates damning anger, which tends to be an irrational emotion, from non-damning anger, which tends to be a rational emotion. Here I will use the term anger to refer to damning anger, and annoyance to refer to its non-damning counterpart.

Inferences

There appear to be three major inference patterns in anger. First, a person may make an inference that a frustrating circumstance exists which serves to block her from achieving goals which she deems important in her personal domain. As

Wessler and Wessler (1980) note: 'The source of frustration can be external or internal, so anger can be directed at other people, the world in general or oneself' (p. 98).

Second, a person may make an inference that another person, an institution, e.g. a company, a tax office or university, or the person herself has transgressed a personal rule deemed important in her personal domain. When the transgressor of the rule is oneself, the rule in anger tends to be non-moral in contrast to guilt when the rule is in the moral domain. While Wessler and Wessler (1980) observe that transgression of personal rules represents a major source of inferred frustration, I prefer to see the rule-transgression inference pattern as separate from inference patterns associated with frustration, since it occurs frequently in counselling practice.

Third, in a certain type of anger that I call 'self-defence' anger, a person makes an inference that the actions of another person, or the responses of an institution, threaten her 'self-esteem' (see 'other issues' below).

Beliefs

Rational-emotive theory states that while inferences of frustration, rule trans-gression or threat to self-esteem tend to be present when the person is angry, they do not, by themselves, account for anger; rather, the person tends to hold irrational beliefs about these inferences, e.g.: 'You must not act in this way and you are damnable for doing so'. It is important to stress then that damning another person, an institution or oneself is an important cognitive dynamic in anger.

Action tendencies and response options

When a person is feeling angry, her major action tendency is to attack either physi-cally or verbally the relevant source of the frustration, rule-breaking or threat to self-esteem in some way. This attack often has a retaliatory intent. If this attack cannot be mounted directly, as strict social rules often restrict the expression of aggression, the person may tend to displace her attack onto another person, usually of lower status or less powerful than the original source, an animal ('kicking the cat') or an object. Another major action tendency associated with anger is with-drawal, as when a person 'storms' out of a meeting.

Typically in anger, a person tends to choose options from her response reper-toire that are characterized by retaliation. The person seeks to get even in some way by choosing, for example, to respond to another person's criticism with damning criticism of that other person in return. When the person's anger is passive-aggressive, this retaliation is expressed indirectly and without the recipient necessarily knowing where the attack has come from e.g., sending anonymous poison-pen letters, since the person tends also to be anxious of attacking the other directly.

While the person who is angry could theoretically choose to engage in productive responses from her response repertoire, e.g. honest non-damning communication, the fact that she is in a 'damning' frame of mind makes this unlikely. This explains why rational-emotive counsellors seek to help clients to work to overcome their anger before helping them to communicate constructively with others (Dryden, 1985 a).

Other issues

It is often difficult to help people to overcome their anger because anger tends to have positive short-term results. Thus anger often helps people to 'feel' powerful and it may, in certain circumstances, help them to get what they want from others, at least initially. However, anger tends also to have negative long-term consequences for the person. Thus anger tends to encourage the deterioration and disintegration of relationships and tends to lead to high blood pressure and other cardio-vascular disorders (Chesney and Rosenman, 1985).

As noted earlier, anger can form an entry point or a 'gateway' to the experience of other emotions such as anxiety or hurt. For example, a client may be angry with her husband for forgetting her birthday, not just because the other person has broken a personal rule and should be punished (although there is that element to the experience), but because she infers that her husband has acted in an uncaring manner. In this example, hurt underpins the experience of anger, i.e. the woman believes that it is terrible to be treated in a way she did not deserve. Another example of anger as a 'gateway' emotion occurred when I once became angry when a friend enquired about the progress of a writing project. I responded with anger not because I believed that my friend should not have made this enquiry, but because he should not have reminded me of my sense of personal inadequacy due to the fact that the project was not going well (threat to my self-esteem). If I was more accepting of myself on that occasion when being reminded of my poor performance, I would still have been annoyed since I would not have liked being reminded of my inadequacy, but I would not have been angry.

Annoyance: The rational alternative to anger

In rational-emotive theory, annoyance is the rational alternative to anger. In annoyance, a person again makes an inference that concerns frustration, rule-breaking or threat to self-esteem, but her beliefs about these are rational e.g. 'I don't like your behaviour and I prefer you didn't act in this way. But there's no reason why you must not act in this bad manner. You are not damnable but a fallible human being who, in my opinion, is acting badly'. Thus acceptance of the other or oneself as 'fallible' is an important cognitive dynamic in annoyance.

When a person is annoyed but not angry, she tends to actualize her tendency to remain in the situation and deal with it constructively by choosing responses from her repertoire that may include assertion and requesting (but not demanding!) behavioural change from others. As in remorse, the person who is annoyed at her own behaviour tends to take responsibility for her own actions, tries to understand her reasons for breaking her own, non-moral rule, and takes corrective action in the future.

Hurt
Inferences

Typically in hurt, a person infers that a significant other has acted towards her in an 'unfair' manner. The other might have ignored the person or disregarded her desires, acted in a non-caring way towards the person, or betrayed the person in some way. Another important inference pattern in hurt which often accompanies the inferences referred to above, involves the person considering that she is undeserving of such treatment.

Beliefs

Rational-emotive theory states that hurt results when a person believes 'The other person absolutely should not have treated me in this unfair manner'. Typical conclusions that follow from this irrational premise can be threefold: (a) 'It's terrible to be treated in this way, particularly as I do not deserve it. Poor me! The world is a rotten place for allowing this to happen'. This can be referred to as 'self-pitying hurt'; (b) 'I'm no good for being treated this way'. This can be referred to as 'depressed hurt'; and (c) 'You are no good for treating me in this way'. This can be referred to as 'angry hurt'. Often in hurt, the person has a blend of these three irrational beliefs.

When deservingness is an issue for the person when she is hurt she tends to believe 'I must get what I deserve' or 'I must not get what I do not deserve'.

Action tendencies and response options

When a person is feeling hurt, her major action tendencies involve withdrawing and closing communication channels with the person who has 'hurt' her (colloquially referred to as 'sulking'), and criticizing the other person normally without disclosing what she feels hurt about. Both often serve the purpose of getting even with the other. Other action tendencies in 'depressed hurt' and 'angry hurt' are similar to those associated with depression and anger.

Typically in hurt, the person, as noted above, often chooses to withdraw from the other who has 'hurt' her. She may also choose responses which are intended to encourage the other person to feel guilty e.g. 'If you really cared about me you would know what you did to hurt me'. Underlying this notion is the person's magical belief that the other person should be able to read one's mind, or know the meaning underlying one's distress. When the person is hurt in a depressed or angry way, she tends to choose response options similar to those selected in depression and anger.

Disappointment: The rational alternative to hurt

In rational-emotive theory, disappointment is the rational alternative to hurt. In disappointment, a person again infers that another has acted unfairly towards her, but her belief about this is rational: 'I prefer to be treated fairly (or not to be treated unfairly), but there's no reason why I must be treated in the way that I prefer (even though I may 'deserve' it). I do not have to get what I deserve'. Typical conclusions that follow from this rational premise are: 'It's bad (but not terrible) to be treated in this way'; 'Being treated in this way does not affect my worth. I'm a fallible human being no matter how I am treated' — here the person's disappointment is tinged with sadness; and 'I don't like your behaviour but you are a fallible human being for acting unfairly. You are not damnable' — here the person's disappointment is tinged with annoyance.

When a person feels disappointment but not hurt about being treated unfairly, she tends to choose options from her response repertoire which actualize her action tendency to influence the other person to act in a 'fairer' manner. She communicates her feelings clearly, directly and assertively to the other person.

Irrational Jealousy

In this section, I will focus on romantic jealousy, since clients are most likely to seek counselling help for this type of jealousy.

Inferences

In irrational jealousy, a person can make a number of inferences including: (a) that the loss of her partner to another is imminent or has occurred; (b) that she does not have the exclusive love or attention of her partner; (c) that she is not the most important aspect of her partner's life; and (d) that her partner is acting in a way that violates her property rights (when she views her partner as her 'property'). These inferences are often linked to inferred threats to the jealous person's self-esteem.

While many people are jealous of their partner's actual or imagined sexual involvement with another person, others allow their partner to have sex with other people and only get jealous when their partner becomes emotionally involved with another person. This suggests that people differ in their jealousy 'rules' (Duck, 1986).

Beliefs

While one or more of the above inferences tend to occur when the person is irrationally jealous, they again do not, by themselves, account for the person's destructive jealous feelings. Rather the person has to hold irrational beliefs about these inferences e.g. when a woman believes 'My husband must only be interested in me. If he shows interest in another woman that would be awful'. She may then conclude either: 'His interest in someone else proves that I am worthless' — (irrational jealousy tinged with depression) or 'He is no good (and/or the other woman is no good) for doing this to me' — (irrational jealousy tinged with anger).

Action tendencies and response options

When a person is irrationally jealous, her action tendencies include monitoring the actions and feelings of her partner, e.g. constantly asking her partner for assurances that she is loved, or phoning her partner at work to check on his movements; searching for evidence that her partner is involved with someone else e.g. checking his car for signs of sexual activity or accusing her partner of engaging in extra-marital affairs; attempting to place restrictions on the movements of her partner, e.g. not allowing her partner to talk to other women at social gatherings; and retaliating, e.g. becoming sexually involved with another person to 'get even' with her partner for his actual or presumed infidelity, or angrily condemning her partner for his 'infidelity'.

As shown above, people who experience irrational jealousy often act in self- and relationship-defeating ways. Because they are anxious about losing their relationship and are yet convinced that this loss is imminent, they often hasten the end of the relationship by their constant checking, accusatory and prescriptive behaviour towards their partner, thus displaying the self-fulfilling prophecy effect commonly found in cases of irrational jealousy.

Rational jealousy: The rational alternative to irrational jealousy

In rational jealousy, the person may again make similar inferences as in irrational jealousy, but her beliefs about these are rational, e.g. 'I want my husband to be only interested in me, but there's no reason why I must have his exclusive interest. If he shows interest in another woman it would be bad, but not awful'. She may then conclude either 'I am still a fallible human being even if he shows an interest in someone else'; or 'He (and/or the other woman) is a fallible human being who is acting against my interests'. Ellis (1985 c) has argued that rational jealousy encourages a person to act and express herself in a loving manner towards her partner rather than taking him for granted; to do something effective to try and win her partner back if that is what she wants; to express her distress assertively and without anger and to ask her partner to set limits on his outside involvements; and to reorganize her life constructively without her partner if he leaves her, or if she decides to terminate the relationship given that it no longer meets her deepest desires.

While there is no research on the subject, rational-emotive theory would predict that the person who experiences rational jealousy is less likely to consider that her partner has outside romantic interests in the absence of such evidence than the person who experiences irrational jealousy.

Problems of Self-discipline

Clients sometimes seek counselling for help with problems of self-discipline such as procrastination, eating disorders and addictions to, say, alcohol or drugs. Also such problems may also be involved in other emotional disorders — for instance, alcoholism is often a feature of aggression.

According to the framework presented in this book, problems of self-discipline are seen here in terms of the conversion of action tendencies into fixed patterns of response which have become habitual. It is important to note that self-discipline problems involve a complex interaction of ego disturbance, discomfort disturbance and responses chosen to actualize action tendencies, the main purpose of which is often to gain relief from immediate feelings of distress. One example will suffice.

People with drink problems often originally have ego anxiety e.g., 'I must do well and I'm worthless if I don't'. They then experience discomfort anxiety about such ego anxiety e.g., 'I can't stand being so anxious' and thence drink to rid themselves of their anxiety. In the next part of the chain they may have irrational beliefs about their drinking and/or about the results of their drinking — since alcohol often disrupts performance e.g., 'I'm no good for doing so poorly' or 'I must not drink this much'. They then make themselves anxious about this ego anxiety and once again drink to rid themselves of these anxious feelings. It should be apparent then that such people set up and maintain a vicious circle of disturbance, while often simultaneously and paradoxically denying that they have a problem. This process of denial probably accounts for the reluctance often shown by such individuals to seek help for their problems.

Wessler and Wessler (1980) have argued that problems of self-discipline serve three major functions:

(1) *a relief function*, whereby the person either abuses alcohol, food or drugs, or procrastinates to gain relief from immediate emotional disturbance, or to prevent such distress occurring

(2) *a self-protective function*, whereby the person uses her self-defeating behaviour as a protection against possible self-condemnation, e.g., the woman who overeats to make herself unattractive to men thus attributing any rejection to her weight rather than to her inherent worthlessness

(3) *a 'spurious' self-enhancement function* whereby a person engages in self-defeating behaviour in order to obtain something positive that she believes she needs, e.g. the man who gambles compulsively in order to finance his entry into an elite social group to which he aspires, and which he thinks he must join.

To this list we can add a fourth function, what I call a *'positive feeling function'* whereby the person engages in self-defeating behaviour, such as alcohol, drugs, etc., in order to get quick intense positive feelings, or a state of relaxation, rather than to avoid negative feelings such as anxiety.

It is apparent, then, that people with problems of self-discipline adhere to a philosophy of low frustration tolerance (LFT) in that they believe they must get what they want, or must not get what they do not want, quickly and easily. Thus a major feature of rational-emotive counselling with such individuals is to help them to raise their level of frustration tolerance.

Additional Issues

I conclude this chapter by considering briefly some additional issues in understanding clients' problems.

A mixture of emotions

Although I have considered emotional problems separately, it is not uncommon in counselling practice for clients to describe a mixture of emotions. For example, some clients report feeling simultaneously depressed and guilty. In practice it is often helpful to separate these emotions and deal with them one at a time. Also clients sometimes report experiencing 'blended' emotions as in 'hurt anger' or 'jealous anger'. Since, as has been shown, there are various types of anger, it is helpful to determine the nature of the emotional blend for assessment purposes, particularly when clients only refer to 'feeling angry', since the cognitions that underpin 'hurt anger' are somewhat different from those underlying 'jealous anger'.

'False' emotions

It is important to bear in mind that clients may report emotions that they do not, in fact, experience, or emotions that are less important to their actual problems than other feelings that they do not disclose. Clients who report emotions that they do not experience sometimes do so because they think that they are supposed to have these emotions (DiGiuseppe, 1984). Clients who report emotions peripheral to their real concerns do so for similar reasons and, in addition, may feel ashamed about their real emotions e.g. clients who report feeling depressed rather than their true feelings of anger.

As Snyder and Smith (1982) have shown, some clients use emotions for impression management purposes. For example, some clients present with 'false' feelings of depression based on self-devaluation in order to elicit pity from other people or to ward off attack from other people. In the latter instance, such clients are often anxious about being criticized and ward off criticism by seeming to put themselves down before they are put down by others (most people will not criticize those who are already criticizing themselves; indeed others are likely to boost the ego of those who are actively condemning themselves). It is difficult for counsellors to identify clients' 'false' emotions, at least initially. However, they should be alert to their existence, particularly when 'something does not seem to ring true' about clients' accounts of their emotional experiences.

Strength versus rationality of negative emotions

Some counsellors who misinterpret rational-emotive theory consider that strong negative emotions are reliable signs that these emotions are irrational. This is not necessarily the case. Thus one can experience mild anger (irrational emotion) and strong annoyance (rational emotion). Strong rational emotions occur when the person does not get what she strongly prefers, or gets what she strongly prefers not to get. Weak irrational emotions occur when the person demands weakly that she gets what she wants, or that she does not get what she does not want.

The clue to whether an emotion is rational or irrational is whether or not the person demands that her desires are met. Thus, counsellors who try to help clients to reduce the strength of their rational emotions make the unfortunate mistake of encouraging them to deny the strength of their desires.

Having covered the main features of rational-emotive *theory*, I now proceed to discuss the *practice* of rational-emotive counselling with individuals in part two of the book.

PART TWO: PRACTICE

5. Counselling Individuals: Rationale and Relationship

Overview

In this chapter, I begin by outlining the indications and contra-indications for individual counselling. I then consider issues concerning the nature of the relationship between counsellor and client in rational-emotive individual counselling. Here I discuss therapeutic conditions, therapeutic style and the personal qualities of effective rational-emotive counsellors.

Contextual Considerations

Prochaska and Norcross (1983) recently carried out a survey of the practices of 410 psychologists belonging to Division 29 (Psychotherapy) of the American Psychological Association (APA) and reported on a similar survey (Norcross and Prochaska, 1982) on a representative sample of psychologists who are members of APA Division 12 (Clinical Psychology). The findings of these two surveys indicated that members of both Divisions spent most of their therapy time practising individual therapy (65.3% — Division 29 members; 63.5% — Division 12 members). While there is no available data on the distribution of working time of therapists and counsellors of different orientations, there is little reason to suggest that a different pattern would be found among rational-emotive counsellors.

I have argued (Dryden, 1984 b) that there are various sources of influence that impinge upon the counsellor and client as they seek to determine in which modality to work. First, counsellors are influenced by the settings in which they work. Such settings may impose practical limitations on the practice of counselling in modalities other than individual counselling. Alternatively different settings may have different norms of practice which favour one particular modality over others. Counsellors who work in private practice usually find that the exigencies of

59

this mode of work mean that individual counselling constitutes the major part of their work-load. Second, counsellors are influenced by the ways in which they account for their clients' disturbances. Since the rational-emotive model of disturbance emphasizes the role played by the individual's belief system upon his or her psychological problems, this may influence practitioners to work more frequently in the modality of individual counselling than in other modalities. Third, clients' preferences are very salient here and these often exert a considerable influence on the choice of therapeutic modality.

In this regard, Ellis (in Dryden, 1984 b, p. 15) has argued 'I am usually able to go along with the basic desire of any clients who want individual, marital, family or group psychotherapy. It is only in relatively few cases that I talk them into taking a form of therapy they are at first loathe to try'. Information is needed concerning the impact of clients' pre-counselling modality preferences on the working practices of RET counsellors. Given that we do not have any data concerning how RET counsellors distribute their working time among the various counselling modalities, what factors determine such decisions, and who is largely responsible for making these decisions, much of my thinking on the issue of when and when not to undertake individual counselling is determined by clinical experience.

Indications for individual counselling

1   Individual rational-emotive counselling, by its nature provides clients with a situation of complete confidentiality. It is indicated therefore when it is important for clients to be able to disclose themselves in privacy without fear that others may use such information to their detriment. Some clients are particularly anxious concerning how others for example, in a group counselling context, would react to their disclosures, and such anxiety precludes their productive participation in that modality. Similarly, clients who otherwise would not disclose 'secret' material are best suited to individual rational-emotive counselling. As in other situations, transfer to other modalities may be indicated later when such clients are more able and/or willing to disclose themselves to others.

2   Individual counselling, by its dyadic nature, provides an opportunity for a closer relationship to develop between counsellor and client than may exist when other clients are present. This factor may be particularly important for some clients who have not developed close relationships with significant people in their lives and for whom group counselling, for example, may prove initially too threatening.

3 Individual rational-emotive counselling can be conducted to best match the client's pace of learning. Thus, it is particularly suited for clients who, due to their present state of mind, or speed of learning, require their counsellor's full undivided attention. This is especially important for clients who are quite confused and who would only be distracted by the complexity of interactions that can take place in other therapeutic modalities.

4 Individual counselling is particularly indicated when clients' major problems involve their relationship with themselves rather than their relationship with other people.

5 Individual counselling may be indicated for clients who wish to differentiate themselves from others, for example, those who have decided to leave a relationship and wish to deal with individual problems that this may involve. Here, however, some conjoint sessions with the partner may also be helpful, particularly in matters of conciliation (Gurman and Kniskern, 1978).

6 It can be helpful for counsellors to vary their therapeutic style with clients in order to minimize the risk of perpetuating the client's problems by providing an inappropriate interactive style. Individual rational-emotive counselling provides counsellors with an opportunity to vary their interactive styles with clients free from the concern that such variation may adversely effect other clients present.

7 Individual counselling is particularly indicated for clients who have profound difficulties sharing therapeutic time with other clients.

8 Individual counselling may also be indicated for negative reasons. Thus, clients may be seen in individual counselling who may not benefit from working in other modalities. Therefore, clients who may monopolize a counselling group, be too withdrawn within it to benefit from the experience, or who are thought too vulnerable to benefit from family counselling are often seen in individual rational-emotive counselling.

Contraindications for individual counselling

1 Individual counselling is contraindicated for clients who are likely to become overly dependent on the counsellor, particularly when such dependency becomes so intense as to lead to client deterioration. Such clients may be more appropriately helped in group counselling where such intense dependency is less likely to develop due to the fact that the counsellor has to relate to several other people.

2 Individual rational-emotive counselling which does not in general advocate close interpersonal relationships between counsellors and clients,

can still be a close interpersonal encounter for the client and as such is less likely to be indicated for clients who may find such a degree of intimacy or the prospect of such intimacy unduly threatening.

3   Individual counselling may be contraindicated for clients who find this modality too comfortable. Based on the idea that personal change is often best facilitated in situations where there is an optimal level of arousal, individual counselling may not provide enough challenge for such clients. Ravid (1969) found that it may be unproductive to offer individual therapy to clients who have had much previous individual therapy, but still require further therapeutic help.

4   Individual counselling may not be appropriate for clients for whom other modalities are deemed to be more therapeutic. For example, clients who are particularly shy, retiring and afraid to take risks are more likely to benefit from group counselling (if they can be induced to join) than from the less risky situation of individual counselling. Second, partners who can productively use the conjoint situation of couples counselling often benefit more from this modality than from working in individual rational-emotive counselling. This is particularly true when they have largely overcome their disturbed feelings about their unproductive relationship and are dealing with issues devoted to enhancement of relationship satisfaction, a situation which particularly warrants their joint participation.

Other issues

Once counsellors and clients have decided to work in a particular modality it is important to stress that this decision is not irrevocable. Clients may move from modality to modality and thus individual counselling, in this context, can be best viewed as part of a comprehensive treatment strategy. This can occur for both positive and negative reasons. Productive movement to and from individual counselling occurs when clients have made therapeutic gains in one modality, but may benefit further from being transferred to a different one. Negative movement in and out of individual counselling occurs when the clients do not improve in a given therapeutic modality.

While I have provided some indications and contraindications for the practice of individual counselling, I conclude by stressing that the state of the art concerning this issue is far from being well developed and would advise RET counsellors thus: Work with clients in the modality which seems to be most productive for them but regard such decisions as tentative and to a large degree experimental. Perhaps the best way of determining whether a client will benefit or not from individual counselling is in fact to work with them in that modality and to monitor their response to it.

I will next consider aspects of the counselling relationship between clients and counsellors in rational-emotive counselling.

The Counselling Relationship

Rational-emotive counselling is an active-directive form of counselling in that its practitioners are active in directing their clients to identify the philosophical source of their psychological problems, and in showing them they can challenge and change their irrational beliefs. As such, rational-emotive counselling is an educational form of counselling. Ellis has sometimes conceptualized the role of the effective RET counsellor as that of an authoritative (but not authoritarian!) and encouraging teacher who strives to teach his or her clients how to be their own counsellor once formal therapy sessions have ended (Ellis, 1979 c, 1984 b).

Therapeutic conditions

Given the above role, RET counsellors strive to unconditionally accept their clients as fallible human beings who often act self-defeatingly, but who are never essentially bad or good. No matter how badly clients behave in counselling, the RET counsellor attempts to accept them as people but will frequently, if appropriate, let them know his or her reactions to their negative behaviour (Ellis, 1973).

Rational-emotive counsellors strive to be as open as therapeutically feasible and do not hesitate to give highly personal information about themselves should their clients ask for it, except when they judge that clients would use such information against them. RET counsellors often disclose examples from their own lives concerning how they experienced similar problems and more importantly how they have gone about solving these problems. Thus, they strive to be therapeutically genuine in conducting sessions.

RET counsellors tend to be appropriately humorous with most of their clients since they think that much emotional disturbance stems from the fact that clients take themselves and their problems, other people, and the world too seriously and thus strive to model for their clients the therapeutic advantages of taking a serious but humorously ironic attitude to life. They endeavour, however, not to poke fun at the clients themselves but at their self-defeating thoughts, feelings and actions (Ellis, 1977 a, 1977 b, 1981 c). In the same vein, and for similar purposes, RET counsellors tend to be informal and easygoing with most of their clients. However, rational-emotive theory opposes therapists unethically indulging themselves in order to enjoy counselling sessions at their clients' expense (Ellis, 1983 b).

RET counsellors show their clients a special kind of empathy. They not only offer them affective empathy (i.e., communicating that they understand how their clients feel), but also offer them philosophic empathy, i.e., showing them that they understand the philosophies that underlie these feelings.

Thus, with certain modifications, they agree with Rogers' (1957) views concerning counsellor empathy, genuineness and unconditional positive regard. However, rational-emotive counsellors are very wary of showing the vast majority of their clients undue warmth. Rational-emotive theory holds that if rational-emotive counsellors get really close to their clients and give them considerable warmth, attention, caring and support, as well as unconditional acceptance, then these counsellors run two major risks (Ellis, 1977 c, 1982 b).

The first major risk is that counsellors may unwittingly reinforce their clients' dire needs for love and approval — two irrational ideas which are at the core of much human disturbance. When this happens clients appear to improve because their counsellors are indeed giving them what they believe they must have. They begin to 'feel better' but do not necessarily 'get better' (Ellis, 1972). Their 'improvement' is illusory because their irrational philosophies are being reinforced. Since they seem to improve, their counsellors have restricted opportunities to identify these ideas, show them how they relate to their problems and help them challenge and change them. Consequently, while such clients are helped by their counsellors, they are not shown how they can help themselves, and are thus vulnerable to future upset.

The second major risk concerns the fact that counsellors may unwittingly reinforce their clients' philosophy of low frustration tolerance (LFT) — a major form of discomfort disturbance. Clients with LFT problems 'almost always try to seek interminable help from others instead of coping with life's difficulties themselves. Any kind of therapy that does not specifically persuade them to stop their puerile whining, and to accept responsibility for their own happiness, tends to confirm their belief that others *must* help them. Close relationship therapy is frequently the worst offender in this respect and thereby does considerable harm' (Ellis, 1977 c, p. 15).

However, since rational-emotive theory is relative in nature and is against the formulation of absolute, dogmatic therapeutic rules, it does recognize that under certain conditions (e.g. where a client is extremely depressed, accompanied by powerful suicidal ideation), distinct counsellor warmth may be positively indicated for a restricted period of time (Ellis, 1985 d).

Therapeutic style

Ellis (1979 d) recommends that RET counsellors adopt an active-directive style with most clients and a particularly forceful version of that style with some very disturbed and resistant clients. However, not all RET counsellors concur with this view. Some recommend a more passive, gentle approach under specific or most conditions with clients (e.g., Garcia, 1977; Young, 1977). Eschenroeder (1979, p. 5) notes that it is important to ask in rational-emotive counselling 'which therapeutic style is most effective with which kind of client?'. In the same vein, recent proponents of eclectic forms of counselling argue that counsellors would be wise to vary their style of therapeutic interaction to meet the special requirements of individual clients (Beutler, 1983; Lazarus, 1981). While this is a scantily researched area in rational-emotive counselling, it may be best for RET counsellors to avoid an overly friendly, emotionally charged style of interaction with 'hysterical' clients; an overly intellectual style with 'obsessive-compulsive' clients; an overly directive style with clients whose sense of autonomy is easily threatened (Beutler, 1983); and an overly active style with clients who easily retreat into passivity. This line of reasoning fits well with the notion of flexibility which rational-emotive counsellors advocate as a desirable therapeutic quality. Varying one's therapeutic style in rational-emotive counselling does not mean departing from the theoretical principles on which the content of this approach to counselling is based. As Eschenroeder (1979, p. 3) points out, in rational-emotive counselling 'there is no one-to-one relationship between theory and practice'.

Finally, the nature of the relationship between counsellor and client often changes during the course of rational-emotive counselling, particularly with respect to the activity of the counsellor. At the outset the client usually does not have much insight into rational concepts and as such the counsellor usually is quite active in helping the client to understand these concepts. Once the client has understood the concepts and has begun to put these into practice the counsellor is usually less active and strives to remind the client of what she already knows whilst encouraging her to work continually to translate this knowledge into practice. At this later stage, the counsellor is usually less active than at the beginning of the counselling process.

Personal qualities of effective rational-emotive counsellors

Unfortunately, no research studies have been carried out to determine the personal qualities of effective rational-emotive counsellors. Rational-emotive theory, however, does put forward several hypotheses concerning this topic (Ellis, 1978), but it is important to regard these as both tentative and awaiting empirical study.

Since rational-emotive counselling is fairly structured, its effective practitioners are usually comfortable with structure but flexible enough to work in a less structured manner when the situation arises.

Rational-emotive counsellors tend to be intellectually, cognitively or philosophically inclined and become attracted to this approach to counselling because the approach provides them with opportunities to fully express this tendency.

Since rational-emotive counselling is often conducted in a strong active-directive manner, its effective practitioners are usually comfortable operating in this mode. Nevertheless, they have the flexibility to modify their interpersonal style with clients so that they provide the optimum conditions to facilitate client change.

Rational-emotive counselling emphasizes that it is important for clients to put their counselling-derived insights into practice in their everyday lives. As a result, effective rational-emotive practitioners are usually comfortable with behavioural instruction and teaching, and with providing the active prompting that clients often require if they are to follow through on 'homework' assignments.

Effective rational-emotive counsellors tend to have little fear of failure themselves. Their personal worth is not invested in their clients' improvement. They do not need their clients' love and/or approval and are thus not afraid of taking calculated risks if therapeutic impasses occur. They tend to accept both themselves and their clients as fallible human beings and are therefore tolerant of their own mistakes and the irresponsible acts of their clients. They tend to have, or persistently work towards acquiring, a philosophy of high frustration tolerance, and do not get discouraged when clients improve at a slower rate than they desire.

Thus effective rational-emotive practitioners tend to score highly on most of the criteria of positive mental health outlined in chapter 3, and serve as healthy role models for their clients.

Rational-emotive counselling strives to be scientific, empirical, anti-absolutist and undevout in its approach to helping people overcome the obstacles to their goals (Ellis, 1978). Thus its effective practitioners tend to show similar traits and are definitely not mystical, anti-intellectual or magical in their beliefs.

Rational-emotive counselling advocates the use of techniques in a number of different modalities: cognitive, imagery, emotive, behavioural and interpersonal. Its effective practitioners are thus comfortable with a multi-modal approach to treatment and tend not to be people who like to stick rigidly to any one modality.

Finally, Ellis notes that some practitioners of rational-emotive counselling often modify its preferred practice according to their own natural personality characteristics (Ellis, 1978). Thus, for example, some helpers practise rational-emotive counselling in a slow-moving passive manner, do little disputing, and focus counselling on the relationship between them and their clients. Whether such modification of the preferred practice of rational-emotive counselling is effective is a question awaiting systematic empirical enquiry.

In the following three chapters I outline the practice of rational-emotive counselling according to the following sequence: induction and assessment — promoting intellectual insight — promoting emotional insight — termination. For the sake of clarity, I will assume in these chapters that the client is seeking counselling help for one major psychological problem. Then, in chapter 9, I draw upon this sequence and outline the more complex practice of rational-emotive counselling, when the client seeks help for a number of psychological problems.

6.   Beginning Rational-Emotive Counselling

Overview

In this chapter, I deal with the beginnings of the rational-emotive counselling process. I have assumed that counsellors will, at some point during the beginning phase of rational-emotive counselling, assess clients' suitability for this type of counselling and have deemed it to be a suitable mode of helping for them (see *Introduction* for a discussion of this issue). First, I discuss how clients can be inducted into RET counselling. Then I cover the basic elements and sequence of rational-emotive assessment of clients' emotional and behavioural problems. I conclude the chapter by outlining some assessment methods that are particularly vivid in nature.

Inducting Clients into RET Counselling

When clients seek help from rational-emotive counsellors they vary concerning how much they already know about the type of therapeutic process they are likely to encounter. Some may approach the counsellor because they know he or she is a practitioner of RET, while others may know nothing about this method of counselling. In any event many rational-emotive counsellors consider that it is beneficial to explore clients' expectations for counselling at the outset of the process. Duckro, *et al.* (1979) have argued that it is important to distinguish between preferences and anticipations when expectations are assessed. Clients' preferences for counselling concern what kind of experience they want, while anticipations concern what service they think they will receive. Clients who have realistic anticipations for the rational-emotive counselling process and have a preference for this process, in general, require far less induction into rational-emotive counselling than clients who have unrealistic anticipations of the process and/or preferences for a different type of therapeutic experience.

Induction procedures, in general, involve showing clients that rational-emotive counselling is an active-directive structured approach which is orientated to discussion about clients' present and future problems, and which requires clients to play an active role in the change process. Induction can take a number of different forms. First, counsellors may develop and use a number of pre-counselling role induction procedures where a typical course of rational-emotive counselling is outlined and productive client behaviours demonstrated (Macaskill and Macaskill, 1983). Second, counsellors may give a short lecture at the outset of counselling concerning the nature and process of rational-emotive counselling. Third, counsellors may employ induction-related explanations in initial counselling sessions using client problem material to illustrate how these problems may be tackled and to outline the respective roles of client and counsellor in rational-emotive counselling.

Albert Ellis, in his therapeutic practice, tends not to initiate any special induction procedures before he focuses on one of his client's major psychological problems. He is prepared to correct any misconceptions about rational-emotive counselling when it becomes clear, through problem-focused dialogue, that his client holds these. His clientele tend to be relatively psychologically sophisticated and thus may not require elaborate induction into rational-emotive counselling. Howard Young (1984 a), on the other hand, found through his work with lower-class clients of Huntington, West Virginia USA, that specific induction procedures facilitated later problem-focused counselling. His clientele would often demand services outside the scope of rational-emotive counselling and he developed a specific sequence for teaching clients the ground rules of counselling to obviate misunderstanding and future disappointment.

Young's sequence was as follows:

1   *Use a biographical data sheet* on which clients can state (amongst other things) the problems that bring them to counselling. This provides counsellors with a good idea concerning what given clients view as appropriate problems for counselling intervention.

2   *Ask the client what he/she expects from counselling.* This direct approach sometimes reveals startling misconceptions. For example, some of Young's clients gave answers ranging from 'a prescription for nerve pills to the removal of warts'. The replies which clients give to this question often provide clear indications concerning how much induction-orientated education they will require before assessment is initiated. While Young (1984 a) does not distinguish between anticipation- and preference-based expectations, it is often helpful to assess both at this phase of induction.

3   *Offer an example.* When it is clear that the client did require education about the counselling process, Young would offer a concrete example

often derived from work with another client and usually tailored to what he believed his client's own problem might be. Young (1984 a, p. 41) provides the following as an illustration: 'Yesterday, a woman came in to see me because she felt depressed — as if life no longer mattered. It seems all her children are grown, her husband works all the time, and she no longer feels needed. I'm helping her figure out how to cope with the situation'.

4   *Advise the client that counselling is primarily a thinking endeavour.* Young found that teaching his lower-class clients that counselling could help them to 'look at problems in another light' helped to counteract their tendency to want to forget or ignore their problems. At this point, I find it helpful to add that thinking about things differently can often help you not only to feel differently but also to deal with life more constructively, i.e., I emphasize that rational-emotive counselling is not just about thinking, but also about feeling and acting.

5   *Use a client-understood analogy.* Young at this point, would offer an analogy with which his clients could identify to reinforce other explanations about what takes place in counselling. I often tell my clients that going to see a rational-emotive counsellor is like going to see a golf professional, as in the following dialogue:

Counsellor: Imagine that many years ago your uncle taught you how to play golf, but taught you badly. Also imagine that you practised diligently the wrong strokes and only realised later that this way of playing was not helping you to lower your scores. If you wanted to improve your game who would you consult?

Client: A golf coach.

Counsellor: What kind of help would you hope to get from him or her?

Client: Well I would hope he would be able to diagnose my errors, point them out to me and show me how to put these right.

Counsellor: Right. And after he had shown you the correct strokes would that be sufficient for you to improve?

Client: No.

Counsellor: What more would be needed?

Client: I'd have to practise to learn the correct strokes.

Counsellor: Right, in order for them to become second nature you would have to practise. Now coming to see me is like going to see that golf pro. My skills are in helping you to diagnose where you've been going wrong psychologically and how to put this right. But just like a golf pro I can't practise for you. Your major task is putting into practice in your daily life what you learn in counselling. Now that process won't go smoothly, just as it won't in golf, and I'll be on hand to help you through the problems of practising. In doing so you'll begin to learn how to diagnose and correct any future psychological problems you may have. But just like in golf where no one player consistently plays perfect golf, you won't become perfectly free from these problems but you'll be able to deal with them.

It should be stressed that analogies are best tailored to the clients' interests. In this respect, it is often helpful to ask questions on biographical data forms about clients' hobbies and interests so that such specially tailored explanatory analogies can be best grasped by the client.

6   *Help the client understand what counselling cannot provide.* Young used to tell his clients that it is unlikely that counselling will cure all their problems such that they can live happily ever after. He also pointed out that 'sometimes therapy makes it easier to bear the problem that cannot be solved. Sometimes I explain it in terms of therapy helping one choose the lesser of two evils and learning to live with the results. It is important that therapy be explained to lower-class clients in this way, as in many cases the solution to their problems involves choosing between negative alternatives' (Young, 1984 a, p. 41).

Rational-emotive counsellors generally make the distinction between practical problems, e.g., poor housing, financial problems, etc., and psychological problems, e.g., depression, anxiety, procrastination, and stress that rational-emotive counselling aims to help people with their psychological problems. While it may encourage people to take productive steps to improve their housing conditions and financial situation by helping them overcome their psychological problems about such practical problems, it cannot directly alleviate the latter.

Finally, when working with individuals it is helpful to stress that rational-emotive counselling cannot directly change other people who are not involved in the counselling process. However, it can help the client try to influence or persuade others to change, if that is deemed to be productive. For example, one of my clients came to me for help with changing her boss who was sexually harassing her. I first helped her overcome her destructive anger towards him and then we considered the relative merits of her behavioural options, most of which centred on influencing the boss to change. None of the options she tried worked in the desired manner and she decided to leave her job, very pleased with my help. The important point here is that early on in counselling I helped her to distinguish between what she could change (her behaviour) and what she could not change (his behaviour).

The principle here is that as rational-emotive counsellors working with individuals you can only help clients change what is in their power to change — *their* thoughts, feelings and actions. If bad events remain unchanged in their lives clients do have a choice concerning how to view these events. Counsellors under such conditions can help the client be unhappy about such events i.e., by thinking rationally about them and experiencing rational negative emotions rather than miserable about them by thinking irrationally about them and experiencing irrational negative emotions.

In conclusion, as a final point about induction, I have often found it helpful to encourage clients to commit themselves to a 'trial' of rational-emotive counselling of about five sessions so that they can learn directly from experience whether or not this approach to counselling will be helpful to them.

Assessment in Rational-Emotive Counselling

As has been mentioned, some RET counsellors like to have their clients fill in a form which provides basic biographical information as well as information concerning the client's presenting problems. In Figure 1 the biographical information form routinely employed by counsellors at the Institute for RET in New York is presented as a representative example of such forms.

In addition, counsellors at the Institute routinely ask clients to fill out a Personality Data Form (see Figure 2) which provides the counsellor with information concerning the irrational beliefs which are likely to underpin the client's problems. However, the use of this form is designed to supplement rather than to replace a thorough assessment of the client's problems.

Most RET counsellors like to structure the therapeutic process at the outset in order to emphasize that therapy will be problem-focused. For example, such questions as, 'What are you bothered most about?' and 'What is your major problem at this time?' are employed to encourage clients to adopt a problem-solving focus. Indeed Albert Ellis routinely reads aloud the information provided by the client on Item 23 of the biographical information form and asks him or her to start talking about what is most bothersome among this list of problems.

Before proceeding to the assessment stage of counselling the RET practitioner often seeks an agreement with the client concerning the first problem to tackle. When this has been achieved the therapist proceeds to help the client to understand his or her problems according to an ABC framework where: 'A' stands for an activating event or inferences about the activating event; 'B' stands for beliefs about the actual or inferred event; and 'C' stands for the emotional and behavioural consequences of holding the belief at 'B'.

Date _____   Name _____
  mo.   day   yr.   (last)   (first)   (middle)

Consultation Center

Institute for Rational-Emotive Therapy
45 East 65th Street • New York, N. Y. 10021

Biographical Information Form

Instructions To assist us in helping you, please fill out this form as frankly as you can. You will save much time and effort by giving us full information. You can be sure that, like everything you say at the Institute, the facts on this form will be held in the strictest confidence and that no outsider will be permitted to see your case record without your written permission. PLEASE TYPE OR PRINT YOUR ANSWERS.

1. Date of birth: _____ Age: _____ Sex: M_____   F_____
                    mo.   day   yr.

2. Address: _____
              street   city   state   zip

3. Home phone: _____ Business phone: _____

4. Permanent address **(if different from above)** _____

_____

5. Who referred you to the Institute? **(check one)**

   ____(1) self ____(2) school or teacher ____(3) psychologist or psychiatrist ____(4) social agency ____(5) hos-

   pital or clinic ____(6) family doctor ____(7) friend ____(8) relative ____(9) other (explain) _____

   Has this party been here?   ____Yes   ____No

6. Present marital status:

   ____(1) never married ____(2) married now for first time ____(3) married now for second (or more) time

   ____(4) separated ____(5) divorced and not remarried ____(6) widowed and not remarried

   Number of years married to present spouse .... Ages of male children .... Ages of female children ....

7. Years of formal education completed (circle number of years):

   1 2 3 4 5 6 7 8 9 10 11 12 13 14 15 16 17 18 19 20   more than 20

8. How religious are you? **(circle number on scale that best approximates your degree of religiosity):**

   very   average   atheist
   1 2 3 4 5 6 7 8 9

9. Mother's age: _____If deceased, how old were you when she died? _____

10. Father's age: _____If deceased, how old were you when he died? _____

11. If your mother and father separated, how old were you at the time? _____

12. If your mother and father divorced, how old were you at the time? _____

13. Total number of times mother divorced _____   Number of times father divorced _____

14. Number of living brothers _____   Number of living sisters _____

15. Ages of living brothers _____ Ages of living sisters _____

16. I was child number _____ in a family of _____ children.

17. Were you adopted? _____ Yes _____ No

18. What kind of treatment have you previously had for emotional problems?

    _____ hours of individual therapy, spread over _____ years, ending _____ years ago.

19. Hours of group therapy _____ Months of psychiatric hospitalization _____

20. Are you undergoing treatment anywhere else now? _____ Yes _____ No

21. Number of times during past year you have taken antidepressants _____

22. Type of psychotherapy you have mainly had **(briefly describe method of treatment—ex., dream analysis, free association, drugs, hypnosis, etc.)** _____

    _____

23. Briefly list (PRINT) your present main complaints, symptoms, and problems: _____

    _____

    _____

    _____

24. Briefly list any additional **past** complaints, symptoms, and problems: _____

    _____

    _____

25. Under what conditions are your problems worse? _____

    _____

    _____

26. Under what conditions are they improved? _____

    _____

    _____

27. List the things you like to do most, the kinds of things and persons that give you pleasure: _____

    _____

    _____

28. List your main assets and good points: _____

    _____

    _____

29. List your main bad points: _____

_____

_____

_____

30. List your main **social** difficulties: _____

_____

_____

31. List your main **love and sex** difficulties: _____

_____

_____

32. List your main **school or work** difficulties: _____

_____

_____

33. List your main life goals: _____

_____

_____

34. List the things about yourself you would most like to change: _____

_____

_____

35. List your chief physical ailments, diseases, complaints, or handicaps: _____

_____

_____

36. What occupation(s) have you mainly been trained for? _____

    Present occupation _____   _____Full time   _____Part time

37. Spouse's occupation _____   _____Full time   _____Part time

38. Mother's occupation _____   Father's occupation _____

39. Mother's religion _____   Father's religion _____

40. If your mother and father did not raise you when you were young, who did? _____

41. Briefly describe the type of person your mother (or stepmother or person who substituted for your mother) was when you were a child and how you got along with her: _____ _____

_____

_____

42. Briefly describe the type of person your father (or stepfather or father substitute) was when you were a child and how you got along with him: _____

_____

_____

43. If there were unusually disturbing features in your relationship to any of your brothers, briefly describe:_____ ___

_____

_____

44. If there were unusually disturbing features in your relationship to any of your sisters, briefly describe: _____

_____

_____

45. Number of close male relatives who have been seriously emotionally disturbed: _____ Number that have been hospitalized for psychiatric treatment, or have attempted suicide: _____ Number of close female relatives who have been seriously emotionally disturbed: _____ Number that have been hospitalized for psychiatric treatment, or have attempted suicide: _____

46. Additional information that you think might be helpful

_____

_____

_____

_____

_____

_____

_____

_____

_____

_____

Figure 1   Biographical information form.

Institute for Rational - Emotive Therapy

45 East 65th Street   New York, N. Y. 10021

Personality Data Form

Instructions: Read each of the following items and circle after each one the word STRONGLY, MODERATELY or WEAKLY to indicate how much you believe in the statement described in the item. Thus, if you strongly believe that it is awful to make a mistake when people are watching, circle the word STRONGLY in item 1; and if you weakly believe that it is intolerable to be disapproved by others circle the word WEAKLY in item 2. DO NOT SKIP ANY ITEMS. Be as honest as you possibly can be.

Acceptance

1. I believe that it is awful to make a mistake when other people are watching   STRONGLY MODERATELY WEAKLY
2. I believe that it is intolerable to be disapproved of by others   STRONGLY MODERATELY WEAKLY
3. I believe that it is awful for people to know certain undesirable things about
    one's family or one's background   STRONGLY MODERATELY WEAKLY
4. I believe that it is shameful to be looked down upon by people for having less
    than they have   STRONGLY MODERATELY WEAKLY
5. I believe that it is horrible to be the center of attention of others who may be
    highly critical   STRONGLY MODERATELY WEAKLY
6. I believe it is terribly painful when one is criticized by a person one respects   STRONGLY MODERATELY WEAKLY
7. I believe that it is awful to have people disapprove of the way one looks or dresses   STRONGLY MODERATELY WEAKLY
8. I believe that it is very embarrassing if people discover what one really is like   STRONGLY MODERATELY WEAKLY
9. I believe that it is awful to be alone   STRONGLY MODERATELY WEAKLY
10. I believe that it is horrible if one does not have the love or approval of certain
    special people who are important to me   STRONGLY MODERATELY WEAKLY
11. I believe that one must have others on whom one can always depend for help   STRONGLY MODERATELY WEAKLY

Frustration

12. I believe that it is intolerable to have things go along slowly and not be settled
    quickly   STRONGLY MODERATELY WEAKLY
13. I believe that it is too hard to get down to work at things it often would be
    better for one to do   STRONGLY MODERATELY WEAKLY
14. I believe that it is terrible that life is so full of inconveniences and frustrations STRONGLY MODERATELY WEAKLY
15. I believe that people who keep one waiting frequently are pretty worthless
    and deserve to be boycotted   STRONGLY MODERATELY WEAKLY
16. I believe that it is terrible if one lacks desirable traits that other people possess STRONGLY MODERATELY WEAKLY
17. I believe that it is intolerable when other people do not do one's bidding or give
    one what one wants   STRONGLY MODERATELY WEAKLY
18. I believe that some people are unbearably stupid or nasty and that one must get
    them to change   STRONGLY MODERATELY WEAKLY
19. I believe that it is too hard for one to accept serious responsibility   STRONGLY MODERATELY WEAKLY
20. I believe that it is dreadful that one cannot get what one wants without making
    a real effort to get it   STRONGLY MODERATELY WEAKLY
21. I believe that things are too rough in this world and that therefore it is
    legitimate for one to feel sorry for oneself   STRONGLY MODERATELY WEAKLY
22. I believe that it is too hard to persist at many of the things one starts, especially
    when the going gets rough   STRONGLY MODERATELY WEAKLY
23. I believe that it is terrible that life is so unexciting and boring   STRONGLY MODERATELY WEAKLY
24. I believe that it is awful for one to have to discipline oneself   STRONGLY MODERATELY WEAKLY

Injustice

25. I believe that people who do wrong things should suffer strong revenge for
    their acts   STRONGLY MODERATELY WEAKLY
26. I believe that wrong doers and immoral people should be severely condemned   STRONGLY MODERATELY WEAKLY
27. I believe that people who commit unjust acts are bastards and that they should
    be severely punished   STRONGLY MODERATELY WEAKLY

Achievement

28. I believe that it is horrible for one to perform poorly   STRONGLY MODERATELY WEAKLY
29. I believe that it is awful if one fails at important things   STRONGLY MODERATELY WEAKLY
30. I believe that it is terrible for one to make a mistake when one has to
    make important decisions   STRONGLY MODERATELY WEAKLY
31. I believe that it is terrifying for one to take risks or to try new things   STRONGLY MODERATELY WEAKLY

Worth

32.	I believe that some of one's thoughts or actions are unforgivable	STRONGLY MODERATELY WEAKLY	
33.	I believe that if one keeps failing at things one is a pretty worthless person	STRONGLY MODERATELY WEAKLY	
34.	I believe that killing oneself is preferable to a miserable life of failure	STRONGLY MODERATELY WEAKLY	
35.	I believe that things are so ghastly that one cannot help feel like crying much of the time	STRONGLY MODERATELY WEAKLY	
36.	I believe that it is frightfully hard for one to stand up for oneself and not give in too easily to others	STRONGLY MODERATELY WEAKLY	
37.	I believe that when one has shown poor personality traits for a long time, it is hopeless for one to change	STRONGLY MODERATELY WEAKLY	
38.	I believe that if one does not usually see things clearly and act well on them one is hopelessly stupid	STRONGLY MODERATELY WEAKLY	
39.	I believe that it is awful to have no good meaning or purpose in life	STRONGLY MODERATELY WEAKLY	

Control

40.	I believe that one cannot enjoy himself today because of his early life	STRONGLY MODERATELY WEAKLY
41.	I believe that if one kept failing at important things in the past, one must inevitably keep failing in the future	STRONGLY MODERATELY WEAKLY
42.	I believe that once one's parents train one to act and feel in certain ways, there is little one can do to act or feel better	STRONGLY MODERATELY WEAKLY
43.	I believe that strong emotions like anxiety and rage are caused by external conditions and events and that one has little or no control over them	STRONGLY MODERATELY WEAKLY

Certainty

44.	I believe it would be terrible if there were no higher being or purpose on which to rely	STRONGLY MODERATELY WEAKLY
45.	I believe that if one does not keep doing certain things over and over again something bad will happen if I stop	STRONGLY MODERATELY WEAKLY
46.	I believe that things must be in good order for one to be comfortable	STRONGLY MODERATELY WEAKLY

Catastrophizing

47.	I believe that it is awful if one's future is not guaranteed	STRONGLY MODERATELY WEAKLY
48.	I believe that it is frightening that there are no guarantees that accidents and serious illnesses will not occur	STRONGLY MODERATELY WEAKLY
49.	I believe that it is terrifying for one to go to new places or meet a new group of people	STRONGLY MODERATELY WEAKLY
50.	I believe that it is ghastly for one to be faced with the possibility of dying	STRONGLY MODERATELY WEAKLY

Figure 2   Personality data form (Ellis, 1968)
Copyright © 1968 by Institute for Rational-Emotive Therapy.

Assessment: Basic elements

Because RET counselling is strongly cognitive, emotive and behavioural it not only assesses clients' irrational beliefs, but also their irrational feelings and self-defeating behaviours. The usual rational-emotive assessment process almost always includes the following:

Clients are helped to acknowledge and describe their irrational negative feelings — anxiety, depression, damning anger and self-hatred, and these are clearly differentiated from their rational negative feelings — concern, sadness, annoyance (or non-damning anger) and disappointment. In doing so, RET counsellors frequently teach clients the rational-emotive language of emotions and help them to distinguish between rational and irrational negative emotions by helping them to identify and distinguish between rational and irrational beliefs.

Clients are helped to acknowledge and delineate their self-defeating behaviours (e.g., compulsions, addictions, phobias and procrastination) rather than to overemphasize idiosyncratic but non-deleterious behaviours (e.g., unusual devotion to socializing, sex, study, or work).

They are asked to point out specific activating events in their lives that tend to occur just prior to their experienced disturbed feelings and behaviours.

Their rational beliefs that accompany their activating events, and that lead to constructive emotive and behavioural consequences, are assessed and discussed.

Their irrational beliefs that accompany their activating events and that lead to disturbed emotive and behavioural consequences are assessed and discussed.

Their irrational beliefs that involve absolutist musts and grandiose demands on themselves, others, and the universe are particularly determined.

Their second-level irrational beliefs that tend to be derived from their absolutist shoulds and musts — e.g., their 'awfulizing', their 'I can't-stand-it-itis', and their 'damning' of themselves and others — are also revealed.

Their irrational beliefs that lead to their disturbance about their disturbance — e.g., their anxiety about their anxiety and their depression about being depressed — are particularly revealed and discussed.

As these specialized RET assessment and diagnostic procedures are instituted, specific treatment plans are made, normally in close collaboration with the clients, to work first on the most important and self-sabotaging emotional and behavioural symptoms that they present and later on related and possibly less important symptoms. Rational-emotive counsellors, however, always try to maintain an exceptionally open-minded, sceptical, and experimental attitude towards the clients and their problems, so that what at first seems to be their crucial and most debilitating ideas, feelings, and actions may later be seen in a different light and the emphasis may be changed to working on other equally or more pernicious irrationalities that might not be evident during the clients' early sessions.

RET counsellors, in general, spend little time gathering background information on their clients, although they may ask them to fill out forms designed to assess which irrational ideas they spontaneously endorse at the outset of counselling (see Figure 2). Rather, they are likely to ask clients for a description of their major problem(s). As clients describe their problems, RET counsellors intervene fairly early to break these down into their ABC components.

Assessment: Basic sequence

In RET, A and C are normally assessed before B, and are usually assessed in the order that the client reports. When A is assessed, RET counsellors usually encourage clients to provide a representative concrete example of the events, actual or inferred, that they are disturbed about. Clients are encouraged to be as specific as they can about A and not to go into unnecessary detail about the event. Clients sometimes jump from event to event or give unnecessary historical material relating to the event at hand. When this happens the counsellor should preferably interrupt them tactfully and bring them back to the original A, or the A which they now see as most relevant.

C refers to both emotional and behavioural consequences of rational and irrational beliefs made at B. Careful assessment of emotional Cs is advocated in RET since they serve as a major indicator of what type of evaluations are to be found at B. In this regard, it is important to reiterate that 'rational' negative emotions are different from 'irrational' negative emotions (as discussed in Chapter 4). To review: emotions such as sadness, regret, annoyance, and concern are termed 'rational' in RET in that they are deemed to stem from rational, preferential beliefs at B and encourage people to attempt to change, for the better, obnoxious situations at A. The 'irrational' versions of the above emotional states are: depression, guilt, anger and anxiety. These are deemed to stem from irrational, *mus*turbatory beliefs at B, and tend to interfere with people's constructive attempts to change undesirable situations.

When emotional Cs are being assessed, it is important to bear in mind the following points. First, clients do not necessarily use affective terminology in the same way as RET counsellors do (as shown in Chapter 4). It is often helpful to inform them about the nature of the unique discriminations made between 'rational' and 'irrational' negative emotional states, so that counsellor and client can come to use a shared emotional 'language'.

Second, emotional Cs are often chained together. For example, anger is frequently chained to anxiety in that one can experience anger to cover up feelings of inadequacy. And one can feel depressed after a threat to one's self-esteem, — the 'anxiety — depression' chain (Wessler, 1981).

Third, rational-emotive counsellors had better realize that clients do not always want to change every 'irrational' negative emotion as defined by rational-emotive theory, i.e., they may not see a particular 'irrational' emotion such as anger as being truly self-defeating. Thus, a good deal of flexibility and clinical acumen is called for in the assessment of emotional Cs to be targeted for change.

Fourth, clients sometimes find it difficult to admit to themselves and/or to their counsellors that they experience certain emotions. This may be due to their belief that they are not supposed to have such feelings and/or that they are worthless for having them. In other words, such clients have second-order problems about their original feelings. If counsellors suspect that this is the case, they can ask the clients how they would feel if they did experience the emotion in question, thus switching their assessment strategy to the second-order problem.

Fifth, clients often become emotional in counselling sessions and when this happens, counsellors have a good opportunity to assess the clients' beliefs that underpin these expressions of affect as they occur.

Sixth, as mentioned in Chapter 4, emotions can sometimes be blended rather than pure. Thus clients talk about feeling 'hurt anger' or a 'guilty depression'. In such cases counsellors can either treat the blended emotion (e.g., 'hurt anger') as C, or separate it into its component parts — hurt and anger — and deal with each accordingly.

Finally, as I also mentioned in Chapter 4, clients' 'emotional problems' at C can be 'false', i.e., not germane to their real problems. It is difficult to determine this immediately in the assessment process and counsellors are urged to keep this in mind as a possibility and to ask themselves whether such emotions may mask serious problems. For example, one of my clients complained of feeling depressed about her marriage. Assessment proceeded in the normal way, but the client wasn't really involved in the process. I then asked her 'If you didn't feel depressed what would you feel?'. She was taken aback and got quite scared in the session. It transpired that what she called 'depression' was really a numbness that served to protect her from feelings of anxiety about coping on her own.

While I have chosen to highlight the assessment of emotional Cs, similar points can be made about the assessment of behavioural Cs. As noted earlier, withdrawal, procrastination, alcoholism, and substance abuse are generally regarded as dysfunctional behaviours and related to irrational beliefs at B (Ellis, 1982 a). Counsellors can thus regard such behaviours as 'Cs' in their own right and thence proceed to an assessment of irrational beliefs at B that underpin them. Another strategy that is often helpful is to remember that such behaviour can be purposive (see Chapter 2) and may serve to prevent clients from an emotional experience, such as anxiety or encourage clients to obtain an emotional experience (e.g., pleasant sensations associated with being 'stoned'). Taking the example of procrastination, which often serves to protect clients from an emotional experience, it is fruitful to view such behaviour as the actualization of an action tendency (see Chapter 2). The client might be taught about action tendencies, and the feelings that occasion them, and be asked to reflect on what possible feelings might have promoted such behaviour. Also the client might be shown that such behaviour is only one of a number of response options available to her in the given situation that she describes. Enquiries might then be directed towards possible emotional Cs that might be experienced if a more productive response option were chosen. Thus the counsellor might say, 'If you decided to sit down to work on that essay rather than deciding to procrastinate what might you have felt?'.

When B is assessed, some rational-emotive counsellors prefer to assess fully the client's inferences in search of the most relevant inference which is linked to the client's irrational beliefs, given that C is self-defeating. This is known as *inference chaining* (Moore, 1983). An example of this procedure is described below:

Counsellor: So what was your major feeling here?

Client: I guess I was angry.

Counsellor: Angry about what? (here the counsellor has obtained C and is probing for A).

Client: I was angry that he did not send me a birthday card (client provides inference about A).

Counsellor: And what was anger-provoking about that? (Probing to see whether this is the most relevant inference in the chain).

Client: Well . . . he promised me he would remember (Inference 2).

Counsellor: And because he broke his promise? (Probing for relevance of Inference 2).

Client: I felt that he didn't care enough about me (Inference 3).

Counsellor: But let's assume that for a moment. What would be distressing about that? (Probing for relevance of Inference 3).

Client: Well, he might leave me? (Inference 4).

Counsellor: And if he did? (Probing for relevance of Inference 4).

Client: I'd be left alone (Inference 5).

Counsellor: And if you were alone? (Probing for relevance of Inference 5).

Client: I couldn't stand that (Irrational Belief).

Counsellor: OK, so let's back up a minute. What would be most distressing for you, the birthday card incident, the broken promise, the fact that he doesn't care, being left by your husband, or being alone? (Counsellor checks to see which inference is most relevant in the chain).

Client: Definitely being alone.

This example shows that not only are inferences chained together but, as mentioned earlier, emotions are too. Here anger was chained with anxiety about being alone. While this rational-emotive counsellor chose then to dispute the client's irrational belief underlying her anxiety he still has to deal with her anger-creating belief. Other rational-emotive counsellors may have chosen to take the first element in the chain (anger about the missing birthday card) and disputed the irrational belief related to anger. Skillful RET counsellors do succeed in discovering the hidden issues underlying the 'presenting problem' during the disputing process. It is important for RET counsellors to assess correctly *all* relevant issues related to a presenting problem. How they do this depends upon personal style and how particular clients react to different assessment procedures.

The above example also shows that for the purposes of getting to B the client is urged to assume that her inferences are correct for the time being. In other dialogues clients are urged to assume the worst about their inferences so that again B can properly be assessed.

Thus, with a client who is scared to fly in an aeroplane because she assumes it might crash, the rational-emotive counsellor would not initially discuss with the client the probabilities of this ever occurring, but would rather encourage the client to assume, for the moment, that this would occur. This leaves the way open for the client to express irrational beliefs about this eventuality or to express further inferences that might be more relevant to her anxiety. In this case, the client was scared not about flying but about surviving a crash as a paraplegic!

After the counsellor has assessed adequately the irrational C and the A, he can then begin to assess B. This is frequently done by asking such questions as: 'What were you telling yourself to make yourself angry?'; 'What did that experience mean to you?'; or even 'What *must* were you telling yourself about the possibility of failure?'. The important point here is for counsellors to employ a variety of questions to elicit clients' irrational beliefs rather than repeating questions which have not yielded statements of irrational beliefs.

In Chapter 3, I mentioned that irrational beliefs occur in the form of a premise, e.g., 'I *must* pass my exam' and a derivative, e.g., 'I'm no good if I fail my exam'. The premise of irrational beliefs occurs in the form of absolute 'musts', shoulds', 'have-to's', etc.; while irrational derivatives may represent examples of 'awfulizing', 'I can't-stand-it-itis' or 'damnation'. When assessing irrational beliefs, I find it helpful, if possible, to assess both the premise and associated derivatives. While Ellis seems to prefer to target 'musts' as a priority for assessing irrational beliefs, he sometimes switches to an assessment of irrational derivatives when 'must assessment' is not productive.

When irrational beliefs are assessed clients are helped to see the link between these irrational beliefs and their 'irrational' affective and behavioural consequences at C. Some rational-emotive counsellors like to give a short lecture at this point on the role of the 'musts' in emotional disturbance, and how they can be distinguished from 'preference'. Ellis, for example, often uses the following teaching dialogue:

Ellis: Imagine that you prefer to have a minimum of £11 in your pocket at all times and you discover you only have £10. How will you feel?

Client: Frustrated.

Ellis: Right. Or you'd feel concerned or sad, but you wouldn't kill yourself. Right?

Client: Right.

Ellis: OK. Now this time imagine that you absolutely *have to* have a minimum of £11 in your pocket at all times. You must have it, it is a necessity. You *must*, you *must*, you *must*, have a minimum of £11, and again you look and you find you only have £10. How will you feel?

Client: Very anxious.

Ellis: Right — or depressed. Right. Now remember it's the same £11 but a different belief. OK, now this time you still have that same belief. You *have to* have a minimum of £11 at all times, you *must*. It's absolutely *essential*. But this time you look in your pocket and find that you've got £12. How will you feel?

Client: Relieved, content.

Ellis: Right. But with that same belief — you *have to* have a minimum of £11 at all times — something will soon occur to you to scare you shitless. What do you think that would be?

Client: What if I lose £2?

Ellis: Right. What if I lose £2, what if I spend £2, what if I get robbed? That's right. Now the moral of this model — which applies to all humans, rich or poor, black or white, male or female, young or old, in the past or in the future, assuming that humans are still human — is: People make themselves miserable if they don't get what they think they must, but they are also panicked when they do — because of the must. For even if they have what they think they must, they could always lose it.

Client: So I have no chance to be happy when I don't have what I think I must — and little chance of remaining unanxious when I do have it?

Ellis: Right! Your *mus*turbation will get you nowhere — except
                  depressed or panicked!

I have stressed that an important goal of the assessment stage is to help clients
distinguish between their primary problems (e.g., depression, anxiety, withdrawal,
addiction) and their secondary problems, that is their problems about their primary
problems (e.g., depression about depression, anxiety about anxiety, shame about
withdrawal, and guilt about addiction). Rational-emotive counsellors often assess
secondary problems before primary problems because these often require prior
therapeutic attention — since, for example, clients frequently find it difficult to
focus on their original problem of anxiety when, for example, they are severely
blaming themselves for being anxious. Secondary problems are assessed in the same
manner as primary problems. If such second-order problems are identified it is
important for the counsellor to help the client to understand why such problems
are assessed and targeted for change *before* the client's primary problems. For
example, a client may be shown that if she is guilty about her anger, she will be less
successful at working on and overcoming her anger problem while she is guilty
about it. However, there are occasions when clients will not accept this rationale
despite the counsellor's explanations. A guiding rule under these conditions is for
the counsellor to work at a level that the client will accept.

Three other points relevant to the assessment stage of RET bear mention. First,
the counsellors had better be alert to problems in *both* areas of disturbance, i.e., ego
and discomfort disturbance. In particular, ego and discomfort disturbance often
interact and careful assessment is required to disentangle one from the other.
Second, RET counsellors pay particular attention to other ways that humans
perpetuate their psychological problems and attempt to assess these carefully in
counselling. Thus, humans often seek to defend themselves from threats to their
'ego' and sense of comfort. Counsellors are often aware that much dysfunctional
behaviour is defensive and help their clients to identify the irrational beliefs that
underlie such defensive dysfunctional behaviour. In addition, psychological
problems are sometimes perpetuated because the person defines their consequences
as payoffs. These payoffs also require careful assessment if productive therapeutic
strategies are to be implemented. Finally, during the assessment process, the
counsellors are also concerned to correct any misconceptions that the clients may
have about the therapeutic enterprise. As in induction procedures, counsellors
endeavour to show their clients that RET counselling is a form of help that is
problem-focused and educational in nature, and that counsellors will often adopt
an active and directive approach. Counsellors also encourage clients to see that
their initial task is to learn to focus on the cognitive determinants of their problems
and, in particular, to learn to search for absolute musts and their derivatives when
they are disturbed at C.

Vivid Assessment Methods

Effective rational-emotive counselling depends initially on the counsellor gaining a clear understanding of the client's problems in cognitive, emotional and behavioural terms, and the contexts in which the client's problems occur. To a great extent the counsellor is dependent on the client's verbal reports to help him gain such an understanding. It is in this area that many obstacles to progress may appear. Some clients have great difficulty identifying and/or accurately labelling their emotional experiences. Other clients are in touch with, and able to report their emotions, but find it hard to relate these to activating events, either external or internal. Yet a further group of clients is easily able to report problematic activating events and emotional experiences but has difficulty seeing how these may relate to mediating cognitions. Vivid methods, i.e., those which are rich, stimulating and arousing can be used in a variety of ways to overcome such obstacles to a valid and reliable assessment of client problems.

Vividness in portraying activating events

With some clients traditional assessment procedures through verbal dialogue do not always yield the desired information. When this occurs, rational-emotive counsellors often use imagery methods. They ask clients to conjure up evocative images of activating events. Such evocative imagery often stimulates the client's memory concerning his or her emotional reactions or indeed in some instances leads to the re-experiencing of these reactions in the session. While focusing on such images, the client can also begin to gain access to cognitive processes below the level of awareness that cannot be easily reached through verbal dialogue.

One particularly effective use of imagery in the assessment of client problems is that of bringing future events into the present. This is illustrated by the following exchange between myself and a client who was terrified that her mother might die, which led her to be extremely unassertive with the mother.

Counsellor: So you feel you just can't speak up to her. Because if you did, what might happen?

Client: Well, she might have a fit.

Counsellor: And what might happen if she did?

Client: She might have a heart attack and die.

Counsellor: Well, we know that she is a fit woman, but let's go along with your fear for the moment. Okay?

Client:	Okay.
Counsellor:	What if she did die?
Client:	I just can't think . . . I . . . . I'm sorry.
Counsellor:	That's okay. I know this is difficult, but I really think it would be helpful if we could get to the bottom of things. Okay? (Client nods). Look, Marjorie, I want you to imagine that your mother has just died this morning. Can you imagine that? (Client nods and begins to shake). What are you experiencing?
Client:	When you said my mother was dead I began to feel all alone . . . like there was no one to care for me . . . no one I could turn to.
Counsellor:	And if there is no one who cares for you, no one you can turn to?
Client:	Oh God! I know I couldn't cope on my own.

Instructing clients to vividly imagine something that has been warded off often leads to anxiety itself. It is important to process this anxiety as it is sometimes related to the client's central problem. Issues like fear of loss of control, phreno-phobia (fear of going mad) and extreme discomfort anxiety are often revealed when this anxiety is fully assessed. However, some clients do find it difficult to spontaneously imagine events and require counsellor assistance.

While imagery methods are now routinely used in cognitive-behavioural counselling (e.g., Lazarus, 1984), there has been little written on how counsellors can stimulate clients' imagery processes. I have used a number of vivid methods to try and help clients utilize their potential for imagining events.

Vivid, connotative counsellor language

One effective way of helping clients to use their imagery potential is for the counsellor to use rich, colourful and evocative language while aiding clients to set the scene. Unless the counsellor has gained prior diagnostic information, he or she is sometimes uncertain about which stimuli in the activating event are particularly related to the client's problem. Thus, it is best to give clients many alternatives. For example, with a socially anxious client I proceeded thus after attempting to get him to use his own potential for imagery without success.

Counsellor: So at the moment we are unclear about what you are anxious about. What I'd like to suggest is that we use your imagination to help us. I will help you set the scene based on what we have already discussed. However, since we have yet to discover detailed factors, some of the things I say might not be relevant. Will you bear with me and let me know when what I say touches a nerve in you?

Client: Okay.

Counsellor: Fine. Just close your eyes and imagine you are about to walk into the dance. You walk in and some of the guys there glance at you. You can see the smirks on their mocking faces and one of them blows you a kiss. (Here I am testing out a hypothesis based on previously gained information). You start to *seethe* inside and . . .

Client: Okay, when you said I was starting to seethe, that struck a chord. I thought I can't let them get away with that, but if I let go I'll just go berserk. I started feeling anxious.

Counsellor: And if you went berserk?

Client: I couldn't show my face in there again.

Counsellor: What would happen then?

Client: I don't know I . . . . It's funny — the way I see it I would never go out again.

Here I was using words like 'smirks', 'mocking', 'blows' and 'seethe' deliberately· in my attempt to stimulate the client's imagination. It is also important for the counsellor to vary his or her tone so that this matches the language employed.

Photographs

I have at times asked clients to bring to interviews photographs of significant others or significant places. These are kept on hand to be used at relevant moments in the assessment process. I have found the use of photographs particularly helpful when the client is discussing an event in the past that is still bothering him or her. Thus, for example, one client who spoke without feeling about being rejected by his father who died seven years hence, broke down in tears when I asked him to look at a picture of him and his father standing apart from one another. Feelings of hurt and anger, with their associated cognitions were expressed, which enabled us to move on to the disputing stage.

Other mementoes

In a similar vein, I have sometimes asked clients to bring in mementoes to counselling sessions. These may include pictures they have drawn, paintings that have meaning for them and poems either written by themselves or by other people. The important point is that these mementoes are to be related to issues that the client is working on in counselling. A roadblock to assessment was successfully overcome with one client when I asked her to bring in a memento that reminded her of her mother. She brought in a bottle of perfume that her mother was accustomed to wearing. When I asked her to smell the perfume at a point in counselling when the assessment process, through verbal dialogue, was again breaking down, the client was helped to identify feelings of jealousy toward her mother, which she experienced whenever her mother left her to go out socializing. Moreover, my client was ashamed of such feelings. This issue was centrally related to her presenting problem of depression.

Another of my clients was depressed about losing her boyfriend. I had great difficulty helping her to identify any related mediating cognitions through traditional assessment procedures. Several tentative guesses on my part also failed to pinpoint relevant cognitive processes. I then asked her to bring to our next session anything that reminded her of her ex-boyfriend. She brought in a record of a popular song that had become known to them as 'our song'. When I played the song at an appropriate point in the interview, my client began to sob and expressed feelings of abandonment, hurt and fear for the future. Again a vivid method had unearthed important assessment material where traditional methods had failed.

It should be noted from the above examples that quite often such dramatic methods lead to the expression of strong affective reactions in the session. This is often an important part of the process because such affective reactions are gateways to the identification of maladaptive cognitive processes that are difficult to identify through more traditional methods of assessment.

The empty chair technique

I see rational-emotive counselling as an example of theoretically-consistent eclecticism whereby techniques are borrowed from other counselling approaches for purposes consistent with rational-emotive theory. Thus, I have sometimes used the empty chair technique, popularised by Gestalt therapists. For example, traditional assessment methods did not reveal important clinical material with one of my clients who suffered from tension headaches after visiting her mother. I thus encouraged her to imagine that her mother was sitting in an empty chair which I placed before her and encouraged her to disclose her feelings to her mother. An example follows:

Client: I feel numb when I'm in your presence . . .

Counsellor: Now sit in the empty chair and talk as your mother to yourself.

Client (as Mother):You're such a child. You've got no backbone. Never have.

Counsellor: Now reply to her from your chair.

Client: Damn it. You're always criticizing me. I hate you.

This technique demonstrates that the client felt angry with her mother. This discovery led to a discussion about her being scared to express negative feelings towards her mother in case her mother disowned her completely.

The 'Interpersonal nightmare technique'

This technique may be best used with clients who are able to identify only sketchily an anticipated 'dreaded' event involving other people, but are neither able to specify in any detail the nature of the event, nor how they would react if the event were to occur. First the client is given a homework assignment to imagine the 'dreaded' event. He or she is told to write a brief segment of a play about it, specifying the exact words that the protagonists would use. The client is encouraged to give full rein to imagination while focusing on what he or she fears might happen. One example will suffice. The following scenario was developed by a fifty-five year old woman with alcohol problems who was terrified of making errors at the office where she worked as a typist.

Scene: Boss's office where he sits behind a very large desk. He has found out that one of the typists has inadvertently filed a letter wrongly and sends for her. She comes in and is made to stand in front of the boss.

Boss: Have you anything to say in this matter?

Typist (me): Only that I apologize and will be more careful in the future.

Boss: What do you mean by saying you will be more careful in the future — what makes you think you have a future? (At this point he starts banging on the desk). I have never yet met anyone less competent or less suited to the job than you are. You mark my words, I will make life so uncomfortable for you that you will leave. When I took over this job I intended to have the people I wanted working for me and you are not on that list. I have already got rid of two typists, and I shall see that you are the third. Now get out of my office you stupid, blundering fool and remember I shall always be watching you and you will never know when I shall be behind you.

I then read over the scene with the client, making inquiries about the tone in which she thought her boss would make these statements and asking her to identify which words the boss would emphasize. I then arranged for a local actor who was the same age as the boss to enact realistically the scene on cassette. In the next session I instructed my client to visualize the room in which the encounter might take place. She briefly described the room, paying particular attention to where her boss would be sitting and where she would be standing. I then played her the cassette, which evoked strong feelings of fear of being physically harmed and humiliated. Again important data had been collected which traditional assessment procedures had failed to uncover.

Rational-emotive problem solving

Knaus and Wessler (1976) have described a method which they call rational-emotive problem solving (REPS). This method involves the counsellor creating conditions in the counselling session that approximate those the client encounters in his or her everyday life and which give rise to emotional problems. Knaus and Wessler contend that this method may be used either in a planned or impromptu fashion and is particularly valuable when clients experience difficulty in identifying emotional experiences and related cognitive processes through verbal dialogue with their counsellors. I employed this method with a male client who reported difficulty in acting assertively in his life, and claimed not to be able to identify the emotions and thoughts that inhibited the expression of assertive responses. During our discussion I began to search around for my pouch of pipe tobacco. Finding it empty, I interrupted my client and asked him if he would drive to town, purchase my favourite tobacco, adding that if he hurried he could return for the last five minutes of our interview. He immediately got up, took my money and walked out of my office towards his car. I rushed after him, brought him back into my office and together we processed his reactions to this simulated experience!

It is clear that this technique must be used with therapeutic judgment and that its use may threaten or even destroy the therapeutic alliance between client and counsellor. However, since rational-emotive counsellors value risk-taking they are often prepared to use such techniques when more traditional and less risky methods have failed to bring about therapeutic improvement. It is further important as Beck *et al.* (1979) have stressed, for the counsellor to ask the client for the latter's honest reactions to this procedure, to ascertain whether it may have future therapeutic value for the client. When a client indicates that he or she has found the rational-emotive problem-solving method unhelpful, the counsellor had better then explain the rationale for attempting such a procedure, and disclose that he or she intended no harm, but was attempting to be helpful. Normally clients respect such disclosures and in fact the counsellor, in doing so, provides a useful model for the client: namely that it is possible to non-defensively acknowledge errors without damning oneself. However, with this method, it is apparent that counsellors cannot realistically disclose their rationale in advance of initiating the method, since this would detract from its potential therapeutic value.

Paradoxical counsellor actions

This method is often best used when clients, through their actions, communicate messages about themselves based on irrational beliefs to the counsellor. For example, I once saw a female client who experienced a lot of rheumatic pain but had an attitude of low frustration tolerance toward it. Her behaviour toward me in sessions indicated the attitude: 'I am a poor soul, feel sorry for me'. This prompted me to adopt an overly sympathetic and diligent stance toward her. Thus, at the beginning of every session I treated her as if she could hardly walk and escorted her by arm to her chair and made frequent enquiries about her comfort. This eventually prompted her to make statements like: 'Don't treat me like a child', 'I can cope', 'It's not as bad as all that', etc. I then helped her to identify some of her implicit irrational messages. Whenever she began to lapse back into her self-pitying attitude, I began to behave in an overly solicitous manner again, which provided a timely reminder for her to attend to the behavioural components of her philosophy of low frustration tolerance, and then to the philosophy itself.

Using the counsellor-client relationship

Wessler (1984) has written that it is important for the rational-emotive counsellor to inquire about the nature of his client's reactions to him or her, that is, to examine some of the client's here-and-now beliefs. Little has been written about this approach in the rational-emotive literature, and thus relatively little is known about its potential as a framework for identifying irrational beliefs. Wessler (1984) also advocates that counsellors give clients frank feedback about the clients' impact on them and to explore whether clients have a similar impact on other people. Such generalizations must of course be made with caution, but such discussion is often a stimulus for clients to become more sensitive to their impact on other people and often leads them to ask other people about their interpersonal impact (Anchin and Kiesler, 1982).

The advantage of using the counsellor-client relationship in this way is that it provides both parties with an opportunity to process the client's beliefs in an immediate and often vivid fashion. For example, one of my clients who complained of loneliness had the habit of putting his feet up on my coffee table. I did not mention this at first, but later on, when I became irritated by his behaviour, I disclosed that I was annoyed by it and wondered if other people had similar reactions to him. I suggested that he get some feedback from other people. He did so and reported that other people reported the same reactions as my own. This led to a discussion concerning his implicit beliefs that underpinned such soundly aversive behaviour and we identified the following irrational belief: 'I must be able to do what I want in social affairs without being criticized'. This belief helped to explain why this client had no friends.

Dreams

Although Albert Ellis has recently written a regular column for Penthouse magazine, providing rational-emotive interpretations of readers' dreams, rational-emotive counsellors are not generally noted for using dream material. However, there is no good reason why dream material cannot be used in rational-emotive counselling as long as it does not predominate in the therapeutic process and the counsellor has a definite purpose in mind in using it.

Freeman (1981, pp. 228–229) has outlined a number of further guidelines for the use of dreams for assessment purposes:

1   The dream needs to be understood in thematic rather than symbolic terms.

2   The thematic content of the dream is idiosyncratic to the dreamer and must be viewed within the context of the dreamer's life.

3   The specific language and imagery are important to the meaning.

4   The affective responses to the dreams can be seen as similar to the dreamer's affective responses in waking situations.

5 The particular length of the dream is of lesser import than the content.

6 The dream is a product of and the responsibility of the dreamer.

7 Dreams can be used when the patient appears stuck in counselling.

I inadvertently stumbled on the usefulness of dream material for assessment purposes when working with a twenty-eight year old depressed student who would frequently reiterate: 'I'm depressed and I don't know why'. I had virtually exhausted all the assessment methods I knew, including those described in this chapter, to help her identify depressogenic thoughts in situations where she experienced depression, but without success. In a desperate last attempt, I asked her if she could remember any of her dreams, not expecting in the least that this line of inquiry would prove fruitful. To my surprise she said yes, she did have a recurring dream. In this dream she saw herself walking alone along a river bank, and when she peered into the river, she saw a reflection of herself as a very old woman. This image filled her with extreme sadness and depression. On further discussion she said that she believed that this dream meant that she had no prospect of finding any happiness in her life, either in love relationships or in her career, and that she was doomed to spend her years alone, ending up as a sad, pathetic, old woman. This account of the dream and subsequent discussion of its meaning enabled me to help her identify a number of irrational beliefs which provided the focus for subsequent cognitive restructuring.

Daydreams may also provide important material for assessment purposes. For some people, particular daydreams occur in response to and as compensation for a negative activating event. Thus, one client reported having the daydream of establishing a multinational corporation after failing to sell insurance to prospective customers. The use of such daydreams by clients may not necessarily be dysfunctional, but may impede them, as in the above example, from getting to the core of their problems. Often daydreams are an expression of our hopes and aspirations, and I have found it valuable to ask clients not only about the content of such material but also what would stop them from actualizing their goals. Much important assessment material is gathered in this manner, in particular concerning ideas of low frustration tolerance.

In vivo counselling sessions

Sacco (1981) has outlined the value of conducting counselling sessions in real-life settings in which clients experience emotional difficulties. I have found moving outside the interview room to such settings particularly useful in gaining assessment material when traditional methods have failed to provide such data. For example, I once saw a male student who complained of avoiding social situations.

He did so in case others would see his hands tremble. Traditional assessment methods yielded no further useful data. To overcome this treatment impasse, I suggested to him that we needed to collect more data and we eventually conducted a counselling session in a coffee shop where I asked him to go and get us both a cup of coffee. He refused because he feared that his hands might tremble, but I firmly persisted with my request. He was able to identify a stream of negative cognitions on the way from our table to the service counter. He returned without our coffees but with valuable information, which we processed later in my office. It is important for counsellors to explain their rationale for conducting *in vivo* sessions in advance in order to gain client co-operation. In addition, obtaining clients' reactions to these sessions is often helpful particularly if *in vivo* sessions are planned for use later in the therapeutic process.

Some cautions about the use of vivid methods in rational-emotive counselling

In this chapter I have introduced the concept of using vivid methods in rational-emotive counselling and will reintroduce the concept in the chapters on 'Promoting Intellectual Insight' and 'Promoting Emotional Rational Insight'. However, I wish at this stage to outline some caution about using such methods in rational-emotive counselling:

> It is important for counsellors to determine the impact on clients of introducing vivid methods into the therapeutic process. Thus, using the guidelines of Beck *et al.* (1979) it is perhaps wise for the counsellor to ask the client at various points to give frank feedback concerning the methods and activities used. While the counsellor may not always agree not to use such techniques just because a client has a negative reaction to them, we had better obtain and understand our clients' negative reactions to our procedures.

> It is important in the use of vivid-dramatic techniques not to overload the client. One vivid and dramatic method carefully introduced into a counselling session at an appropriate time is much more likely to be effective than several dramatic methods employed indiscriminately in a session.

> It is also important that rational-emotive counsellors be clear about the rationale for using vivid methods and not see the use of such methods as a goal in itself. The important thing to remember is that vivid methods are to be used as a vehicle for promoting client attitude change and not to make the therapeutic process more stimulating for the counsellor. It is also extremely important to ascertain what the client has learned from the vivid methods the counsellor has employed. The client will not magically

come to the conclusion the counsellor wants him or her to. It is also important that counsellors do not promote 'false' change in their clients. Change is 'false' when the client feels better as a result of some of these vivid methods but does not get better. Ellis (1972) has written an important article on such a distinction. Thus, counsellors should invariably ask questions like: 'What have you learned from doing this vivid method?' and 'How can you strengthen this learning experience for yourself outside of counselling?'.

Dramatic and vivid methods are not appropriate for all clients. They are particularly helpful for those clients who use intellectualization as a defence and/or who use verbal dialogue to tie rational-emotive counsellors in knots. While there is no data at the moment to support the following hypothesis, I would speculate that dramatic and vivid methods had better not be used with clients who have overly dramatic and hysterical personalities. It is perhaps more appropriate to assist such clients to reflect in a calm and undramatic manner on their experiences than to over-stimulate an already highly stimulated personality.

With these words of caution, I leave the issue of assessment and consider the issue of 'promoting intellectual rational insight' in the following chapter.

7. Promoting Intellectual Rational Insight

Overview

In this chapter, I deal with issues concerning the promotion of intellectual rational insight. First, I distinguish between two forms of rational insight: intellectual and emotional. Then I cover standard and vivid methods of disputing irrational beliefs (premises and derivatives) which are designed to help clients achieve intellectual insight. I conclude the chapter by discussing various homework aids that clients can use to facilitate this process.

Rational Insight: Intellectual and Emotional

Once the client can see clearly and agree that her emotional or behavioural problem C is based on an irrational belief B and in order to get over her problem at C, she needs to change her irrational belief at B, then the therapeutic stage is set for the counsellor to help the client to change this belief. The counsellor tries to effect this change by disputing the client's belief, i.e., asking for evidence to support or refute it. The major goal of the disputing process at this stage of counselling is to help the client understand and acknowledge that there is no evidence that exists to support her irrational belief but that there *is* evidence to support its rational equivalent. When the client can acknowledge this, i.e., see that it is true, then it is assumed that she has achieved intellectual rational insight, which is defined here as 'weak and occasional conviction that an irrational belief is false and a rational belief is true'. Here the rational belief is lightly and occasionally held. Intellectual rational insight, in general, does not lead to significant emotional and behavioural change. In this chapter I describe rational-emotive techniques designed to help clients achieve intellectual rational insight.

Intellectual rational insight is distinguished from emotional rational insight, which is defined here as 'strong and frequent conviction that an irrational belief is false and a rational belief is true'. Here the rational belief is strongly and frequently held. Emotional rational insight does often lead to significant emotional and behavioural change. In the next chapter I consider rational-emotive techniques designed to help clients move from intellectual to emotional rational insight. At this point, it should be noted that intellectual rational insight very frequently precedes emotional rational insight. It is extremely rare for a client to relinquish an irrational belief and immediately believe in its rational alternative with such conviction that she will be able to act on it straight away.

Disputing Irrational Beliefs

When disputing irrational beliefs, rational-emotive counsellors attempt to engage their clients in a socratic dialogue. This involves asking clients questions about the validity of their irrational beliefs, helping them to see why their wrong answers are incorrect, and then asking again for evidence supporting the validity of the same irrational belief. This process is continued until the client can acknowledge that there exists no evidence in favour of the irrational belief, but that evidence does exist in favour of the rational belief. In other words the process continues until the client achieves intellectual rational insight.

Debating and discriminating

Disputing involves two major activities: debating and discriminating (Phadke, 1982). Debating consists of the counsellor asking a variety of questions designed to help the client examine the validity of her irrational belief. Questions that are frequently employed include: 'Where is the evidence that . . .?'; 'Where is the law of the universe that . . .?'; 'Where is the proof that . . .?'; 'How does it follow that . . .?'. Discriminating involves the counsellor helping the client to distinguish clearly between her rational belief (want, preference, desire, etc.) and her irrational belief (must, absolute should, have-to, etc.). These two activities are frequently used in concert as the counsellor strives to teach the client the differences between rational and irrational beliefs, and that there exists no evidence in favour of irrational beliefs. An example of this process follows:

> *Counsellor:* So can you see that your anxiety is based on your belief that you must achieve, in the academic arena anyway, whatever you set your sights on.

Client: Yes.

Counsellor: So if you want to get over your anxiety what would it be advisable for you to change?

Client: That belief.

Counsellor: Right. So now I'm going to ask you some questions to help you assess the validity of that belief. Why *must* you achieve whatever you set your sights on? (Debating intervention).

Client: Because its important to me to do so.

Counsellor: No, that's why it's desirable. Note that I didn't ask you the question why is it desirable for you to achieve your academic goals but why do you absolutely have to do so. Can you see the difference between your belief 'I want to achieve my academic goals' and your belief 'I must achieve my academic goals'? (Discriminating intervention).

Client: Not really.

Counsellor: Well, the belief 'I want to achieve my academic goals' is relative. It allows for the possibility that you won't achieve them. That belief, if fully stated, is really: 'I want to achieve my goals, but there is no law in the universe which states that I absolutely have to'. Whereas the belief 'I absolutely have to achieve my goals' is an absolute one. If that belief were true there would be no way for you to fail. That's the difference. Do you see that?

Client: Yes I do.

Counsellor: Fine, but I want to be sure that I've made myself clear. Can you put into your own words the differences between the two beliefs?

Client: Well, my belief 'I want to achieve my goals' is an expression of what's important to me, but doesn't mean that I necessarily will achieve them. The belief 'I must achieve my goals' means that no matter what I will achieve them.

Counsellor: That's right. Now let me ask you again. Where's the evidence that you *must* achieve what it's important for you to achieve? (Debating intervention).

Client: There isn't any.

Counsellor: That's it and if you really work on convincing yourself that there is no evidence that you must achieve your goals, and stick rigorously with your rational belief that you really want to achieve them but don't have to, then you'll still be concerned about failing, but not anxious about it. And that concern will motivate you to try your best, whereas if you do as some of my clients do, jump to 'It doesn't matter if I pass or fail' then (a) you'll be lying to yourself because you really do care, and (b) you won't be motivated to try to do your best, since it won't matter to you.

Client: So desire is helpful and the *must* will lead to anxiety, which will interfere with me achieving my goals.

Counsellor: Yes, and indifference?

Client: That won't help me either.

Note from this exchange that when it is clear that a client doesn't understand the difference between his rational and irrational beliefs, the counsellor gives a brief explanation to clarify the difference between the two beliefs. Rational-emotive counsellors routinely employ socratic disputing and didactic explanation where appropriate. In this exchange the counsellor does not persist in using a strategy (i.e. socratic disputing) which does not appear to help the client. When the counsellor uses a didactic explanation to clarify a rational concept, note that his explanation is brief and concise and that he requests feedback from the client that the latter understands the difference between a rational belief and an irrational belief by asking the client to state his understanding of this point in his own words.

Note also that the counsellor helps the client to see the links between B and C. He stresses that the client's irrational belief leads to anxiety and that his rational belief will lead to concern — a rational emotion which is more likely to encourage the client to reach his goals than the irrational emotion of anxiety. This is an important point. When disputing clients' irrational beliefs it is often desirable to help them understand that rational alternatives to these irrational beliefs will lead to less debilitating negative emotions and will often encourage clients to persist in goal-directed activities and to make a constructive adjustment when these goals can no longer be achieved. On this latter point it is likely that the client would feel depressed if he did not achieve his academic goals and clung to his irrational belief, whereas if he adhered to his rational belief in a rigorous manner he would feel disappointed about his future. Disappointment would encourage his constructive adjustment to a situation where he could not achieve his goals, whereas depression would discourage such adjustment.

The final point to note from this interchange is that the counsellor helps the client to discriminate between his rational belief based on desire and a belief based on indifference. Clients often consider that the only alternative to an irrational belief is one that is based on indifference, e.g., I don't care if I don't reach my academic goals. Here the counsellor attempts to forewarn the client about this possibility which the client appears to understand.

As has already been noted, an irrational belief has a premise and one or more derivatives. Disputing can therefore be targeted at the premise form of the irrational belief or at the derivative form or, of course, at both forms. I personally find it effective to dispute *both* the premise *and* derivative forms of clients' irrational beliefs.

Disputing irrational premises

Disputing irrational premises involves challenging the validity of clients' irrational beliefs expressed in the form of 'musts', 'absolute shoulds', 'oughts', 'have-to's' etc. As above, the purpose of disputing 'musts', etc., is to show clients that there is no evidence in support of such absolute beliefs. Thus, if there was a law of the universe that states, for example, that I must achieve my goals in life, I would have to achieve them *no matter what*. Thus absolute musts go against reality and in this context it is often useful to help clients understand that when they believe in such dogmatic attitudes they are demanding that what exists absolutely *must not exist*. Indeed the *empirical* form of the word 'must' indicates that if I do not achieve my goals then conditions exist so that I must not achieve them, i.e., what does not exist, must not exist.

Another helpful strategy in disputing absolute musts, etc., is to help clients understand that the evidence that they provide in support of absolute musts constitutes, in reality, evidence in favour of their rational beliefs. For example, in a disputing sequence with one of my female clients, she listed the following as evidence in support of her irrational belief, 'I must be loved by my husband': (a) I would feel better if he did love me, (b) we would get on better if he loved me, and (c) his love means more to me than most other things in life. In response to my question 'Why do you want very much your husband's love?', she listed the same reasons. This helped her to see that she hadn't yet provided any support in favour of the irrational form of her belief.

When disputing clients' irrational beliefs expressed in the form of musts it is important to ascertain first that the 'must' is indeed irrational, in the sense of being unconditional. As noted above not all musts are irrational and some musts are in fact conditional as in the phrase 'If I want to pass my examination I must learn the material'. Here passing the examination is conditional on learning the material. It is thus an error to dispute conditional musts.

The same point can be made when considering the word 'should' in that not all 'shoulds' are dogmatic and unconditional, and thus irrational in nature. In particular when disputing irrational beliefs expressed in the form of 'shoulds' it is important for the counsellor to help the client discriminate between 'preferably should' (rational belief) and 'absolutely should'. I recommend that when disputing irrational 'shoulds' the counsellor use the qualifier 'absolutely'. If the qualifier is not used the client may think that the counsellor is asking for evidence in support of the preferential form of the word 'should', and not the absolute form of the word. In such cases therapeutic impasses frequently ensue. As with other terms employed in rational-emotive counselling, it is important for the counsellor and client to share a commonly agreed meaning framework in the course of the therapeutic work (Dryden, 1986).

Finally, it is important for the counsellor to discover which form of the irrational premise the client best understands as reflecting a statement of absolutism. Thus, with some clients, disputing 'have-to's' is more effective in this respect than disputing 'musts', etc., because for these clients the term 'have-to' best captures the meaning of absolutism and personal dogma.

Disputing irrational derivatives

As shown in Chapter 3, there are three major derivatives from irrational premises: 'awfulizing', 'I-can't-stand-it-itis' and 'damning'.

Disputing 'awful'. In rational-emotive theory, the term 'awful', when it stems from an irrational belief, means '101 per cent bad' or 'worse than it absolutely must be'. In this sense it is not a synonym of the term 'very bad', although it is often judged to be so in everyday language. Thus, it is important for rational-emotive counsellors to help clients discriminate between such phrases as 'very bad' and the word 'awful'. When this is done clients are shown that whatever they evaluate as 'awful' could, in reality, be worse; and that the concept of 101 per cent badness is a magical one that does not exist except by definition. A good way of reinforcing this is to ask clients to rate what is evaluated as 'awful' on a 0–100 scale of badness, as in the following example:

> *Counsellor:* So you're saying that being rejected by Harry is awful, right?
>
> *Client:* Right.
>
> *Counsellor:* So on a scale from 0–100 of badness how bad would being rejected by Harry be?
>
> *Client:* 100 per cent.

Counsellor:	So if you are going to rate that as 100 per cent then how would you rate being rejected by Harry *and* losing a leg?
Client:	(laughs). I hadn't thought of it like that. I guess that would be 100 per cent.
Counsellor:	OK. Now where would you rate being rejected by Harry, losing a leg and having a very large rates bill that you couldn't pay?
Client:	That would be 100 per cent too . . . Oh, now I see what you're getting at. Looking at it like that being rejected by Harry wouldn't be that bad.
Counsellor:	Right, but it still would be very bad. Now can you see the differences between very bad and awful?
Client:	Yes I see that now.
Counsellor:	Right, awful doesn't really exist, unless we invent it because we can keep adding bad things to the list and if we do that when will we ever get to 100 per cent badness?
Client:	Never, I guess, because things could always be worse.
Counsellor:	That's exactly it. Now awful really stems from the belief 'It mustn't be as bad as it is'. Now granted that being rejected by Harry is bad why *must* that not be as bad as it is? . . .

Ellis (personal communication) has argued that the method whereby clients are encouraged to rate events as 'bad' rather than 'awful' should be used with caution. This is because a person could rate a situation as 40 per cent bad and still believe that it *must not* be as bad as it is and thus make herself disturbed. Thus when using this method it is important *also* to dispute any remaining irrational premises, as in the example presented.

In addition, when clients are encouraged to rate events as bad rather than awful, counsellors should be careful to stress the distinction between these two terms (e.g. 'Right, so if you continue to show yourself that it was *bad* that it happened, *but not awful*, then you will get over your depression').

An interesting way of disputing 'awfulizing' beliefs has been described by Young (1984 a) in his work with lower-class clients in West Virginia.

'I usually accomplish this by using a sheet of paper on which I put two columns. One column I label "Pain in the neck — HASSLE" and the other column I label "End of the world-HORRORS". Next I encourage the client to tell me exactly what is wrong in his problem. Then, after we list all the disadvantages and inconveniences involved, I will ask the client in which column the problem belongs — the hassle column or the horror column. Clients always see the point and admit that their problems belong in the hassle column. I ask them how they would feel if they could see their problem as a hassle instead of a horror. Clients usually admit that they would feel much less upset. I then inform them that their job is constantly to tell themselves the truth — that the problem is a pain-in-the-neck, nothing more and nothing less' (Young, 1984 a, p. 47).

Note in this example that Young does not overtly deal with the philosophical issue that nothing merits inclusion in the 'End of the world horror' or 'awful' column. Young probably did not do this because his clientele would not grasp this point. This raises another important principle in rational-emotive counselling: *Work at a level that your client can understand.* My own preference in this regard is to assume that my client will be able to grasp the full meaning of rational concepts until I obtain evidence to suggest otherwise.

Disputing 'I-can't-stand-it-itis'. The purpose of disputing 'I-can't-stand-it-itis' beliefs is to help clients see that this term, when it stems from an irrational premise, means 'I will never experience happiness again' and is thus rarely true. Indeed I find it helpful to encourage clients to see that even when they believe and tell themselves 'I can't stand it' they are, in fact, 'standing it', albeit not very well. The discussion can then shift to helping clients explore ways of tolerating it better. Another way of demonstrating to clients that they can stand what they believe they can't is to ask them if there are circumstances under which they could stand 'it' as is shown in the following interchange:

Counsellor: So you're saying that you can't stand that feeling of jelly legs when you go out and that's why you don't go out. Is that right?

Client: Yes, that's right.

Counsellor: Now as we've seen, as long as you believe that you can't stand that feeling you won't go out. But let's see if that belief is true. Let's suppose that your sister has been kidnapped and the only way the kidnappers will release her is if you delivered the ransom money on your jelly legs, or else they would kill her. Now under these conditions, should we arrange for her funeral or would you go?

Client: I'd go and deliver the money.

Counsellor: But how could you if you couldn't stand having these feelings of jelly legs?

Client:	Well, I'd do it even though I couldn't stand it.
Counsellor:	But if you couldn't stand it you'd collapse in the attempt — that's what you've been saying about the feeling isn't it?
Client:	Well, I wouldn't focus on it in that instance.
Counsellor:	You mean you could stand it enough not to dwell on it?
Client:	I suppose so.
Counsellor:	Now if you'd go out on jelly legs to save your sister will you do it for the sake of your recovery, even though it's damned uncomfortable?
Client:	I see your point.
Counsellor:	Now as you do this, really work on convincing yourself that you can stand these uncomfortable feelings even though you'll never like them. And don't forget to remind yourself that you're choosing to stand them for a reason — your mental health.

Here, as elsewhere, rational-emotive counsellors can use the methods of general semantics to show clients that when they say 'I can't stand it' they really mean, as in the above example 'I haven't learned to stand it yet' and 'I am having great difficulty standing it at the moment, but that doesn't mean that I never will'.

Disputing 'damning' beliefs. When applied to people the process of damning implies that a person can be given a global rating, that this is negative and that the person is damnable, i.e., sub-human. The purpose of disputing damning beliefs, which again tend to be derivatives from irrational premises, is to show the client that a person is too complex to be given a single rating; a person's traits, behaviours or thoughts are part of the person, but never equal to the person; and the essence of the person is fallibility, being capable of good and bad, rather than goodness or badness. Below, I provide one example to demonstrate each principle in action. Although they each refer to irrational beliefs about the self, similar points apply to irrational beliefs about others.

1   The 'self' is too complex.

Counsellor:	OK, so you say that you're worthless for cheating on your wife, is that right?
Client:	Yes that's what I believe.
Counsellor:	OK, but let's test that our. Are you saying that you are worthless, or what you've done is worthless?

Client: I'm saying that I'm worthless, not just what I did.

Counsellor: OK, but let's see if that is logical. You know when you say 'I'm worthless' you are giving you, your personhood or your essence, a single rating. Can you see that?

Client: Yes.

Counsellor: But let's see if you warrant that. You're 35. How many thoughts have you had from the day you were born till now.

Client: Countless, I guess.

Counsellor: Add to that all your actions and throw in all your traits for good measure. From that time till now how many aspects to you are there?

Client: Millions, I guess.

Counsellor: At least now when you say that Y-O-U ARE WORTHLESS you can see that you're implying that you are about as complex as a single cell amoeba, and that this cell is worthless. Now is that true from what we've just been discussing?

Client: No, of course it's not.

Counsellor: So do you, in all your complexity, merit a single rating?

Client: No, but I did do a pretty worthless thing and it was serious.

Counsellor: Agreed, but what has greater validity, the belief, 'I'm worthless in all my essence' or the belief, 'I am too complex to be rated, but I did do something lousy which I regret'.

Client: The second.

Counsellor: Right and if you really worked on believing that would you still feel suicidal as you do now?

Client: No I wouldn't. I see what you mean.

2.   **I equal what I do (think, feel).**

This example is taken from Young's (1984 a) work with a lower-class client who is convinced that you are what you do.

Counsellor: Maybe I can show you a better way to think about yourself. (I pointed at her hand). Is that your hand?

Client: (laughing) Yes!

Counsellor: Is it important to you?

Client: Yes.

Counsellor: Tell me why. Suppose you didn't have that hand?

Client: It would handicap me. There would be lots of things I couldn't do. It would be pretty bad for me.

Counsellor: So your hand's important! Now let me ask you this: Is that hand part of you or is it you? Now really think for me. Does that important hand equal you? Could you describe yourself simply as a hand?

Client: No.

Counsellor: Why not? You gave the right answer. Now tell me why it is the right answer.

Client: Because my hand is only part of me.

Counsellor: Do you have any other part, such as your eyes, ears, nose, or big toe that is your whole self? Is there any part of your body, inside or out, that you could say is you?

Client: No, I guess I'm made up of a lot of parts.

3. The essence of the self is fallibility

In order to make the point that the essence of a person is fallibility I draw three big circles on a sheet of paper and show this to the client. I say that these three circles represent three people: A, B and C. First I take circle A and stick as many small gold stars within the circle as I can. Next I stick as many black dots as I can within circle B. Finally I stick a mixture of gold stars and black dots in circle C. I explain to the client that the gold stars represent good deeds, thoughts, feelings and traits; and the black dots represent bad deeds, thoughts, feelings and traits.

Then I ask my client what we generally call someone who only has the equivalent of gold stars; who only has the equivalent of black dots; and who has a mixture of the two. I usually get such replies as: perfect, a saint, an angel; bad, the devil, evil; and human, normal, ordinary, respectively. Then I ask the client two more questions: whether she really knows anyone like the people represented by circles A and B, to which the answer is almost always no; and which circle best represents her, to which the answer is invariably 'C'. In this manner clients can see that the essence of human beings is a mixture of good and bad (or fallibility) and that she also belongs in the category: 'fallible human being'.

A final note on language. As with irrational premises clients use different words to damn themselves and others. For example, Young (1984 b) has shown that clients can be 'bad me' thinkers, 'less me' thinkers or 'damn me' thinkers. As elsewhere, I recommend that the counsellor use the client's language in disputing sequences unless there are sound reasons to do otherwise.

Dissonance-inducing interventions

According to cognitive dissonance theory (e.g. Festinger, 1957), when a person is confronted with information that conflicts with one of his importantly held beliefs, a state of cognitive dissonance, a form of psychological tension, is induced. In order to reduce dissonance the person *may* change his belief. I stress the word *may* in the above sentence because in order to reduce dissonance the person may change other features of the dissonant situation, e.g., he may cast doubt on the validity of the conflicting information or on the credibility of the source of the new information. Thus although rational-emotive counsellors employ dissonance-inducing interventions to promote intellectual rational insight, they do so with caution.

One dissonance-inducing intervention that is commonly used in rational-emotive counselling is one which attempts to show clients that they have already engaged in adaptive behaviour which is inconsistent with their maladaptive belief. Thus clients who believe that they are 'failures' are asked to provide evidence of their successes; those who believe that they are unloveable are asked for evidence that they have been loved. Since clients frequently append 'but that doesn't count' to their evidence I have often found it helpful to say something like: 'Of course I realize that any evidence that you give you will immediately dismiss in some way, but let's hear it anyway', before letting the client answer. I do this to reduce in advance the potency of their attempts to maintain their irrational belief by denying the importance of their evidence. The success of this type of dissonance-inducing intervention often depends on the wealth of evidence the client provides and then it is important to keep asking for more and more evidence until a healthy portfolio of evidence which conflicts with the client's irrational belief has been assembled.

Another dissonance-inducing intervention concerns the counsellor demonstrating that the client's irrational belief is incongruent with one of the client's cherished ideas as in the following example.

> *Counsellor:* So you're furious with Bill because he upset your friend and you believe he absolutely should not have done that. Is that right?
>
> *Client:* Yes, indeed.

Counsellor: I remember you said on your biographical form that one of your pet hates is totalitarianism. Have I remembered correctly?

Client: That's right, but what's that got to do with it?

Counsellor: I'm coming to that, bear with me for a moment. Why are you against state control?

Client: Because it restricts the individual's freedom.

Counsellor: His or her freedom to act?

Client: Yes.

Counsellor: So even if the individual acts really badly he or she, in your opinion, should preferably have that choice.

Client: Yes. Of course there have to be laws and consequences for the individual, but basically yes.

Counsellor: So I guess you're saying all people have the right to act badly except Bill because aren't you demanding, in a totalitarian way, that he absolutely should not have acted badly towards your friend.

Client: (Laughs loudly) OK, Doc, you've got me. I give in.

Counsellor: Now what would a non-totalitarian attitude towards Bill sound like?

A final dissonance-inducing strategy that is often quite powerful concerns showing the client that her attitude towards herself conflicts with her attitude towards her best friend, e.g.:

Counsellor: So you say that you're a bad person for having those evil thoughts. Is that right?

Client: Yes.

Counsellor: Well let's test that out. Now we'll agree for the moment that those thoughts of stabbing your child are evil. But how are you evil for having evil thoughts?

Client: Well, it's obvious isn't it?

Counsellor: Is it? Aren't you saying that because part of you is evil that you are thoroughly evil?

Client: Yes.

Counsellor: Well, does that follow?

Client: Well . . .

Counsellor: Let's put it another way. Who's your best friend?

Client: Cathy.

Counsellor: Well, let's suppose that Cathy came to you and said: 'Sue, I'm evil because I've had thoughts of stabbing my child.' Would you say to her 'Get out of my sight you evil person?'

Client: No I wouldn't.

Counsellor: Would you think it?

Client: No.

Counsellor: Why not?

Client: Because she isn't evil.

Counsellor: Even though she's had evil thoughts?

Client: I see what you mean.

Counsellor: Now do you think there should be one rule for Cathy and a different one for you? Does that make sense?

Client: No, I guess not.

Counsellor: So why not work at applying your attitude towards Cathy to you?

Here, as elsewhere, rational-emotive counsellors should guard against clients giving themselves second-order problems as a consequence of the counsellors' interventions. Thus some clients may conclude from the last example 'Oh, I am treating my friend more compassionately than myself as I must not. That really proves how worthless I am'. Questions like: 'How do you feel about the fact that you seem to be harsher on yourself than you are on your best friend' should preferably be asked after the intervention to determine the existence of such second-order problems.

Goals and rational beliefs

As I have already noted, an important part of the disputing process involves helping clients to discriminate between irrational and rational beliefs. As these distinctions are clarified it is advisable for counsellors to encourage clients to see that rational beliefs are related to more functional rational emotions which are often negative in nature. For example, imagine that a client is anxious about performing well in her driving test, because she is demanding that she must pass the test. In the process of helping this client to dispute this belief, the counsellor will show her that her rational belief is 'I very much want to pass the test but I don't have to', and that if she adopted this belief she would feel concerned, but not anxious, about driving well. However, if the client's goal is to be calm and not concerned about the prospect of failing the test, she will resist adopting the new rational belief. Thus rational-emotive counsellors often discuss clients' emotional and behavioural goals during the process of disputing their irrational beliefs to ensure that their goals can be achieved by adopting rational beliefs. In the example I have provided, the counsellor would attempt to show the client that concern is a rational negative emotion, based on a rational belief that will motivate her to do well, whereas calmness, which can only be achieved by the client lying to herself by telling herself 'It doesn't matter if I do well or not', hardly provides her with the motivational base to do as well as she can. Thus while rational-emotive counsellors often elicit their clients' emotional and behavioural goals they do not accept un-critically clients' stated goals and are particularly sceptical of the functionality of goals which signify attitudes of indifference.

The above example also highlights another feature of the disputing process; namely that counsellors attempt to help clients to understand the logical con-sequences of holding rational and irrational beliefs. Thus, here the counsellor might say, 'As long as you believe that you must do well you will be anxious, and this anxiety may interfere with your driving performance. However, if you work at believing that while it is important to you to do well, you don't have to, you'll be concerned, and thus be in a better frame of mind to do well'. This part of the dis-puting process, which can be done socratically as well as didactically, as above, is often referred to as 'pragmatic disputing' in that it draws the client's attention to the pragmatic consequences of holding rational and irrational beliefs.

Vivid Disputing Methods

In this section, I outline various vivid methods of disputing clients' irrational beliefs which rational-emotive counsellors (including myself) have employed with good results. As with the other vivid methods described in this book, these tend to be used after the more traditional disputing methods, outlined in the previous section, have proved unsuccessful. Vivid techniques do need to be employed selectively and I refer the reader to the previous chapter for cautions about the use of such methods in rational-emotive counselling.

Biographical information

Before initiating the vivid disputing process I often find it helpful to gather certain information about the client. I often find it helpful to find out about my client's interests, hobbies, and work situation. I have found this information often helps me adapt my interventions, using phrases that will be meaningful to my client given his or her idiosyncratic life situation. Thus, if my client is passionately interested in boxing, a message utilizing a boxing analogy may well have greater impact than a golfing analogy.

I also find it helpful to discover who my client admires. I do this because later I may wish to ask my client how he or she thinks these admired individuals might solve similar problems. This prompts the client to identify with a model to imitate. Lazarus (1984) has employed a similar method with children. For example, I asked a male client to imagine that his admired grandfather experienced public speaking anxiety and inquired how he would have overcome it. This helped him to identify a rational belief which he used to overcome his own public speaking anxiety problem. This approach is best used if the client can also acknowledge that the admired individual is fallible and thus prone to human irrationality. In addition it is important that the client sees the feasibility of imitating the model.

I find it invaluable to ask my clients about their previous experience of attitude change. I try and discern the salient features of such change for possible replication in my in-session disputing strategies. For example, one anxious female client told me she had changed her mind about foxhunting after reading a number of personal accounts offering arguments against foxhunting. As part of my disputing plan, I directed this client to autobiographies of people who had overcome anxiety. Another client claimed she had in the past experienced help from speaking to people who had experienced problems similar to her own. I arranged for this client to speak to some of my ex-clients who had experienced but overcome comparable problems.

I now propose to outline a number of ways in which rational-emotive counsellors can employ vivid disputing techniques. The importance of tailoring interventions to meet the specific, idiosyncratic requirements of clients should be borne in mind throughout.

In the previous chapter I outlined a number of ways of vividly portraying activating events to help clients identify their emotional reactions and the cognitive determinants of these reactions. I outlined various visual, auditory and olfactory methods. These same methods can be used as context material in the disputing process. For example, one client brought along a drawing of herself and her mother. She portrayed her mother as a very large, menacing figure and herself as a small figure crouching in fear in front of her mother. I asked the client to draw another picture where she and her mother were of the same height standing face-to-face looking each other in the eye. When she brought in this drawing, I inquired how her attitude toward her mother differed in the two pictures. This not only provided her with a demonstration that it was possible for her to evaluate her mother differently, but also led to a fruitful discussion in which I disputed some of her irrational beliefs inherent in the first drawing while having her focus on the second.

Imagery methods

One very effective imagery method that can be used in the disputing of irrational beliefs is that of time projection (Lazarus, 1984). When a client makes grossly exaggerated negative evaluations of an event, she often stops thinking about it and therefore cannot see beyond its 'dreaded' implications. The purpose of time projection is to enable clients to see vividly that time and the world continue after the 'dreaded event' has occurred. Thus, for example, a Malaysian student whose tuition fees were paid for by his village concluded that it would be terrible if he failed his exams because he couldn't bear to face his fellow villagers. I helped him to imagine his return to his village while experiencing shame; I then gradually advanced time forward via imagery. He began to see that it was likely that his fellow villagers would eventually come to adopt a compassionate viewpoint toward him, and even if they did not, he could always live happily in another part of the country, or in another part of the world.

The rational-emotive counsellor as raconteur

Rational-emotive counsellors often capitalize on the therapeutic value of relating various stories, parables, maxims and aphorisms to clients. Each one, of course, is designed to teach a rational concept to clients. For example, Wessler and Wessler (1980, p. 126) relate the story of Nathan Leopold to illustrate the concepts of human complexity and the futility of evaluating oneself and others.

> Nathan Leopold . . . along with Richard Loeb committed the 'Crime of the Century' in the 1920s by kidnapping and killing a young boy. Years later, Leopold was pardoned as a changed person, became a social worker, married, and spent much of the rest of his life doing good works. After telling or reminding the client of Leopold's story we ask, 'Now was Nathan Leopold a good man or a bad man?'. Again we get a variety of answers. The one we are looking for is 'He was neither. He was a man who did both good and bad things'. Leopold is an extreme case (which makes him a good example) and leads to a discussion of human fallibility.

The important factor about telling such stories is that the counsellor modifies the content of these to fit the client's idiosyncratic situation. Telling identical stories to two different clients may well have two different effects. One client may be deeply affected by the story, while for another the story may prove meaningless. It is important that rational-emotive counsellors become acquainted with a wide variety of these stories and be prepared to modify them from client to client without introducing unwarranted distortions.

Active-visual methods

Active-visual methods combine therapist or client activity with a vivid visual presentation. Young (1984 b) has outlined one such method, which he uses to help clients see the impossibility of assigning a global rating to themselves. He asks a client to describe some of his behaviours, attributes, talents, interests, etc. With every answer the client gives, Young writes the attribute on a white sticky label, and sticks the label on the client. This continues until the client is covered with white sticky labels and can begin to see the impossibility of assigning one global rating to such a complex being. Wessler and Wessler (1980) outline similar active-visual methods to communicate a similar point. For example, they ask their clients to assign a comprehensive rating to a basket of fruit on a desk. Clients are encouraged to actively explore the components of the fruit basket while attempting to assign a global rating to it. They soon come to realize that they can rate components of the basket but not its essence.

Visual models

I have designed a number of visual models, each of which demonstrates a rational message. For example, I employ a model called the 'LFT Splash'. In the model a young man is seated at the top of a roller coaster with a young woman standing at the bottom. I tell clients that the young man does not move because he is telling himself that he can't stand the splash. Clients are asked to think what the young man would have to tell himself in order to reach the woman. This model is particularly useful in introducing to clients the idea of tolerating acute time-limited discomfort which, if tolerated, would help them achieve their goals.

Flamboyant counsellor actions

A common disputing strategy that rational-emotive counsellors use in verbal dialogue when clients conclude they are stupid for acting stupidly is to ask some variant of the question 'How are you a stupid person for acting stupidly?' Alternatively, instead of asking such questions, the counsellor could suddenly leap to the floor and start barking like a dog for about thirty seconds and then resume his or her seat, then ask the client to evaluate this action. Clients usually say that the action is stupid. The counsellor can then ask whether that stupid action makes him or her a stupid person. Such flamboyant actions often enable clients to more easily discriminate between global self-ratings and ratings of behaviours or attributes.

Counsellor self-disclosure

Some clients find self-disclosure by the counsellor an extremely persuasive method while for others it is contraindicated. One way of attempting to ascertain a client's possible reactions to counsellor self-disclosure is to include an appropriate item in a pre-counselling questionnaire. It may well be wise for counsellors to avoid using self-disclosure with clients who respond negatively to the item. In any case, the counsellor had better ascertain the client's reaction to any self-disclosing statements that he or she might make. The research literature on this topic indicates that counsellors had better not disclose personal information about themselves too early in the therapeutic process (Dies, 1973).

When counsellors do disclose information about themselves it is my experience that the most effective forms of self-disclosure are those in which they portray themselves as coping rather than mastery models. Thus, for example, it is better for the counsellor to say to the client: 'I used to have a similar problem, but this is how I overcame it' rather than to say: 'I have never had this problem, because I believe . . .'. Occasionally I tell clients with shame-based anxieties how I overcame my anxiety about stammering in public. I tell them that I used to believe: 'It would be terrible if I stammered in public and it would prove I was worthless if I did'. I then disclose how I changed my belief to 'I don't like stammering in public but if I do I do, too bad! I can accept myself with my stammer even if others put me down'.

Rational humorous songs

Ellis (1977 a) has written about the use of his now famous rational songs in counselling. For example, the counsellor can hand a client a song sheet and sing, preferably in an outrageous voice, a rational song that has been carefully selected to communicate the rational alternatives to the client's target irrational belief. Since Ellis tends to favour songs that have been written many years ago, it may be more productive for the counsellor to re-write the words to more up-to-date and popular songs for clients not familiar with some of the 'old favourites'.

The following is a rational humorous song written by me to the tune of 'God save the Queen':

> God save my precious spleen
> Send me a life serene
> God save my spleen
>
> Protect me from things odious
> Give me a life melodious
> And if things get too onerous
> I'll whine, bawl and scream

Once clients can identify their own irrational belief in the lyrics I then help them to re-write the words of the song to reflect a rational philosophy.

Reduction to absurdity

Here the counsellor assumes temporarily that the client's irrational belief is true and carries it to its logical extreme thus illuminating its absurdity. For example, Richard Wessler, once Director of Training at the Institute for RET in New York, related the following episode when he was working with a client who irrationally demanded a guarantee that bad things wouldn't happen in his life. Wessler suddenly jumped up and hid under his desk inviting his client to join him there. His puzzled client enquired why and was told by Wessler that this was the only way to guarantee that the ceiling would not fall on them. The client refused to join Wessler having understood the point of his intervention. Note how Wessler, in this example, combined a reduction to absurdity intervention with a flamboyant counsellor action to illustrate an appropriate rational concept.

I urge readers to be creative and devise novel vivid disputing methods which should preferably be tailored to help individual clients. It has been my experience that effective rational-emotive counsellors are creative in this respect and tend to avoid the slavish replication of vivid techniques devised by others.

Homework Aids in Promoting Intellectual Rational Insight

While I have focused thus far on counsellor's in-session interventions, which aim to promote clients' intellectual rational insight, an important part of this process is carried out by clients between sessions. These are frequently embodied in 'homework' assignments negotiated between client and counsellor.

Listening to audiotapes of sessions

It sometimes occurs that clients become confused during the disputing process in counselling sessions. This may happen, for example, when clients become emotionally distracted in the sessions, and/or counsellors work too quickly for the clients' level of understanding. In such cases clients often supplement their learning about rational concepts by listening to audiotapes of their sessions. This has the advantage that clients can replay segments of the tape as many times as they find valuable to clarify their understanding of what transpired between them and their counsellors. When this technique is suggested counsellors should preferably encourage clients to write down any issues they wish to discuss in their following counselling session, and in particular to make a note of any doubts they may have about the invalidity and self-defeating nature of their irrational beliefs.

Some clients do not find listening to tapes of their therapy sessions very useful. These are often clients who blame themselves for their lack of understanding as demonstrated in the session, or for the sound of their voice. While it is sometimes helpful to suggest that such clients use the tapes as stimuli to dispute their irrational beliefs about these two features, counsellors should preferably not insist that clients listen to these tapes when doing so is not helpful for them.

Structured disputing

There exist a number of forms that structure the disputing process for clients to use between counselling sessions. A good example is *DIBS* (Disputing Irrational Beliefs) and Ellis (1979 c, pp. 79–80) has outlined its form thus:

Question 1: What irrational belief do I want to dispute and surrender?

Answer: I must be as effective and sexually fulfilled as most other women.

Question 2: Can I rationally support this belief?

Answer: ....

Question 3: What evidence exists of the truth of this belief?

Answer: ....

Question 4: What evidence exists of the falseness of my belief that I must be as orgasmic as other women are?

Answer: ....

Question 5: What are the worst possible things that could actually happen to me if I never achieved the orgasm that I think I must achieve?

Answer: ....

Question 6: What good things could happen, or could I make happen, if I never achieved the heights of orgasm that I think I must achieve?

Answer: ....

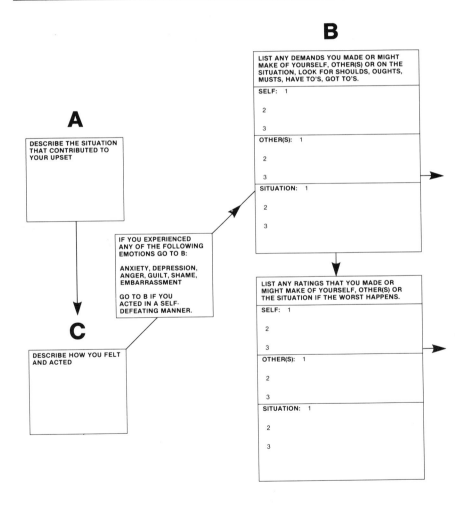

A

DESCRIBE THE SITUATION
THAT CONTRIBUTED TO
YOUR UPSET

IF YOU EXPERIENCED
ANY OF THE FOLLOWING
EMOTIONS GO TO B:

ANXIETY, DEPRESSION,
ANGER, GUILT, SHAME,
EMBARRASSMENT

GO TO B IF YOU
ACTED IN A SELF-
DEFEATING MANNER.

C

DESCRIBE HOW YOU FELT
AND ACTED

B

LIST ANY DEMANDS YOU MADE OR MIGHT
MAKE OF YOURSELF, OTHER(S) OR ON THE
SITUATION, LOOK FOR SHOULDS, OUGHTS,
MUSTS, HAVE TO'S, GOT TO'S.

SELF: 1

2

3

OTHER(S): 1

2

3

SITUATION: 1

2

3

LIST ANY RATINGS THAT YOU MADE OR
MIGHT MAKE OF YOURSELF, OTHER(S) OR
THE SITUATION IF THE WORST HAPPENS.

SELF: 1

2

3

OTHER(S): 1

2

3

SITUATION: 1

2

3

As a homework exercise DIBS is best used after a general socratic and/or didactic disputing sequence has been successfully completed, and after the counsellor demonstrated the use of DIBS in the session taking the irrational belief that has been successfully disputed as an example.

Apart from DIBS, there exist a number of structured disputing exercises that can be suggested for use as cognitive homework assignments. Two examples of these appear in Figures 3 and 4. The major purpose of these forms is to help clients to identify, challenge and change their irrational beliefs and they appear to have a number of shared components. They encourage clients to identify: activating

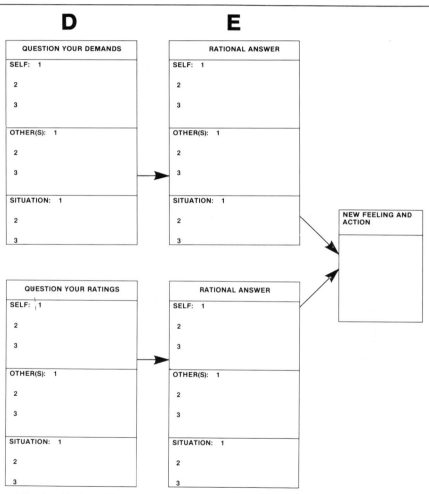

Figure 3 A guide for solving your emotional and behavioural problems by re-examining your self-defeating thoughts and attitudes (Dryden 1982).

RET SELF-HELP FORM

Institute for Rational-Emotive Therapy
45 East 65th Street, New York, N.Y. 10021
(212) 535-0822

(A) ACTIVATING EVENTS, thoughts, or feelings that happened just before I felt emotionally disturbed or acted self-defeatingly: _____

(C) CONSEQUENCE or CONDITION—disturbed feeling or self-defeating behaviour—that I produced and would like to change: _____

(B) BELIEFS—Irrational BELIEFS (IBs) leading to my CONSEQUENCE (emotional disturbance or self-defeating behaviour). Circle all that apply to these ACTIVATING EVENTS **(A).**	**(D) DISPUTES** for each circled IRRATIONAL BELIEF. Examples: "Why MUST I do very well?" "Where is it written that I am a BAD PERSON?" "Where is the evidence that I MUST be approved or accepted?"	(E) EFFECTIVE RATIONAL BELIEFS (RBs) to replace my IRRATIONAL BELIEFS (IBs). *Examples: "I'd PREFER to do very well but I don't HAVE TO." "I am a PERSON WHO acted badly, not a BAD PERSON." "There is no evidence that I HAVE TO be approved, though I would LIKE to be."*
1. I MUST do well or very well!		
2. I am a BAD OR WORTHLESS PERSON when I act weakly or stupidly.		
3. I MUST be approved or accepted by people I find important!		
4. I am a BAD, UNLOVABLE PERSON if I get rejected.		
5. People MUST treat me fairly and give me what I NEED!		
6. People who act immorally are undeserving, ROTTEN PEOPLE!		
7. People MUST live up to my expectations or it is TERRIBLE!		
8. My life MUST have few major hassles or troubles.		
9. I CAN'T STAND really bad things or very difficult people!		
10. It's AWFUL or HORRIBLE when major things don't go my way!		

11. I CAN'T STAND IT when life is really unfair!		
12. I NEED to be loved by someone who matters to me a lot!		
13. I NEED a good deal of immediate gratification and HAVE TO feel miserable when I don't get it!		
Additional Irrational Beliefs:		
14.		
15.		
16.		
17.		
18.		

(F) FEELINGS and BEHAVIOURS I experienced after arriving at my EFFECTIVE RATIONAL BELIEFS: _____

I WILL WORK HARD TO REPEAT MY EFFECTIVE RATIONAL BELIEFS FORCEFULLY TO MYSELF ON MANY OCCASIONS SO THAT I CAN MAKE MYSELF LESS DISTURBED NOW AND ACT LESS SELF-DEFEATINGLY IN THE FUTURE.

Figure 4   RET self-help form (Sichel and Ellis, 1984).

Joyce Sichel, Ph.D. and Albert Ellis, Ph.D.

events (or inferences about these events); irrational feelings and/or self-defeating actions that occur in the context of these events; and their mediating irrational beliefs. Furthermore these forms invite clients to ask for evidence that supports their irrational beliefs and provide spaces for them to identify rational alternatives to that irrational belief; and likely emotional and/or behavioural effects of these new rational beliefs. It is recommended that rational-emotive counsellers demonstrate the use of these forms in counselling sessions before asking clients to use them in their daily lives.

Rational self-help material

Rational-emotive counsellors frequently suggest that clients read or listen to self-help materials between sessions in order to build upon and reinforce the rational intellectual insight that clients gain within sessions. Since there is a wide range of such aids available, counsellors are recommended to monitor clients' reactions to these so that they can suggest material that is most appropriate to the client's level of understanding of rational concepts. Frequently suggested books include Ellis and Harper's (1975) *A New Guide to Rational Living* and Ellis and Becker's (1982) *A Guide to Personal Happiness*. When using these books, counsellors, in the first instance, are advised to assign chapters that reinforce the message that beliefs determine emotions and actions, and thereafter recommend particular chapters relevant to the client's problem(s). It is helpful to encourage clients to note points for future discussion in counselling sessions, particularly those which they do not understand and those with which they disagree. If clients find the two books mentioned difficult to understand, they can be asked to read less complex material like Young's (1974) *A Rational Counseling Primer* or Kranzler's (1974) *You Can Change How You Feel*.

In addition, RET-orientated books are available which are devoted to particular client problems, such as depression, anger, anxiety, procrastination, etc., and in this regard Paul Hauck's books in the Sheldon Press, *Overcoming Common Problems* series are particularly popular with British clients.

In addition to reading material, there exist numerous audiotapes on general and specific applications of rational-emotive theory which clients can use for the same purposes as the books I have mentioned. Again counsellors are advised to elicit clients' reactions to such material, paying particular attention to doubts and disagreements which can then be discussed in regular sessions.

While the achievement of rational *intellectual* insight is an important stage for clients in the counselling process, as noted earlier, it is rarely sufficient for meaningful psychological change to occur. For such change to take place clients need to achieve *emotional* rational insight, and the next chapter is devoted to its promotion.

8. Promoting Emotional Rational Insight

Overview

In this chapter, I deal with issues concerning the promotion of emotional rational insight. First I note that helping clients to achieve this type of insight is difficult and list a number of reasons why this is so. Then I highlight standard and vivid techniques which are used during this stage of rational-emotive counselling. Thus I describe cognitive, imagery and behavioural techniques most of which have a decided emotive quality. Finally, I outline a number of vivid cues that counsellors can use to encourage clients to initiate the process of promoting emotional rational insight.

Promoting Emotional Rational Insight is Difficult

When clients have achieved intellectual but not emotional insight into rational concepts, they typically make such statements as, 'Yes, I see that what you say makes sense, but I don't believe it yet', or 'I understand it up here in my head, but not down here in my gut'. It is important to explain to clients that gaining intellectual rational insight is an important step in the change process but one which is usually insufficient to bring about meaningful emotional and behavioural change. Rational-emotive counsellors further explain that in order to achieve significant attitude change that affects feelings and actions, i.e., emotional rational insight, clients will usually have to employ repeatedly and persistently a variety of cognitive, emotive and behavioural techniques.

As rational-emotive practitioners note (e.g., Grieger, 1985) helping clients to move from intellectual to emotional rational insight is often a difficult painstaking process. This is so for a number of reasons. First, as Ellis (1976) in particular has argued, humans have a distinct tendency towards irrational thinking and often have a hard time working against this tendency.

Second, even those rational-emotive counsellors who adopt a social learning perspective, rather than a biological perspective on human irrationality, acknowledge that changing irrational beliefs is a difficult process. Such theorists (e.g., Grieger, 1985) note that once clients have learned to think irrationally and to act in accordance with their irrational beliefs, they become habituated to these ideas and 'changing anything so well learned, therefore, requires repeated energetic efforts, even for those who are willing and committed to change'. (Grieger, 1985, p. 144).

Third, many clients have a philosophy of low frustration tolerance (LFT) and believe that they shouldn't have to work so hard to effect meaningful psychological change and as Grieger (1985, p. 145) notes 'left to their own devices, they drift, goof and act on their acknowledged irrational, self-defeating beliefs even though they know better'. Attacking clients' LFT beliefs is a prominent feature of promoting emotional rational insight.

Fourth, and related to the above, clients often become habituated to their problems and become used to the 'comfortable discomfort' that these problems bring. They fear that change may bring more acute discomfort and therefore will not risk changing. Rational-emotive counsellors need to help clients understand that they may indeed feel more uncomfortable in the short-term, but if they work at tolerating such discomfort the long-term rewards will usually outweigh the short-term rewards of avoiding discomfort.

Fifth, as Fransella (1985) has shown, clients often give their psychological problems a central position in their sense of identity (e.g., a person who stammers sees himself as 'a stammerer') and they cannot imagine how they would lead their lives if they did not, for example, stammer. Here rational-emotive counsellors need to use general semantic methods, for example, helping such clients to employ precise and accurate language (changing 'I am a stammerer' to 'I am a person who stammers under certain conditions and not under other conditions) and to help such clients construct a view of what life might be like if they did not stammer as often.

Sixth, clients may experience sources of secondary gain as a result of having their problems. Thus a woman who wishes to lose weight in order to be more attractive to men might find, if she is successful, that she has to be assertive in declining to sleep with men, which she would find difficult. An advantage of being fat for this woman then is that she doesn't place herself in situations where she might become promiscuous, which she would evaluate very negatively. It is clear then that rational-emotive counsellors need to focus particular attention on assessing potential obstacles to the change process and deal with these as they become relevant during this stage of counselling. This issue will be discussed more fully in Chapter 10.

Seventh, as Grieger, among others has noted, clients often make unrealistic predictions of what their lives might be like if they adhered to a rational philosophy of life: these include 'fear of losing one's identity or becoming a phony . . . . ; fears of becoming emotionally dulled or machine-like by thinking rationally; and fears of becoming mediocre and losing one's specialness by giving up perfectionistic ideas'. (Grieger, 1985, p. 144). One of my clients recently announced that she didn't think much of life according to rational-emotive philosophy because it meant never falling in love! It is important that rational-emotive counsellors be aware that clients may well misinterpret rational-emotive philosophy and be ready to correct such misconceptions. I advise rational-emotive counsellors to ask clients directly about how they would construe their lives if they indeed achieved what they hoped to gain from counselling rather than to wait for clients to disclose such constructions. In such exploration counsellors should pay particular attention to misinterpretations of rational-emotive philosophy and deal with them accordingly.

Finally, clients may find it difficult to put their intellectual rational insights into consistent practice because the balance of their outside relationships would be disturbed if they did. For example, asserting oneself with one's spouse may lead to marital problems, getting over one's depression may be a trigger for one's partner to become depressed, etc. Rational-emotive counsellors need to be sensitive to the fact that clients in individual counselling have a wide variety of interpersonal relationships in their daily lives which may exert a positive or negative influence on their attempts to achieve their counselling goals. Rational-emotive counsellors may indeed suggest to clients that they involve their significant others in counsel-ling, particularly if these others may wittingly or unwittingly sabotage clients' attempts to change. Since this book is concerned with counselling individuals I refer the reader to Ellis and Dryden (1987) for a discussion of the practice of RET in its other modalities. In the final analysis, however, if significant others do react negatively to clients' attempts to change and do not want to become involved in counselling, then rational-emotive counsellors encourage their clients to view this situation as another troublesome A in the ABC framework to be coped with using rational thinking.

Techniques to Promote Emotional Rational Insight

The remainder of this chapter will focus on methods and techniques that clients can use to achieve emotional rational insight. In addition to using repeatedly and persistently the disputing methods outlined in the previous chapter, clients are encouraged to use a variety of cognitive, behavioural and emotive assignments in the service of achieving emotional and behavioural changes. I will especially focus on methods and techniques which are most frequently used in rational-emotive counselling and those which are particularly vivid. In this latter respect, Ellis (1958, p. 45, italics added) from RET's inception strongly recommended that clients undertake 'some kind of activity which itself will act as a *forceful* counterpropagandist agency against the nonsense they believe'. Ellis continues to stress that for clients who will agree to do them, *dramatic, forceful* and *implosive* activities remain the best forms of promoting emotional insight. This is due to the fact that since clients, according to Ellis, have a pronounced tendency to think irrationally, they need to counter this tendency forcefully and repeatedly.

Cognitive techniques

Clients are encouraged to use cognitive techniques to convince themselves outside counselling sessions that rational philosophies, which they can acknowledge as correct in counselling, are indeed correct and functional for them. The emphasis here is particularly on clients weakening their adherence to irrational beliefs and strengthening their adherence to rational beliefs. I have found that encouraging clients to provide evidence in favour of rational beliefs is particularly helpful at this stage of rational-emotive counselling and these will be discussed first.

Building your rational portfolio: Here, as noted above, counsellors encourage clients to focus on evidence in favour of rational beliefs. Thus a client who can see that there is no evidence in support of her irrational belief 'I *must* control my emotions in public' is asked to explain in detail why it would be better but not essential if she could control her emotions in public. The role of the counsellor in this process is to encourage the client to find a variety of different reasons in support of the rational belief and to suggest others when the client has exhausted her own supply. I call this technique 'Building your rational portfolio'.

Devil's advocate disputing: Once a client has sufficiently built up her portfolio in the above manner and shows some skill at disputing her irrational beliefs, the counsellor can adopt the role of a devil's advocate and attack the client's rational thinking. The client's role is to point out flaws in the reasoning of the devil's advocate and destroy his arguments, thus strengthening further her rational belief:

> *Counsellor:* But how can you possibly say that you don't need a man in
> *(as Devil's* your life? Look at all your friends, they do and they're
> *Advocate)* normal. Aren't you abnormal for trying to deny your needs?
>
> *Client:* Just because my friends believe they need a man in their life
> doesn't mean that I have to believe the same. Most of them are
> anxious when they don't have a man and anxious when they
> do in case he leaves them. I don't want that for myself. Also

> I'm not denying my need, I'm trying to challenge it and if I
> am abnormal in this regard I'm abnormally healthy, not sick
> as you seem to imply.

In devil's advocate disputing the counsellor looks for issues that the client doesn't deal with and feeds this back into the discussion. Thus in the above example if the client did not deal with the issue of abnormality the counsellor in his role of devil's advocate would have raised this issue again.

When beginning devil's advocate disputing, the counsellor should preferably raise one issue at a time until the client shows some skill at this procedure. The example provided above is with a client who has previously demonstrated a high level of skill at this form of disputing. Thus, the counsellor, in the example, can raise two or three issues at once.

Another major counsellor goal in devil's advocate disputing is to find vulnerable points in the client's rational thinking so that these can be dealt with. Here the counsellor presents irrational beliefs to the client to which she experiences difficulty in responding. When this occurs it is best to stop the procedure and discuss the new irrational belief in a more traditional manner.

Devil's advocate disputing is one example of what Kassinove and DiGiuseppe (1975) call *Rational Role Reversal*, where the counsellor adopts an irrational role and the client adopts a rational role. While I have focused on devil's advocate disputing where the counsellor attacks the client's thinking, rational role reversal can take different forms. For example, the counsellor plays the irrational part of the client and supplies the client with irrational messages. The client's task is to respond rationally to these irrational messages. In another version the counsellor plays a naive client with an emotional problem that is usually similar to the client's and presents an irrational belief identical to the one targeted for change. The client is encouraged to adopt the role of the rational-emotive counsellor and help the 'client' to dispute his or her irrational belief.

It should be reiterated that all versions of rational role reversal are best used when the client has demonstrated a fair measure of skill at disputing her own irrational beliefs using more traditional methods, as described in the previous chapter. As noted above, they can also all be used to identify weaknesses in the clients' rational arguments in response to irrational beliefs articulated in 'reversed role' by counsellors.

The courtroom evidence technique. In the courtroom evidence technique the client is asked to play the roles of prosecuting attorney and defence attorney providing evidence in favour and against the client's rational belief in one 'trial', and doing the same with the client's irrational belief in another 'trial'. The goal, of course, is to provide more compelling evidence in favour of the rational belief and to contradict the 'evidence' in favour of the irrational belief. At the end of this procedure the client is asked to play the role of judge and sum up all the evidence presented and provide a verdict which hopefully is: 'I thus conclude that the rational belief is valid and the irrational belief is invalid'. If the client concludes otherwise the counsellor is provided with useful information concerning the client's doubts and reservations about the relevant rational belief. These are then discussed once the 'trial' has been concluded. After these have been discussed the counsellor calls for an appeal against the previous verdict and the procedure is repeated.

Rational essays. Another technique that can be used under the heading of strengthening rational beliefs is to suggest that the client write an essay on a theme suggested by a rational belief, e.g., 'Why I cannot legitimately give myself a global rating'. Here is an extract from an essay written by one of my clients on the above theme:

> 'I have many different roles in my life. But let me take one, 'mother', to show how complex this role is. Breaking this role down into its component parts, I find there are many different aspects of mothering. But let me take one, 'disciplining'. Even this has different components including 'setting limits', 'working with my husband', 'voice tone', etc. Let me take one: voice tone. Even this has different components including firmness, gentleness, harshness, etc. Yesterday, in the space of an hour I used what I consider to be a good voice tone (firmness) with my child and a bad voice tone (harshness). Can I say I have a good voice tone? Hardly. How stupid it is then for me to say 'I'm a good or bad disciplinarian with my child'. If that is stupid how even more stupid for me to say 'I'm a good or bad mother'. Looking at it this way how can I possibly say that I'm a good or bad person? Obviously I can't. As Dr Dryden suggested I will undertake to use the sentence 'I am a person who . . . . .' whenever I can. But if I don't and I do rate myself, I won't rate *myself* badly for rating myself'.

Rational proselytizing (Bard, 1973). Here clients are encouraged to teach rational-emotive principles to their friends and relatives. In teaching others to live more rationally it is hypothesized that clients will become more convinced of rational-emotive philosophy and in my experience this often happens. In the process of teaching these principles to significant others clients learn to counter their objections and thus learn to think 'on their feet' when confronted with their own irrational beliefs. In addition, when clients report being unable to counter objections from significant others these are discussed further in regular counselling sessions. This technique, however, is best used with caution and clients should be warned against playing the role of unwanted counsellor to friends and relations.

Tape-recorded disputing. In this technique clients are encouraged to put a disputing sequence on tape and instructed to play both the rational and irrational parts of themselves. They are further encouraged to try and make the rational part more persuasive and more forceful in responding to the irrational part. Clients then play excerpts of these tapes to their counsellors who check whether their clients have indeed successfully disputed their irrational beliefs and listen carefully to the tone of the dialogue. When clients do not dispute their irrational beliefs forcefully and persuasively this may be attributed to two factors. First, this may indicate their difficulties in responding to certain elements of their irrational philosophy, in which case their doubts and lack of intellectual insight should be targets for discussion in sessions. Second, it may indicate that clients find it difficult to be forceful in adopting the rational role. When clients experience such difficulty, counsellors should model appropriate ways of disputing forcefully and encourage clients to practise responding to their irrational beliefs in similar ways.

Passionate rational self-statements. Clients who are intellectually unable to do cognitive self-disputing in the traditional sense can be encouraged to use passionate rational self-statements instead. Here clients and counsellors work together to develop appropriate rational self-statements which clients can use in their daily lives. Clients are then encouraged to repeat these statements in a very forceful manner instead of in their normal voice tone. Another variation of this technique is to encourage clients to say rational self-statements to their reflection in a mirror using a passionate tone and dramatic gestures to reinforce the rational message.

Encouraging clients to go against their irrational action tendencies

In Chapter 2, I introduced the concepts of action tendencies and response options. In Chapter 4 I argued that different emotions lead to different action tendencies and that given a certain tendency to act a person will choose certain response options and avoid others. I also argued that irrational emotions lead to irrational action tendencies which in turn influence individuals to choose responses which tend to be self-defeating. It follows that if clients are to be encouraged to act rationally then counsellors need to encourage them to go against irrational action tendencies. Also, as is argued in the next section, behavioural change is often the best way of encouraging clients to change their irrational beliefs. In order to encourage such behavioural change rational-emotive counsellors often have first to help clients to dispute their irrational beliefs that are implicit in their irrational action tendencies.

For example, one of my clients experienced anxiety about asking girls to dance at a discotheque. His irrational belief in this situation was 'I would be worthless if they refused to dance with me'. I successfully helped this client to dispute this belief and to achieve intellectual rational insight. However, he still would not ask any girls to dance and work toward rational emotional insight due to his tendency to avoid anxiety (irrational action tendency). Implicit in this action tendency was another irrational belief . . . 'I must be comfortable when I ask girls to dance'. Thus in order to help this client to achieve emotional rational insight I had first to help him to challenge this latter belief and change it to 'I prefer being comfortable when I ask girls to dance but I can still do so even though I feel uncomfortable'. Then I had to help him to push himself to act on this latter belief and choose a different option from his response repertoire i.e., ask girls to dance rather than avoid the situation. He did this repeatedly and achieved emotional rational insight on both the aforementioned beliefs.

When action tendencies encourage clients to avoid situations rather than to confront them constructively, activities which help them to reverse this trend have been called 'stay in there' activities by Grieger and Boyd (1980). Another example: one of my clients wanted to overcome her car-driving phobia. One of the things she feared was that her car would stall at a set of traffic lights and she would be exposed to the wrath of motorists who were stuck behind her. After eliciting and disputing her irrational ideas in traditional verbal dialogue, I encouraged her to turn off her engine at a set of lights and to stay there for about twenty minutes, thus creating the impression that her car had broken down. Fortunately, the other car drivers did react in an angry fashion and she was able to practise disputing her dire needs for approval and comfort in a situation in which she remained for fully half an hour.

The same methods can be used when action tendencies encourage clients to act in self-defeating ways other than avoidance. However, whatever action tendencies are involved in clients' problems, the following principle can be recommended: Whenever clients find it difficult to choose appropriate options from their repertoire, and in fact choose to act in accordance with their irrational action tendencies, look for their low frustration tolerance (LFT) ideas — since clients often have these in such situations.

Behavioural techniques

As shown above, one of the best ways of encouraging clients to achieve emotional rational insight is to have them change their self-defeating behaviour in relevant situations. I wish to reiterate this point since many people believe wrongly that rational-emotive counsellors only employ cognitive techniques to help clients change irrational beliefs. However, ideally behaviour change should be enacted while clients are simultaneously working cognitively to change their irrational beliefs. Thus in the example I introduced in the previous section the client asked girls to dance while convincing himself: 'I can do this even though I feel uncomfortable and I'm not a worm if I'm rejected'. With this point in mind I will discuss in this section certain behavioural techniques that rational-emotive counsellors particularly favour.

Ellis (1983 c) has criticized some popular behavioural techniques on the grounds that they do not necessarily encourage clients to achieve emotional rational insight as efficiently as possible. In particular he criticizes those methods that encourage clients to confront dreaded events in a gradual manner. He argues that gradualism may indeed reinforce some clients' low frustration tolerance ideas, e.g., 'I do need to go slowly, you see even my counsellor believes I can't stand feeling anxious'. Wherever possible then, rational-emotive counsellors encourage their clients to act in dramatic and vivid ways because they believe significant attitude change is more likely to follow the successful completion of such tasks. In addition, dramatic behavioural assignments are recommended to help clients overcome their LFT beliefs. Here the focus is orientated toward clients changing their irrational beliefs concerning their internal experiences of anxiety or frustration.

Shame-attacking exercises. Here clients are encouraged to act in a manner which they regard as 'shameful' while disputing their shame-creating beliefs. Clients are encouraged to act in ways that will encourage other people in the environment to pay attention to them and criticize them negatively without bringing harm to themselves, or the other people, and without unduly alarming others. Clients are encouraged in particular to engage simultaneously in vigorous disputing such as, 'They may think I'm an idiot but I choose to accept myself even though I may be acting stupidly'. Examples of shame-attacking beliefs that some of my clients have undertaken include: asking for directions to a street along which one is already walking, asking for a bar of chocolate in a hardware store and wearing clothes back to front. One of the difficulties with shame-attacking exercises for clients is actually eliciting the aversive responses from others that clients predict will occur. For example, if a client is anxious about a shopkeeper laughing at him for acting stupidly, then the client may have to carry out shame-attacking exercises several times before he encounters such a shopkeeper. However, this actual encounter is important if the client is going to have the experience of disputing his shame-inducing belief in the context of the feared event. Otherwise the client may make an inferentially-based change i.e., he may come to learn 'it is unlikely that shopkeepers will laugh at me when I act stupidly'. While this change is not to be decried it is less preferable than evaluative belief change e.g., 'If shopkeepers laugh at me, I can still accept myself'.

Risk-taking exercises. In risk-taking exercises clients are encouraged to do something they regard as being 'too risky'. These exercises are particularly helpful in encouraging clients to dispute discomfort-related irrational beliefs relating to certainty. For example, a client may be encouraged to take the risk of acting in an unpredictable manner not knowing how others will respond while disputing his belief 'I can stand the uncertainty of not knowing what will happen'.

Step-out-of-character exercises. Wessler (1984) has modified this exercise from

Kelly (1955). Clients are encouraged to identify desired behavioural goals which are not currently enacted with frequency and are encouraged to practise these behaviours while tolerating the accompanying feelings of 'unnaturalness' and to continue doing this until the new behaviour becomes habitual. For example, one of my clients chose the goal of eating more slowly, which for him was a desirable, nonshameful, nonrisky exercise, but one that involved monitoring of eating habits and cognitive disputing of low-frustration-tolerance ideas.

In vivo desensitization. These methods require clients to repeatedly confront their fears in an implosive manner. For example, clients with elevator phobia are asked to ride in elevators twenty to thirty times a day at the start of treatment instead of gradually working their way up to this situation either in imagery or in actuality. Again simultaneous cognitive disputing is urged. Neuman (1982) has written on and presented tapes of short-term group-orientated treatment of phobias. In his groups, clients are encouraged to rate their levels of anxiety. The most important goal is for clients to experience a 'level 10', which is extreme panic. Neuman continually points out to people that it is important to experience 'level 10' because only then can they learn that they can survive and live through such an experience. Similarly, if inroads to severe phobic conditions are to be made, it is important for rational-emotive counsellors to work toward helping clients tolerate extreme forms of anxiety before helping clients to reduce this anxiety.

There are occasions when clients refuse to undertake such assignments. When this occurs, compromises should preferably be made, as discussed in Chapter 10.

Repetition of behavioural assignments. Some clients tend to do dramatic exercises once or twice and then drop them from their repertoire. Counsellors are often so glad and so surprised that their clients will actually do these assignments that they do not show them the importance of continuing to do them. One of the reasons for continued practice has already been mentioned, namely that clients are more likely to make inferential changes than belief changes by doing these assignments infrequently. This is largely because the 'dreaded' event has a far lower probability of occurring than clients think. However, sooner or later, if clients consistently and persistently put into practice the above assignments, they may well encounter such events that will provide a context for disputing of irrational beliefs. Thus, if counsellors really want to encourage clients to make changes at B as well as at A, they had better be prepared to consistently encourage clients to do these dramatic assignments over a long period of time.

Rewards and penalties. Ellis (1979 c) has consistently employed rewards and penalties to encourage clients to take responsibility for being their own primary agents of change. Here clients are encouraged to identify and employ positive reinforcements for undertaking assignments, and penalties when they do not do so. While not all clients require such encouragement, difficult and resistant clients, whose resistance is due to low-frustration tolerance ideas, can be encouraged to take full responsibility for not putting into practice assignments that would stimulate change. Thus, dramatic experiences like burning a ten pound note, throwing away an eagerly awaited meal, and cleaning a dirty room at the end of a hard day's work are experiences that are designed to be so aversive that clients would choose to do the assignment previously avoided rather than undergo the penalty. Of course clients can, and often do, refuse to do the assignment and refuse to employ operant-conditioning methods. However, many clients who have been resistant in this part of the change process have, in my experience, begun to move when the counsellor adopts this no-nonsense approach.

Imagery techniques

Lazarus (in press) has criticized rational-emotive counselling for underemphasizing the imagery modality in working with clients. This criticism does have some merit in that RET practitioners prefer, whenever possible, to encourage clients towards emotional rational insight through action rather than through imagination, believing action to be a more powerful medium for promoting such insight than imagery. Perhaps the exception to this is the technique known as rational-emotive imagery (REI) which was pioneered by Maultsby (1975) and modified by Ellis. The purpose of REI is to promote emotional rational insight while vividly imagining troublesome events at A.

REI (Ellis version). In Ellis' version of REI the client is asked to imagine a vivid example of the context A in which the client's emotional problems occur and to 'get in touch with' her irrational emotion at C. She is then asked to change her irrational emotion to its rational alternative (e.g., anxiety to concern) while still vividly imagining the same situation at A. When the client executes the procedure successfully, she does so by changing her irrational belief to its rational alternative. However, counsellors are recommended to check this since clients can achieve this feeling change by modifying inferences or by distraction. When this occurs, the counsellor encourages the client to repeat the exercise, but this time without changing inferences and without using distractions. Once the client has learned how to execute REI in the counselling session she is instructed to practise it for thirty days (three times a day for a minimum of ten minutes on each occasion).

REI (Maultsby version). In Maultsby's version of REI, the client is again asked to imagine vividly the situation at A, but this time she is instructed to repeat forcefully the relevant rational belief at B in order to experience a rational emotion at C. Repeated practice is again recommended after the client has understood the procedure.

It is worthwhile noting that some clients experience difficulty creating images and may have to be trained in stepwise fashion to utilize this ability. Furthermore, while helpful, it is probably not necessary for clients to imagine with clarity in order to benefit from both versions of REI.

Imagery rehearsal. Imagery rehearsal can be used in rational-emotive counselling to build a bridge between the client's intellectual insight into a rational concept and the client's attempt to act on that insight in the world. For example, one of my clients gained intellectual insight into her shame-based philosophy and understood intellectually, but not emotionally, that she is not a fool for acting foolishly; rather she is a fallible human being who has acted foolishly. In order for her to begin to act on and internalize this rational belief, I encouraged her to act foolishly in public while practising the new rational philosophy *in situ*. Imagery rehearsal was used with this client, as with others, prior to the behavioural assignment because she doubted her ability to execute the assignment in the real world. Thus:

> *Counsellor:* OK. You say that you see the sense of doing that (Here the assignment was for her to go into a confectionery shop and ask for one brand of chocolate bar, leave the shop and return to exchange the bar for another brand. She was to practise simultaneously the rational belief: 'I'm a fallible human being even though I may appear stupid to others').
>
> *Client:* Yes, but I don't know whether I can do it.
>
> *Counsellor:* OK, but let's see. Let's try it out in your mind's eye first. Do you think imagining yourself doing it will help you to do it?
>
> *Client:* It might.
>
> *Counsellor:* OK. Now close your eyes and imagine that you've begun the exercise by going into the shop and buying the first bar. Can you picture that?
>
> *Client:* Yes.
>
> *Counsellor:* OK, and how do you feel in this image?
>
> *Client:* Fine at this point.
>
> *Counsellor:* Good. Now imagine you've bought the bar and you've left the shop. Picture yourself deciding to go back to exchange the bar. How do you feel now?
>
> *Client:* Anxious.
>
> *Counsellor:* OK. Now see yourself using that anxiety as a cue to vigorously say to yourself your new rational belief: 'I'm a fallible

human being even though I may appear stupid to the shop-keeper'. Can you imagine yourself doing that?

Client: (Pause) Yes.

Counsellor: Now keep that new belief in mind and picture yourself going into the shop and see yourself ask for a swap and imagine that the shopkeeper's attitude implies that he thinks you are stupid. Really work on keeping the new philosophy in the front of your mind even in the face of his critical attitude and even though it's a struggle. Now really work on doing that. (Pause). Can you do that?

Client: (Pause). Yes, but it's difficult.

Counsellor: Now go over that scene in your mind's eye several times a day. Keep on assuming that the shopkeeper's attitude will be critical and see yourself accept yourself in the face of his attitude. Do you think that will help you to do that in reality?

Client: Yes, I think that may well help.

It is important to offer clients a coping rather than a mastery model of themselves in imagery rehearsal. Thus note that I stressed both that it was a struggle to keep the new belief in her mind's eye and that she could do it even though it was difficult.

Constructing a new attitude

I have found it helpful to draw upon Kelly's (1955) 'fixed role therapy' method to help clients to construct a new attitude. Let us assume that a client has once again gained intellectual insight into the rational concept of unconditional self-accept-ance rather than the irrational concept of conditional self-esteem. What I do is to have the client select a relevant situation in which she can practise the new rational philosophy. I then say the following:

'Now imagine someone with whom you can identify, who is like you in many ways apart from the fact that, at the moment, she is more self-accepting than you. What kind of thoughts will the person have about herself, others, and the situation she finds herself in? What will she say in this situation, what will she be feeling and what will she be doing?'

After this material has been collected and modified to represent a realistic rational model, i.e., one that isn't perfectly rational and thus outside the client's scope, I suggest that the client imagines in her mind's eye for a week or two that she is that person to see how the role fits. When the client has done this, we discuss her reactions and make appropriate adjustments to the new rational role. I then suggest that the client practises in imagery the modified role for a further week. Assuming that no further adjustments are necessary, I suggest that the client tries out the new role in action as an experiment. The client's reactions to this experiment are then discussed in counselling, with the counsellor helping the client to dispute any further irrational beliefs and suggesting modifications to the role as appropriate.

A variation of this method is to use the client as her own model and to contrast her present irrational self with a perfectly rational self and a fallible, i.e., imperfect, rational self. I particularly emphasize the latter distinction with clients who demand that they must be perfectly rational.

Vivid Cues for Encouraging Clients to Initiate the Process of Promoting Emotional Rational Insight

While some clients conscientiously do the homework assignments that they and their counsellors have negotiated, other clients do not. It is true that some clients do not follow through on these assignments because of low frustration toleration ideas; still other clients do not follow through, particularly early on in the promoting of emotional rational insight process, because they require some vivid reminders to initiate this process. With such clients, I have found it particularly helpful to ask them what they generally find memorable in everyday life experiences. For example, some people find the printed word memorable while others have visual images on which they cue. Yet others focus primarily on auditory stimuli. I find that it is profitable to capitalize on whatever channel the client finds most memorable.

Vivid visual cues

There are a number of ways clients can remind themselves to initiate the disputing process. A number of rational-emotive counsellors encourage clients to carry around small cards with rational self-statements written on them to which clients can refer at various times. Other counsellors have encouraged clients to write reminders to themselves either to initiate a homework assignment or to refer to a rational message. These clients are encouraged to pin up such messages at various places around the home or in their work situation.

I find it helpful to encourage those clients who find visual images powerful to associate a particular dysfunctional feeling with a visual image that would enable them to initiate the disputing process. Thus one client found it helpful to conjure up a sign in her mind that said 'Dispute' when she began to feel anxious. Another client, who was depressed, began to associate the onset of depression with a road sign on which was written 'Act Now'.

Another strategy I have used is to ascertain from clients what, if any, in-session experiences they have found particularly memorable. I try to help them encapsulate some of these experiences as a cue either to initiate the disputing process or to remind themselves of the relevant rational principle to which this experience referred. One client who was prone to thinking himself an idiot for acting idiotically found it memorable when I made strange faces at him to help him get the point that concluding he was an idiot for acting idiotically was an overgeneralization. Whenever he began to make such an overgeneralization in everyday life, he would get the image of my making faces and quickly remember to what this referred. This helped him accept himself for any idiotic act he actually made or thought he might make in the future.

Another client who did virtually no cognitive disputing or behavioural assignments outside the sessions was helped in the following manner: first, this issue was made the focus of counselling. Instead of asking her traditional disputing questions, I asked her to imagine what I would say to her were I to respond to her irrational beliefs. She in fact had understood rational principles because her answers were very good. Her problem was that she would not employ these principles. I then asked her if there was any way she could conjure up a picture of me giving her rational messages at various emotionally vulnerable times in her everyday life. She hit on the idea of imagining that I was perched on her shoulder whispering rational messages into her ear. Additionally she began to carry around a small card that said 'Imagine that Dr Dryden is on your shoulder'. This proved a particularly effective technique where all else had failed.

Vivid language

Wexler and Butler (1976) have argued in favour of counsellors using expressive language in counselling. I have found that one of the major benefits of using vivid nonprofane language is that clients remember these vivid expressions, or catch phrases and use them as shorthand ways of disputing irrational beliefs in their everyday lives.

For example, several of my clients find phrases like 'just too bad', 'tough luck', 'hard cheese' as helpful vivid reminders to practise the rational philosophy of high frustration tolerance. Concerning self-worth problems I helped one of my clients who was ashamed of urinating in public toilets to move from intellectual to emotional insight by encouraging him to remind himself that he was a 'fallible human peeing' while he was urinating.

In a related technique, the counsellor can ask the client to give his or her own distinctive name to a faulty psychological process. Wessler and Wessler (1980) give such an example where a client came to refer to himself as 'Robert the Rule Maker' to describe his tendency to make demands on himself and other people. A knowledge of clients' subcultural values is particularly helpful here. I used to work in a working-class area in Birmingham, England, and one word my clients frequently used which was unfamiliar to me, was the word 'mather'. (This is pronounced 'my-the' and means to be worried or bothered). I helped one client who was angry with her mother to see that her mother was a fallible human being with a worrying problem, and that she could be accepted for this rather than be damned for it. My client suddenly laughed and said, 'Yes! I guess my mother is a matherer'. I encouraged her to remember this catchy phrase whenever she began to feel angry toward her mother.

Auditory cues

As has been shown, rational-emotive counsellors often make tape recordings of their sessions for clients to replay several times between sessions. This serves to remind clients of rational principles they have understood in the session but may have since forgotten. Using personal recording systems, clients can also be encouraged to develop auditory reminders to initiate either cognitive or behavioural homework assignments. In addition, they can be encouraged to put forceful and emphatic rational statements on cassettes and play these while undertaking behavioural assignments. For example, I once saw a client who was anxious about other people looking at her for fear they might think her strange. I suggested that she do something in her everyday life that would encourage people to look at her so that she could dispute some of her underlying irrational beliefs *in situ*. She decided to wear a personal stereo system in the street which she thought would encourage people to look at her. I suggested that while walking she play a tape on which she had recorded the rational message 'Just because I look strange doesn't mean that I am strange'.

The use of rational songs in counselling has already been described. Several of my clients have found that singing a particular rational song at an emotionally vulnerable time has been helpful for them. It has reminded them of a rational message they might not ordinarily have been able to focus on while being emotionally distressed. Another client told me that her sessions with me reminded her of a particular song and whenever she hummed this song to herself it helped bring to mind the fact that she could accept herself even though she did not have a man in her life. The song ironically was 'You're No One Till Somebody Loves You'. In fact she rewrote some of the words and changed the title to 'You're Someone Even Though Nobody Loves You'.

Olfactory cues

It is possible for clients to use various aromas as cues to remind themselves to do a homework assignment or to initiate the disputing process. One client said that she found my pipe tobacco particularly aromatic and distinctive. Since we were both seeking a memorable cue, I suggested an experiment whereby she purchased a packet of my favourite tobacco and carried this around with her to smell at various distressing times. This aroma was associated in her mind with a particular rational message. This proved helpful and indeed my client claimed that by saying to herself the phrase 'Pipe up' she now no longer has to take the tobacco out of her handbag to smell. Just the phrase is enough to remind her of the rational message.

While I have outlined a number of techniques in this chapter which encourage clients to initiate and sustain the process of moving from intellectual to emotional insight, once again I wish to stress that it is important for counsellors to use their own creativity in devising and implementing new techniques to help their own clients to initiate the change process.

9. Case Management

Overview

In this chapter I deal with a number of issues concerning general case management issues in rational-emotive counselling. First, I deal with issues of structuring counselling sessions and dealing with a variety of client problems throughout the counselling process. In particular I discuss the use of problem lists, problem and summary matrices and session agendas. Second, I present a handout developed by Ellis (1984 c) which provides advice to clients on how they can maintain and enhance their therapeutic gains. Third, I discuss a number of issues that are relevant to working towards termination of counselling. Finally, I present a typical session of rational-emotive counselling, and a typical case of rational-emotive counselling to demonstrate the process of case management in action.

Introduction

Chapters 6, 7 and 8 have dealt with a given sequence of intervention when a client seeks help with *one* major problem, i.e., induction — assessment — promotion of intellectual rational insight — promotion of emotional rational insight.

However, what if the client has a number of different psychological problems? The first point to keep in mind here is that the assessment — intellectual rational insight — emotional rational insight sequence is common to all of the psychological problems that the client may have. The second point I wish to stress is that unless there are good reasons for doing otherwise, the counsellor would be wise to focus, at the beginning of any counselling session, on the problem that the client most wishes to discuss. This may mean that discussion of the previous week's homework assignment is postponed until later in the session. The major exception to this rule concerns client avoidance. When the counsellor suspects that the client is choosing to discuss issues in order to avoid discussion of more important issues, the counsellor should preferably raise this as a possibility with the client.

It has been my experience that if a counsellor tries to begin a session by focusing on an issue which conflicts with what the client wishes to discuss, then the client is likely to become distracted and irritated. If the counsellor considers it to be important to begin a session by discussing the client's reactions to the previous week's homework assignment, while the client wishes to start elsewhere, then the counsellor is advised to provide the client with a clear rationale for beginning with the assignment and to elicit the client's agreement to begin with that issue. If the counsellor cannot elicit such agreement he is advised to begin with the client's priority.

Beck *et al.* (1979) are particularly helpful on case management issues in suggesting the development of a problem list and an agenda for the session.

Problem list

A problem list is an inventory of problems for which the client is seeking help during counselling. It is often developed in initial sessions, although additions to and subtractions from the list are likely throughout the counselling process. Ideally, the list should exist in written form and a copy be kept by both client and counsellor.

When the counsellor and client are ready to start focusing on a problem, the client is invited to choose from the problem list to begin the counselling process. This problem may be the client's most pressing problem, the problem which is easiest to solve, or one which if progress is achieved, engenders most hope for the client. The guiding principle here is that counsellor and client should preferably collaborate on problem selection and agree on the chosen issue, which, in practice, tends to be the client's most pressing problem.

In addition, I recommend that counsellors develop a *summary matrix* for each client which shows the client's problems (as written on the problem list) and the counselling stage that has been reached for each problem. An example of such a summary matrix appears in Figure 5. This figure shows that the client has chosen, so far, to discuss problems 1, 3 and 4. The counsellor considers that the client has achieved: (a) partial intellectual insight into the irrationality on problem 1; (b) good intellectual insight and partial emotional insight on problem 4; but (c) no intellectual insight into the cognitive underpinnings of problem 3. It is important to stress that frequent modifications are usually made to such matrices. Just because a client has achieved a level of intellectual insight at one time in counselling does not preclude the possibility that she may 'lose' such insight later in the process. For this reason I also keep an up-to-date *problem matrix* for each of the client's problems

Problem List	Assessment	Intellectual Rational Insight	Emotional Rational Insight
1. Anxious about shopping	Yes	Yes (4)	No
2. Anger at husband	No	—	—
3. Depressed about financial situation	Yes	No	—
4. Lack of confidence at social events	Yes	Yes (8)	Yes (4)

A scale from 0–10 is used where:

> 0 = None
> 5 = Fair
> 10 = Excellent

The scale represents the counsellor's subjective clinical judgment.

Figure 5.   Client F: Summary Matrix (at end of session 8)

(see Figure 6). It should be noted from this that counsellors may well have to 'go over old ground' with their clients and repetition of assessment and discussion of rational concepts is a regular feature of rational-emotive counselling.

When a client wishes to discuss a particular problem then, the summary and problem matrices help the counsellor to see which stage the client has reached on that problem so far. The counsellor then undertakes a quick assessment to determine whether the client has maintained, enhanced or lost her gains on a particular issue and starts accordingly. The guiding principle here is: 'start where the client is at *now*'.

Lack of confidence at social events

Session 1	A
Session 2	A; II (3)
Session 3	II (5)
Session 4	Not discussed
Session 5	II (6); EI (3)
Session 6	Not discussed
Session 7	II (4); EI (2)
Session 8	A; II (8); EI (4)

A = Assessment
II = Intellectual Insight
EI = Emotional Insight

A scale of 0–10 is used where:

> 0 = None
> 5 = Fair
> 10 = Excellent

The scale represents the counsellor's subjective clinical judgment.

Figure 6.   Client F: Problem Matrix

As clients make progress on one problem, it does happen that they begin to make progress on their other unrelated problems, although as noted in the previous chapter, it should not be assumed that generalization will naturally occur. Thus, at the end of counselling, client F was able on her own to assess the irrational beliefs underlying her anger and achieved excellent intellectual and emotional rational insight on the problem even though we only discussed the issue once.

The problem list is an important tool when reviews of client progress are carried out. I use such reviews, which can occupy part of a counselling session or an entire session, as opportunities for my clients and I to reflect on their progress and the problem list is used as a basis for such discussion. The list can also be used when client follow-up sessions are held after formal termination of counselling.

Session agenda

It was noted earlier in this chapter that it is wise for counsellor and client to be in accord concerning what to discuss in counselling sessions and that it is important for this agreement to occur at the beginning of sessions. Setting an agenda is particularly helpful in this respect (Beck *et al.*, 1979). An agenda lists the topics which counsellor and client have agreed to discuss during a given session. As such, the agenda helps to structure counselling sessions but should be used flexibly and not slavishly. In particular a long list of items should be avoided particularly if it is clear that any one item will occupy a large proportion of session time.

Some counsellors prefer to use the agenda informally while others like to develop a more formal arrangement with clients. An example of an informal agenda occurred when I agreed with client F at the beginning of session six that we would spend most of the session discussing her most pressing issue of the week (depression about her family's financial situation) and if we had enough time we would discuss her previous week's homework assignment. In fact the entire session was devoted to her problem of depression and we postponed discussion of the assignment until session seven. An example of a formal agenda appears below, the order of which reflects the client's priorities.

Session 9.   Client Z: Therapist Y

(1)   Last night's panic attack
(2)   Last week's homework
(3)   Josh's illness
(4)   Hypochondria

The advantage of a formal agenda is that it helps to prevent some counsellors from switching unhelpfully from problem to problem. Thus if client Z suddenly stops discussing her panic attack and switches to discussing Josh's illness, the counsellor can check whether or not this is a productive shift. If not, the counsellor can bring the client back to the panic attack and/or discuss what prompted the shift, e.g., the issue provoked too much anxiety. The major disadvantage of a formal agenda is that it may encourage both client and counsellor to believe that an agenda *must be* covered in any session.

Helping Clients to Maintain and Enhance their Gains

When clients have made progress on their psychological problems it is helpful for counsellors to educate them on how to maintain their improvement, deal with backsliding, and generalize from working on one emotional problem to others. Ellis (1984 c) has produced a valuable handout which summarizes concisely the advice which clients are given on each of these three points. This handout is reproduced below (with minor modifications).

How to maintain your improvement

1 When you improve and then fall back to old feelings of anxiety, depression, or self-downing, try to remind yourself and pinpoint exactly what thoughts, feelings, and behaviours you once changed to bring about your improvement. If you again feel depressed, think back to how you previously used rational-emotive principles to make yourself undepressed. For example, you may remember that:

  a You stopped telling yourself that you were worthless and that you couldn't ever succeed in getting what you wanted.
  b You did well in a job or in a love affair and proved to yourself that you did have some ability and that you were lovable.
  c You forced yourself to go to interviews instead of avoiding them and thereby helped yourself overcome your anxiety about them.

  Remind yourself of thoughts, feelings, and behaviours that you have changed and that you have helped yourself by changing.

2 Keep thinking, thinking and thinking rational beliefs or coping statements, such as: 'It's great to succeed but I can fully accept myself as a person and enjoy life considerably even when I fail!'. Don't merely parrot these statements but go over them carefully many times and think them through until you really begin to believe and feel that they are true.

3 Keep seeking for, discovering, and disputing and challenging your irrational beliefs with which you are once again upsetting yourself. Take each important

irrational belief — such as, 'I have to succeed in order to be a worthwhile person!' — and keep asking yourself: 'Why is this belief true?', 'Where is the evidence that my worth to myself, and my enjoyment of living, utterly depends on my succeeding at something?', 'In what way would I be totally unacceptable as a human if I failed at an important task or test?'.

Keep forcefully and persistently disputing your irrational beliefs whenever you see that you are letting them creep back again. And even when you don't actively hold them, realize that they may arise once more, bring them to your consciousness, and preventively — and vigorously! — dispute them.

4 Keep risking and doing things that you irrationally fear — such as riding in elevators, socializing, job hunting, or creative writing. Once you have partly overcome one of your irrational fears, keep acting against it on a regular basis. If you feel uncomfortable in forcing yourself to do things that you are unrealistically afraid of doing, don't allow yourself to avoid doing them — and thereby to preserve your discomfort forever! Often, make yourself as uncomfortable as you can be, in order to eradicate your irrational fears and to become unanxious and comfortable later.

5 Try to clearly see the difference between rational negative feelings — such as those of sorrow, regret, and frustration, when you do not get some of the important things you want — and irrational negative feelings — such as those of depression, anxiety, self-hatred, and self-pity, when you are deprived of desirable goals and plagued with undesirable things. Whenever you feel *overconcerned* (panicked) or *unduly* miserable (depressed) acknowledge that you are having a statistically normal but a psychologically unhealthy feeling and that you are bringing it on yourself with some dogmatic *should*, *ought*, or *must*. Realize that you are invariably capable of changing your irrational (or *mus*turbatory) feelings back into rational (or preferential) ones. Take your depressed feelings and work on them until you *only* feel sorry and regretful. Take your anxious feelings and work on them until you *only* feel concerned and vigilant. Use rational-emotive imagery to vividly imagine unpleasant activating events even before they happen: let yourself feel irrationally upset (anxious, depressed, enraged, or self-downing) as you imagine them; then work on your feelings to change them to rational emotions (concern, sorrow, annoyance, or regret) as you keep imagining some of the worst things happening. Don't give up until you actually do change your feelings.

6 Avoid self-defeating procrastination. Do unpleasant tasks fast — today! If you still procrastinate, reward yourself with certain things that you enjoy — for example, eating, vacationing, reading, and socializing — only *after* you have performed the tasks that you easily avoid. If this won't work, give yourself a

severe penalty — such as talking to a boring person for two hours or burning a hundred dollar bill — every time that you procrastinate.

7 Show yourself that it is an absorbing challenge and something of an adventure to maintain your emotional health and to keep yourself reasonably happy no matter what kind of misfortunes assail you. Make the uprooting of your misery one of the most important things in your life — something you are utterly determined to steadily work at achieving. Fully acknowledge that you almost always have some choice about how to think, feel, and behave: and throw yourself actively into making that choice for yourself.

8 Remember — and use — the three main insights of rational-emotive counselling:

Insight No. 1: You largely *choose* to disturb yourself about the unpleasant events of your life, although you may be encouraged to do so by external happenings and by social learning. You mainly feel the way you think. When obnoxious and frustrating things happen to you at point A (activating events), you consciously or unconsciously *select* rational beliefs that lead you to feel sad and regretful and you also *select* irrational beliefs that lead you to feel anxious, depressed and self-hating.

Insight No. 2: No matter how or when you acquired your irrational beliefs and your self-sabotaging habits, you now, in the present, *choose* to maintain them — and that is why you are now disturbed. Your past history and your present life conditions importantly *affect* you; but they don't *disturb* you. Your present *philosophy* is the main contributor to your *current* disturbance.

Insight No. 3: There is no magical way for you to change your personality and your strong tendencies to needlessly upset yourself. Basic personality change requires persistent *work and practice* — yes, *work and practice* — to enable you to alter your irrational beliefs, your inappropriate feelings, and your self-destructive behaviours.

9 Steadily — and unfrantically! — look for personal pleasures and enjoyments — such as reading, entertainment, sports, hobbies, art, science, and other vital absorbing interests. Take as your major life goal not only the achievement of emotional health but also that of real enjoyment. Try to become involved in a longterm purpose, goal, or interest in which you can remain truly absorbed. For a good, happy life will give you something to live *for*; will distract you from many serious woes; and will encourage you to preserve and to improve your mental health.

10 Try to keep in touch with several other people who know something about RET counselling and who can help go over some of its aspects with you. Tell them about problems that you have difficulty coping with and let them know how you are using rational-emotive principles to overcome these problems. See if they agree with your solutions and can suggest additional and better kinds of disputing methods that you can use to work against your irrational beliefs.

11 Practise using rational-emotive methods with some of your friends, relatives, and associates who are willing to let you try to help them with it. The more often you use it with others, and are able to see what their irrational beliefs are and to try to talk them out of these self-defeating ideas, the more you will be able to understand the main principles of RET counselling and to use them with yourself. When you see other people act irrationally and in a disturbed manner, try to figure out — with or without talking to them about it — what their main irrational beliefs probably are and how these could be actively and vigorously disputed.

12 When you are in rational-emotive counselling try to tape record many of your sessions and listen to these carefully when you are in between sessions, so that some of the rational-emotive ideas that you learned in counselling sink in. After counselling has ended, keep these tape recordings and play them back to yourself from time to time, to remind you how to deal with some of your old problems or new ones that may arise.

13 Keep going back to the rational-emotive reading and audio-visual material from time to time, to keep reminding yourself of some of the main rational-emotive findings and philosophies.

How to deal with backsliding

1 Accept your backsliding as normal — as something that happens to almost all people who at first improve emotionally and who then fall back. See it as part of your human fallibility. Don't feel ashamed when some of your old symptoms return: and don't think that you have to handle them entirely by yourself and that it is wrong or weak for you to seek some additional sessions of counselling and to talk to your friends about your renewed problems.

2 When you backslide look at your self-defeating behaviour as bad and unfortunate; but work very hard at refusing to put yourself down for engaging in this behaviour. Use the highly important rational-emotive principle of refraining from rating *you*, your*self*, or your *being*, but of measuring your *acts*, *deeds*, and

traits. You are always a *person who* acts well or badly — and never a *good person* nor a *bad person*. No matter how badly you fall back and bring on your old disturbances again, work at fully accepting yourself with this unfortunate or weak behaviour — and then try, and keep trying, to change your behaviour.

3 Go back to the ABCs of rational-emotive counselling and clearly see what you did to fall back to your old symptoms. At A (activating event), you usually experienced some failure or rejection once again. At rB (rational belief) you probably told yourself that you didn't *like* failing and didn't *want* to be rejected. If you only stayed with these rational beliefs, you would merely feel sorry, regretful, disappointed, or frustrated. But when you felt disturbed again, you probably then went on to some irrational beliefs (iBs) such as 'I *must* not fail! It's *horrible* when I do!' 'I *have to* be accepted, because if I'm not that makes me an *unlovable worthless person!*' Then, after convincing yourself of these iBs, you felt, at C (emotional consequence) once again depressed and self-downing.

4 When you find your irrational beliefs by which you are once again disturbing yourself, just as you originally used disputing (D) to challenge and surrender them, do so again — *immediately* and *persistently*. Thus, you can ask yourself: 'Why *must* I not fail? Is it really *horrible* if I do?' And you can answer: 'There is no reason why I *must* not fail, though I can think of several reasons why it would be highly undesirable. It's not *horrible* if I do fail — only distinctly *inconvenient*'. You can also dispute your other irrational beliefs by asking yourself, 'Where is it written that I *have* to be accepted? How do I become an *unlovable, worthless person* if I am rejected?' And you can answer: 'I never *have to be* accepted, though I would very much *prefer* to be. If I am rejected, that makes me, alas, a *person who* is rejected this time by this individual under these conditions, but it hardly makes me an *unlovable, worthless person* who will always be rejected by anyone for whom I really care'.

5 Keep looking for, finding and actively and vigorously disputing your irrational beliefs which you have once again revived and that are now making you feel anxious or depressed once more. Keep doing this, over and over, until you build intellectual and emotional muscle (just as you would build physical muscle by learning how to exercise and then by *continuing* to exercise).

6 Don't fool yourself into believing that if you merely change your language you will always change your thinking. If you neurotically tell yourself: 'I *must* succeed and be approved' and you sanely change this self-statement to 'I *prefer* to succeed and be approved', you may still really be convinced: 'But I really *have to* do well and *have got to be* loved'. Before you stop your disputing and before you are satisfied with your answers to it (which in rational-emotive counselling we call E, or an effective philosophy), keep on doing it until you

are *really* convinced of your rational answers and until your feelings of disturbance truly disappear. Then do the same thing many, many times — until your new E (effective philosophy) becomes hardened and habitual — which it almost always will if you keep working at arriving at it and re-instituting it.

7   Convincing yourself lightly or 'intellectually' of your new effective philosophy or rational beliefs often won't help very much or persist very long. Do so very *strongly* and *vigorously* and do so many times. Thus, you can *powerfully* convince yourself, until you really *feel* it: 'I do not *need* what I *want*! I never *have* to succeed, no matter how greatly I wish to do so! I *can* stand being rejected by someone I care for. It won't *kill* me — and I *still* can lead a happy life! *No* human is damnable and worthless — including and especially *me*!'.

How to generalize from working on one emotional problem to working on other problems

1   Show yourself that your present emotional problem and the ways in which you bring it on are not unique and that virtually all emotional and behavioural difficulties are created by irrational beliefs. Whatever your irrational beliefs are, moreover, you can overcome them by strongly and persistently disputing and acting against these irrational beliefs.

2   Recognize that you tend to have three major kinds of irrational beliefs that lead you to disturb yourself and that the emotional and behavioural problems that you want to relieve fall into one of these three categories:

   a   'I *must* do well and *have to* be approved by people whom I find important'. This irrational belief leads you to feel anxious, depressed, and self-hating; and to avoid doing things at which you may fail and avoiding relationships that may not turn out well.

   b   'Other people *must* treat me fairly and nicely!' This irrational belief contributes to your feeling angry, furious, violent, and over-rebellious.

   c   'The conditions under which I live *must* be comfortable and free from major hassles!' This irrational belief tends to create your feelings of low frustration tolerance and self-pity; and sometimes those of anger and depression.

3   Recognize that when you employ one of these absolutist *musts* — or any of the innumerable variations on it that you can easily slide into — you naturally and commonly derive from them other irrational conclusions, such as:

a 'Because I am not doing as well as I *must*, I am an incompetent worthless individual!' (Self-damnation).

b 'Since I am not being approved by people whom I find important, as I *have to be*, it's *awful* and *terrible!*' (Awfulizing).

c 'Because others are not treating me as fairly and as nicely as they *absolutely should* treat me, they are *utterly rotten people* and deserve to be damned!' (Other-damnation).

d 'Since the conditions under which I live are not that comfortable and since my life has several major hassles, as it *must* not have, I can't stand it! My existence is a horror!' (Can't-stand-it-itis).

4 Work at seeing that these irrational beliefs are part of your *general* repertoire of thoughts and feelings and that you bring them to many different kinds of situations that are against your desires. Realize that in just about all cases where you feel seriously upset and act in a distinctly self-defeating manner you are consciously or unconsciously sneaking in one or more of these irrational beliefs. Consequently, if you get rid of them in one area and are still emotionally disturbed about something else, you can always use the same rational-emotive principles to discover your irrational beliefs in the new area and to eliminate them there.

5 Repeatedly show yourself that it is almost impossible to disturb yourself and to remain disturbed in any way if you abandon your absolutist, dogmatic *shoulds*, *oughts*, and *musts* and consistently replace them with flexible and unrigid (though still strong) *desires* and *preferences*.

6 Continue to acknowledge that you can change your irrational beliefs by rigorously (not rigidly!) using the scientific method. With scientific thinking, you can show yourself that your irrational beliefs are only theories or hypotheses — not facts. You can logically and realistically dispute them in many ways, such as these:

a You can show yourself that your irrational beliefs are self-defeating — that they interfere with your goals and your happiness. For if you firmly convince yourself: 'I *must* succeed at important tasks and *have to* be approved by all the significant people in my life', you will of course at times fail and be disapproved — and thereby inevitably make yourself anxious and depressed instead of sorry and frustrated.

b Your irrational beliefs do not conform to reality — and especially do not conform to the facts of human fallibility. If you always *had to* succeed, if the universe commanded that you *must* do so, you obviously *would* always succeed. And of course you often don't! If you invariably *had* to be approved by others, you could never be disapproved. But obviously you frequently are! The universe is clearly not arranged so that you will always get what you demand. So although your desires are often realistic, your godlike commands definitely are not!

c Your irrational beliefs are illogical, inconsistent, or contradictory. No matter how much you *want* to succeed and to be approved, it never follows that therefore you *must* do well in these (or any other) respects. No matter how desirable justice or politeness is, it never *has to* exist.

Although the scientific method is not infallible or sacred, it efficiently helps you to discover which of your beliefs are irrational and self-defeating and how to use factual evidence and logical thinking to rid yourself of them. If you keep using scientific analysis, you will avoid dogma and set up your hypotheses about you, other people, and the world around you so that you always keep them open to change.

7 Try to set up some main goals and purposes in life — goals that you would like very much to reach but that you never tell yourself that you absolutely must attain. Keep checking to see how you are coming along with these goals; at times revise them; see how you feel about achieving them; and keep yourself goal-orientated for the rest of your days.

8 If you get bogged down and begin to lead a life that seems too miserable or dull, review the points made here and work at using them. Once again: if you fall back or fail to go forward at the pace you prefer, don't hesitate to return to counselling for some booster sessions.

Working Towards Termination

As counsellor and client work together on particular problems over time, the counsellor endeavours to help the client to internalize the following process. First, the client identifies troublesome emotions and behaviours, links them to activating events, and thence identifies his or her major irrational beliefs. The client then disputes those beliefs and then puts the alternative rational beliefs into practice by executing relevant assignments. Thus, in this phase of rational-emotive counselling the counsellor is not only concerned with helping clients to solve their emotional and behavioural problems but also with helping them to internalize the scientific methods of rational-emotive problem identification and problem solution.

As clients make progress on their major problem it often happens that the degree of counsellor directiveness fades as the counsellor encourages them to practise self-therapy. In addition, the counsellor strives to help clients see that they can tackle similar problems that may occur in different contexts. Thus, counsellors often plan and work to help clients achieve therapeutic generalization across situations. This process should preferably not be seen as occurring naturally. Thus, the client who believes 'I must be perfect at passing examinations' and is successful in challenging this belief and acting on the alternative rational belief may not in fact be successful at challenging a similar belief with relevance to love relationships.

Thus, after the client has made some progress on her major problem, the counsellor encourages her to see the links between this and related problems, which are underpinned by similar irrational beliefs. The counsellor continually looks for opportunities to encourage the client to use the skills that he or she has successfully demonstrated in helping to solve problem number one which can then be used to solve problem number two.

Whereas at the outset the counsellor is usually responsible for making sugges- tions concerning homework assignments, at the later stages of counselling the counsellor encourages clients to set their own homework assignments and also helps them to learn the effective ingredients which are involved in the selection of effective homework assignments (to be discussed in Chapter 10).

Another major concern of the RET counsellor in this phase is to assess adequately the reasons for therapeutic change and to help the client to understand and learn from these. Clients can make progress on their emotional and behav- ioural problems for a variety of reasons. Thus, a client may show therapeutic progress because he or she has successfully changed A, has effected an inferen- tially-based change, a behaviourally-based change or, as is the ideal in rational- emotive counselling, a change in underlying philosophy, i.e., clients have success- fully challenged their irrational beliefs and replaced these with rational beliefs. When changes can be attributed to one or more of the sources mentioned above (other than the philosophic source) the counsellor uses this information to help the client see that the core of emotional or behavioural problems has not been success- fully tackled and encourages the client to address herself to the philosophic core of her problem.

When the client has made significant progress on her major and related problems the counsellor seeks to prepare her to be her own future counsellor. In other words the counsellor seeks to make himself redundant. Individual rational- emotive counselling is terminated not when clients have necessarily solved all their problems, but when they feel prepared to solve their remaining problems on their own and are confident in their ability to solve any future difficulties. The counsel- lor may work towards termination by either decreasing the frequency of sessions over time or by setting a definite termination date. In both cases most RET counsellors do schedule follow-up sessions to monitor client progress. In advance of termination the counsellor can productively use session time to help the client to anticipate future problems and to imagine how he or she would productively handle those problems by using the skills of rational-emotive self-counselling that have now, hopefully, been internalized to a considerable degree.

Additionally, the counsellor elicits and deals with any dependency needs that the client may have about terminating counselling. Some clients who have made considerable progress still believe that they need the continued help of a counsellor in order to maintain their progress. Such problems may become manifest when clients, who have made considerable progress, are reluctant either to set a termination date or to decrease the frequency of sessions. However, there are a minority of quite disturbed clients who do seem to find it hard to cope on their own and in this case counsellors can productively schedule infrequent 'booster' sessions of rational-emotive counselling for such people.

Some counsellors may be reluctant to terminate counselling with clients who have shown considerable progress. They may believe that they need the continued evidence of client progress to prove that they are competent practitioners and therefore worthwhile people. Needless to say, it would be highly desirable for such counsellors to identify and challenge such competency needs using the methods of rational-emotive counselling outlined in this book.

Terminating clients should preferably be able to acknowledge that they experience 'irrational' negative emotions which cause them to act dysfunctionally; detect the irrational beliefs which underpin these experiences; discriminate their irrational beliefs from their rational alternatives; challenge these irrational beliefs; and counteract them by using cognitive, emotive and behavioural self-change methods.

A Typical Session of Individual Rational-Emotive Counselling

I wish now to give the reader an idea of how a 'typical' session of individual rational-emotive counselling is conducted. It is important to note that the following is meant to be a flexible guide rather than a rigid framework.

The counsellor asks the client what she most wishes to discuss in the session and indicates that he wishes to discuss her experiences in carrying out the previous week's homework assignment. They decide to start with the client's priority item (which in this case has not been previously discussed), leaving the homework assignment till later in the session. The counsellor encourages the client to describe briefly the nature of this problem and uses an early opportunity to assess the problem using the ABC framework.

Using inference chaining the counsellor helps the client to identify the most relevant inference that provided the context for her emotional and/or behavioural problem. The counsellor temporarily encourages the client to assume that her inference is correct. Before progressing to the disputing stage the counsellor checks whether the client has a secondary problem about the primary problem (e.g., a depression about feeling depressed or anxiety about feeling anxious). If a secondary problem does exist and is likely to interfere with the solution of the primary problem the counsellor gives a persuasive rationale concerning why it is important to devote therapeutic time to this problem before moving to the primary problem. If the client agrees, assessment of the secondary problem begins. If no secondary problem exists the counsellor can reiterate the problem in ABC form and proceed to help the client to see the connections between A factors, B factors and C factors, paying particular attention to helping her to see the connection between B and C. (This framework can also be used if the counsellor is spending time on the client's secondary problem). When the client can see the connection between B and C the counsellor then helps the client to understand that if she wishes to achieve her emotional and/or behavioural goals at C (which are determined at this stage) she had better dispute her irrational beliefs. The counsellor then disputes the client's major irrational belief by asking for any evidence that supports it, e.g., 'Where is the evidence that . . . ?'. The counsellor helps the client to see that any 'evidence' that she provides is virtually always in support of her rational belief and not of her irrational belief, e.g., there is evidence that it is preferable for her to do well and be approved, but not that therefore she must do well or be approved.

The counsellor goes over this process until the client acknowledges that evidence can only be provided for the existence of the rational belief, but not for the irrational belief (intellectual rational insight). The counsellor then helps the client to see the relationship between the rational belief and the constructive and desired emotional and behavioural changes and emphasizes that the client should preferably continue to dispute her irrational beliefs in the setting outlined in A.

After this has been done, the counsellor negotiates a homework assignment with the client which will give her the opportunity to dispute the irrational belief and act on the new rational belief. The counsellor works carefully to ensure that the client can see the sense of doing the assignment and helps her to overcome any doubts that she may have concerning the practice of the assignment. The counsellor encourages the client to be specific in determining when and where the assignment will be executed, and generally trouble-shoots possible obstacles to the successful completion of each task before it is undertaken. If relevant, the counsellor conducts in-session practice in which the client can rehearse the assignment using imagery or simulated exercises, e.g., role play.

If time allows and it is relevant, the counsellor can help the client to identify and correct any distorted inferences which were assumed to be true when the ABC analysis was first conducted. In addition, and again if time allows, the counsellor can engage clients in constructive skills training if they are deficient in any skills which are relevant to the problem outlined.

The above framework indicates clearly that the typical session of rational-emotive counselling is sequentially structured. It is important to reiterate that it is highly desirable that the client can make sense of and agrees to participate actively in this structure.

Whenever possible the counsellor attempts to individualize the therapy session for the client using the therapeutic strategies and techniques which are assumed to be of particular benefit to this particular client at this particular time (see Chapter 10). If any written homework assignment or tape material is to be suggested, it is important that it meets the therapeutic requirements of the client. Thus, for example, for clients who do not often read books or do not profit from reading, the counsellor may suggest that they listen to a tape. If a client often reads but is not used to complex material, the counsellor may suggest a book such as Young's (1974) *A Rational Counseling Primer* instead of Ellis and Harper's (1975) *A New Guide to Rational Living*.

If any time remains it is devoted to the client's homework assignment that was executed during the previous week. If no time exists for this purpose the counsellor makes a mental note to check on this at a later date. If the assignment has been carried out successfully it is important to investigate whether the client has achieved the success by making changes in her irrational beliefs, her distorted inferences, or whether she has changed her behaviour or the activating event. If the client has not achieved change by modifying her irrational beliefs then it is important for the counsellor to help her to realize this and to understand the importance of carrying out a similar assignment in order to bring about such philosophically-based change. If any problems with the homework emerge, the counsellor had better spend some time on trouble-shooting these problems. In particular, the counsellor can help the client to become aware of the existence of any irrational beliefs that prevented her from executing the task. If this is the case, then the counsellor spends some time disputing these beliefs and re-assigning the task, if appropriate.

I wish to stress that the amount of therapeutic material discussion in RET counselling sessions varies tremendously and it is important that novice counsellors do not demand that they must cover everything that has been discussed above. I will now discuss a typical case example of rational-emotive counselling.

A Typical Case of Rational-Emotive Counselling

Mrs. Haynes (pseudonym), at the time that I saw her, was a 35-year-old professional married woman who had recently discovered that her husband had been having an affair and had decided to leave her for his other woman. There were no children in this marriage. Mrs. Haynes was referred to me for counselling by her general practitioner for depression and anxiety. In the initial session she made it clear to me that she did not want to involve her husband in counselling but rather she wanted an opportunity to focus on her own problems. She further did not think that joining a group would give her sufficient time or privacy to discuss her problems in as much depth as she considered to be most productive for her. We thus decided on a course of individual rational-emotive counselling.

In the initial session, Mrs. Haynes reported having had a previous spell of individual counselling with a marriage counsellor who, from her description, appeared to practise a kind of non-directive psychoanalytically-orientated counselling. She felt that she did not benefit from this approach, mainly because she was confused and put off by the counsellor's passivity and seeming lack of active involvement. I gave her a thumb-nail sketch about what she might realistically expect from rational-emotive counselling and her initial reaction was favourable. We agreed to meet initially for five sessions. I like to make an initial time-limited contract to enable clients to make a more informed decision about whether or not they think that they will benefit from rational-emotive counselling.

Mrs. Haynes saw depression as more of a pressing problem for her than anxiety, and it was the one that she wanted to make a start on. She was particularly depressed about her own failure to make her marriage work and blamed herself for her husband's preference for another woman. I helped her to see that it wasn't his preference for another woman which made her depressed, but her belief about the situation which was, 'I must make my marriage work and I am a failure if I don't!'. Before proceeding to help her to dispute this belief in the initial session, I worked patiently with her to enable her to see the connections between A, B and C.

I only started to dispute her irrational belief when she said that she saw clearly that it was this belief that caused her depression rather than her husband leaving her and that in order to overcome her depression she needed to change her belief. While disputing her belief I helped her to develop a list of self-disputes that she could ask herself in the coming week whenever she felt depressed about her presumed failure in marriage. I gave her a copy of *A New Guide to Rational Living* (Ellis and Harper, 1975) and suggested that in particular she read Chapter 2 (You feel the way you think) and Chapter 11 (Eradicating dire fears of failure). I also offered her an opportunity to take away a tape of our session which she accepted gratefully.

At the beginning of the following session I asked her for her reactions to both the tape and the reading material. It transpired from this that she had a positive response to both the tape and reading material and she commented that she particularly liked the method of bibliotherapy. Her depression had lifted considerably since our first session and she was able to use her own self-disputes to come up with plausible answers. In order to reinforce her progress I asked her if she would find it helpful to use one of the written self-help forms that exist for this purpose and showed her three. She decided to start off with the one which I invented (See Figure 1, Chapter 7). We first worked on an episode of depression — even though she had progressed on that since our initial session — after we had decided that it was better to get closure on her depression before we tackled her anxiety. We spent the rest of session two filling out this form and at the end I gave her a number of these forms and suggested that she read Chapter 15 of *A New Guide to Rational Living* (Conquering anxiety) and to use such insights to fill in a form whenever she became anxious.

At the beginning of session three, she reported that she benefitted from reading the chapter on anxiety, but had experienced some difficulty in zeroing in on the irrational beliefs which underpinned her anxiety. Using the inference chaining procedure, I helped her to see that she was anxious about ever finding another man again and ending up an old spinster. As is typical in rational-emotive counselling, I encouraged her to assume the worst and to imagine that she was an old spinster and asked her for her feelings about that. Her reply was instructive: 'Oh God, I couldn't stand the thought of living like that'. I disputed her belief that she needed a man in her life in order to be happy and helped her to see that she could in fact gain a fair measure of happiness in her life being single even though she would prefer to be married and have a family. This led on to a discussion of her immediate anxiety, i.e., her feeling that she could not go out on her own because this would be shameful.

Often feelings of shame are related to feelings of anxiety and assuming this to be the case with Mrs. Haynes I helped her to see that she was saying: 'If I go out on my own then other people will think that I am alone and that would prove that I am worthless'. The rest of the session was spent putting this into A, B, C, D, E form using the self-help form. I then suggested that we try rational-emotive imagery as a bridge between changing her attitude in her mind's eye and putting into practice her new belief: 'I have every right to go out on my own and if other people look down on me, then I refuse to look down on myself'. Mrs. Haynes had a great deal of difficulty in using rational-emotive imagery (Ellis' version) in the session, and between sessions three and four.

At the beginning of session four I went over the rational-emotive imagery and suggested instead that she say her new rational belief quite vigorously to herself. She was able to do this, first of all out loud and then internally and felt a mood shift which was much more profound than that she was able to achieve by using Ellis's version of rational-emotive imagery. Let me add that her feelings of depression were no longer considered by her to be a problem since session one.

At the end of session four we negotiated an assignment whereby she would go out socially on her own on two occasions, on one occasion to a local evening class and secondly to a dance hall, while vigorously repeating the rational self-coping statements we developed. This apparently was very helpful to Mrs. Haynes for she reported that she was able to go out on both occasions without undue anxiety. This was our fifth session, the last of our therapeutic contract and I discussed progress with Mrs. Haynes and how she wished to proceed in the future. She said that she felt very pleased with her progress and wanted to continue to have sessions every two weeks rather than weekly.

From sessions five to ten Mrs. Haynes made great progress. She had a number of dates with men and was able to resist the sexual advances of two of them which to her was a great stride because in the past she had had great difficulty saying 'No' to men and had for a period prior to her marriage been quite promiscuous, out of desperation rather than out of choice. Between sessions five and ten, I gave her *Why Do I Think I Am Nothing Without A Man* by Penelope Russianoff (1981) and *Living Alone and Liking It* by Lynn Shahan (1981) to read. She also continued to listen to the tapes of her sessions, although I suggested that she reviewed them only once, rather than her accustomed three times, because I wished to encourage her to rely on her own resources rather than to rely on my direction, albeit secondhand, through the tapes. She also continued going out on her own and used vigorous self-disputing to increasingly good effect.

As counselling progressed to what I thought would be termination, Mrs. Haynes got quite anxious. She said that she felt she had become quite dependent upon my help and was anxious about whether or not she could cope on her own. First of all I disputed her belief that she needed my help, and, second, I encouraged her to view a break from counselling as an experiment and suggested a six week gap between our tenth and eleventh sessions, stressing that she rely more on self-disputing rather than on bibliotherapy. I also suggested that she should not listen to any of the past tapes, so that we could conduct a fair experiment of her inference that she could not cope on her own.

The experiment proved to be a success because she came in and wondered why she even thought that she could not cope on her own since she had managed the six week gap very well. I commented that I was pleased with her progress, to which she replied: 'That's nice to know but even if you weren't, I am. I don't need your approval'. Having been firmly put in my place in this regard, we discussed whether she needed any future sessions and finally agreed that we would have a six month follow-up, although I did suggest that she could contact me if she wanted to in the interim, on the condition that she used her own skills for a two-week period and if she could not cope with any emotional problems which came up in that period then she could contact me.

At the six-months follow-up session Mrs. Haynes had attained and enhanced her therapeutic gains. She was productively involved in many social and voluntary activities and had on-going casual relationships with three men, one of which included sex out of choice and not out of desperation. Her relationship with her husband was reasonably cordial and they were proceeding towards an amicable divorce. In my keenness to encourage her to cope on her own, I made the error of moving toward termination without helping her to anticipate future problems and encourage her to see that she could use her new coping methods to deal with these problems. Although this was an error at the time, Mrs. Haynes was able to do this in the intervening period. In addition, I had to do very little work in helping her set goals for increased satisfaction since she was able to do this on her own.

10.   Obstacles to Client Progress

Overview

In this chapter I discuss the major obstacles to client progress in rational-emotive counselling. I mainly deal with common counsellor errors in the practice of rational-emotive counselling as covered in Chapters 6–9. I also briefly discuss client factors, relationship factors and environmental factors that serve as obstacles to client progress. I conclude the chapter by considering how rational-emotive counselling can be individually tailored to the unique requirements of clients.

Sources of Obstacles to Client Progress: Counsellor Factors

In this section I discuss obstacles to client progress that can be attributed to the counsellor. I emphasize errors that are commonly made by counsellors in the beginning phase of rational-emotive counselling (induction and assessment); in attempting to promote intellectual rational insight; in attempting to promote emotional rational insight; and in general management of cases. It is of course desirable for RET counsellors to strive continually to improve their skills by involving themselves in ongoing supervision and training activities (Dryden, 1983; Wessler and Ellis, 1980, 1983).

Finally I discuss the major irrational beliefs held by counsellors that appear to interfere with the practice of effective rational-emotive counselling.

Beginning rational-emotive counselling

Rational-emotive counsellors can obstruct the progress of their clients by committing the following errors in the induction and assessment stages of beginning counselling:

Failing to explore clients' anticipations and preferences for counselling. A common result of this failure is that misconceptions that clients may have about the process of rational-emotive counselling remain unchecked. Clients may 'resist' the counsellor's interventions when they 'expect' a different type of help from that provided.

Failing to assess clients' problems correctly. This may mean that counsellors proceed to work on 'problems' that clients do not have.

Failing to identify relevant second-order problems (i.e., problems about problems). When these problems are not identified and assessed clients may not be helped because they may be distracted with their second-order problem when their first order problems are being discussed.

Failing to explain why counsellor and client had better work on the secondary problem first. When this occurs the client often becomes puzzled when the counsellor proceeds to work on the secondary problem without giving an adequate rationale for doing so.

Failing to identify clearly and specifically negative emotional and behavioural consequences (Cs). Here counsellors often fail to clarify vague emotional Cs such as 'upset' or 'unhappy' and may thus assume wrongly that these emotions are irrational when they may in fact be rational. I refer readers to Chapter 4 for a full discussion of how to distinguish between irrational and rational emotions.

Failing to help the client understand the dysfunctional nature of his/her self-defeating emotions and behaviours at C. When this point is omitted counsellors often assume that their clients will want to change these 'self-defeating problems' when in fact the clients do not necessarily define them as self-defeating (a common example here is irrational anger). Before moving to the disputing stage of counselling it is important that clients are helped to view them as targets for change. Just because an emotion or action is deemed irrational by rational-emotive theory does not mean that clients wish to change them. As Golden (1983, p. 34) has shown clients often 'resist' working on self-defeating Cs if this means confronting a higher-order anxiety, e.g. 'an overweight client fearing that if she lost weight she would then have to deal with her social and sexual anxieties about dating'. Thus higher-order anxieties often need to be assessed in rational-emotive counselling.

Spending too much time listening to irrelevant background data on activating events (As). When counsellors make this error they unwittingly train their clients to talk about irrelevances and thus practise inefficient counselling. As noted earlier, clients should preferably be encouraged to specify activating events as briefly as possible.

Spending too much time focusing on the historical determinants of clients' problems. Doing this may encourage clients to believe that such material is very important in understanding their current problems; whereas rational-emotive theory emphasizes that it is the client's current beliefs that should ideally be the focus of enquiry.

Gaining a total picture of the client's past and present problems before assessing specific problems. While collecting such data may be helpful, in practice it does not add very much to the assessment of specific problems. Counsellors who make this error often like to place clients in relevant diagnostic categories believing (wrongly in my opinion) that doing so will aid the treatment process.

Failing to use inference chaining to identify the most relevant inference in the inference chain. (See Chapter 6). Thus, a man may be angry with his wife for forgetting to collect his suit from the cleaners not because she is forgetful *per se*, but because her forgetfulness will get him into trouble at work, trouble which he dreads. The correct use of inference chaining often helps counsellors to identify significant problems which are not immediately apparent from clients' accounts of their problems.

Failing to show clients that the ideology of their problems is most fre-quently expressed in the form of devout, absolutist 'musts' or one of the three main derivatives of 'musturbation'. Inexpert rational-emotive counsellors tend to assume that clients' anti-empirical, or inferentially distorted thinking, 'causes' their emotional and/or behavioural problems.

Failing to uncover clients' relevant irrational beliefs. Here counsellors may identify irrational beliefs which are either incorrect or too general in nature. An example of the latter occurred when a counsellor identified the general irrational belief 'I must be approved by everyone' whereas the client's actual irrational belief was more specific 'I must be approved by significant others in my life'.

Failing to explain the B — C connection. When this explanation is not made clients are often puzzled when their counsellors begin to dispute their irrational beliefs. They cannot fully understand that changing their beliefs will lead to their desired emotional and/or behavioural goals.

Failing to assess clients' emotional and behavioural goals. When counsellors fail to assess their clients' goals, they often assume that clients have goals which they do not in fact have. Here, as elsewhere, rational-emotive counsellors may assume wrongly that their clients will function according to RET theory, e.g., that they will want to be concerned rather than anxious.

Promoting intellectual rational insight

The following errors are often committed by inexpert rational-emotive counsellors in this stage of the counselling process.

Assuming that clients will automatically change their irrational beliefs once

they have identified them. Inexpert RET counsellors either fail to dispute irrational beliefs at all or use disputing methods sparingly and with insufficient vigour.

Disputing distorted inferences before disputing irrational beliefs. Inexpert RET counsellors tend to eschew the preferred rational-emotive strategy of assuming temporarily that distorted inferences are true so that irrational beliefs maybe challenged. They tend to dispute distorted inferences because they are distorted and fail to realize that while such inferential distortions are implicated in clients' problems they are not central to their existence. The danger of disputing distorted inferences before irrational beliefs is that while clients may improve, this improvement is temporary and the ideological evaluative roots of their problems still need to be addressed.

Failing to focus disputing interventions on clients' actual irrational beliefs. Here counsellors tend to stray from specific irrational beliefs that they correctly assessed earlier. The most common error here is to shift to disputing general beliefs as noted in the previous section.

Failing to help clients to understand the difference between rational and irrational beliefs. Helping clients to understand this difference is important since in response to questions asking for evidence in favour of their irrational beliefs, they will provide evidence in support of their rational beliefs. Clarifying the distinction between rational and irrational beliefs helps to refocus clients on challenging the latter.

Failing to use socratic-type disputing with clients who can benefit from this method. As such, counsellors deprive these clients of the opportunity to think for themselves and impede them from becoming their own future counsellors.

Failing to lecture didactically when it is clear that clients do not understand a concept through socratic disputing. While rational-emotive counsellors prefer to use socratic disputing whenever possible, rigid adherence to this method can be counterproductive. Didactic presentations have their place in rational-emotive counselling and can be fruitfully employed when clients do not benefit from socratic disputing. When material is presented didactically it is important for counsellors to be concise in their explanations and to check whether or not they have made themselves understood.

Philosophizing in an abstract manner. While effective rational-emotive counsellors do engage in philosophical discussions with their clients these debates are focused on clients' actual irrational beliefs and reminders of the relevance of these discussions for the clients' problems at C are provided. Inexpert RET counsellors tend to engage their clients in abstract philosophical discussions divorced from the latter's problems. As such both counsellor and client lose a productive therapeutic focus.

Failing to use appropriate examples, metaphors, stories, etc., while

disputing. Effective disputing sequences are characterized by a variety of examples, metaphors, stories, etc., tailored to the client's own idiosyncratic situation. When these are omitted disputing can lose its desired impact.

Failing to remind clients of the dysfunctional consequences of adhering to irrational beliefs. A good way of encouraging clients to work on relinquishing their irrational beliefs is to provide them with frequent reminders of the dysfunctional consequences of such beliefs. Thus a counsellor may say 'OK, so you keep maintaining that you must achieve your certificate, but where is that belief getting you other than anxious and depressed?'.

Failing to counter the illogicalities that clients express during the process of disputing. Clients often express a variety of illogicalities in defence of their irrational beliefs while responding to the disputing interventions of their counsellors (Edelstein, 1976; Guinagh, 1976). Ineffective rational-emotive counsellors may not even identify these illogicalities or when they do identify them they may not address them successfully. Commonly-expressed illogical defences include:

a   *Statements of indifference.* Here clients think that rational alternatives to irrational beliefs are expressions of indifference, e.g., 'I don't care if . . . rather than I prefer that . . .'. I recommend that counsellors help their clients to distinguish among irrational beliefs, rational beliefs and 'indifferent' beliefs.

b   *'My belief is true because I feel it to be true'.* This is an example of emotional reasoning (Burns, 1980). Clients should be shown that feeling something to be true is often not a good guide to its validity.

c   *'I can't change my belief because that's the way I am'.* Here clients wrongly consider that their irrational belief is part of their unalterable identity. Distinctions between thinking and identity should be made and instances of clients changing important beliefs should be sought to counter this notion.

d   *Appeals to authority.* Here clients point to respected authorities as the source of irrational beliefs and consider that such beliefs are true because such authorities have credibility, e.g., 'My father taught me that I must do well in life. That's why it's true'. Here clients can be shown that such authorities probably intended to indicate relative rather than absolute values and that even if absolute values were being taught, such respected authorities probably didn't want the clients to have dysfunctional results, e.g., 'Do you think your father wanted you to be miserable? Would he prefer you to be miserable and cling to your belief, or do you think he would want you to give up the exaggerated quality of your belief if it meant you weren't miserable?' It is often not productive however to cast the respected authority in a negative light since counsellors who attempt this may be viewed negatively themselves.

e *Evading the issues.* Clients will often evade the issue by changing the subject or by bringing up other problems. They do this to try to distract counsellors from their purpose. Effective rational-emotive counsellors succeed in bringing clients back to the issue at hand while acknowledging that focusing on difficult problems is uncomfortable. In some cases, counsellors may need to dispute clients' LFT beliefs about tolerating the pain of focusing on their problems.

Promoting emotional rational insight

The following errors are often committed by inexpert rational-emotive counsellors while attempting to promote emotional rational insight:

Failing to show clients the differences between intellectual rational insight and emotional rational insight. It is very important for rational-emotive counsellors to help clients understand that gaining intellectual rational insight is rarely sufficient for them to solve their emotional and behavioural problems. Rather clients should be shown that they need to challenge their irrational beliefs repeatedly and vigorously using cognitive, emotional and behavioural methods, if they are to achieve lasting change.

Failing to uncover and address client's blocks to working hard to achieve emotional rational insight. Clients refuse to work hard to achieve emotional rational insight for a number of reasons. These include: (a) a philosophy of low frustration tolerance (LFT) where clients believe, for example, that 'It's too hard to work to achieve lasting change. Change must not be that hard'; (b) cognitive-emotive dissonance whereby clients feel 'unnatural' as they work towards strengthening their rational beliefs, and believe that they must feel natural at all times (Maultsby, 1984). Grieger and Boyd (1980) note that this phenomenon can take a number of forms: 'I won't be me' whereby clients fear that they will lose their identity if they relinquish their irrational beliefs, and, 'I'll become a robot' whereby clients believe that rationality means becoming devoid of all feeling rather than experiencing appropriate negative emotions, e.g., sadness, regret, etc. — see Chapter 4.

Failing to experiment with a broad range of cognitive, emotional and behavioural techniques. Clients vary in their response to rational-emotive techniques. It is recommended that counsellors adopt an experimental attitude in attempting to discover which techniques best suit which clients. Counsellors who only employ a limited range of techniques at this stage are generally less effective than counsellors who are willing to use a broad range of techniques.

Insisting that clients employ implosion methods of change. Rational-emotive theory states that implosive techniques of behavioural change are more effective than gradual methods of behavioural change. Also, Ellis (1979 b, 1980 a) has argued that many clients perpetuate their problems and deprive themselves of learning experiences because they believe that they *must* be comfortable. Thus rational-emotive counsellors prefer to encourage their clients to fully confront their anxieties, for example, while tolerating their uncomfortable feelings. While this is a sound strategy, it often needs to be modified for pragmatic purposes since some clients stubbornly refuse to employ such implosive methods. Rational-emotive counsellors who insist that such clients use these methods are likely to damage the therapeutic alliance. For example, while it may be desirable for a client who is anxious about eating in public to go to an expensive restaurant and challenge her anxiety-creating cognitions in a situation where her worst fears may be realized, many clients will not do this. When I provide a rationale for homework assignments I do so in a way which incorporates a principle I call 'challenging but not overwhelming' and contrast it with gradual desensitization and implosion methods (Dryden, 1985 b):

> 'There are three ways you can overcome your fears. The first is like jumping in at the deep end; you expose yourself straightaway to the situation you are most afraid of. The advantage here is that if you can learn that nothing terrible will happen then you will overcome your problems quite quickly. However, the disadvantage is that some people just can't bring themselves to do this and get quite discouraged as a result. The second way is to go very gradually. Here, on the one hand, you only do something that you feel comfortable doing, while on the other you don't really get an opportunity to face putting up with discomfort, which in my opinion is a major feature of your problem. Also treatment will take much longer this way. The third way is what I call 'challenging but not overwhelming'. Here you choose an assignment which is sufficiently challenging for you to make progress, but not one which you feel would be overwhelming for you at any given stage. Here you are likely to make progress more quickly than with the gradual approach, but more slowly than with the "deep end" approach'.

I find that when clients are given an opportunity to choose their own rate of progress, the therapeutic alliance is strengthened. Most clients who will not employ implosive methods of change choose the 'challenging but not overwhelming' approach and only very rarely do they opt for gradual desensitization therapy.

When they do so I try to dissuade them and frequently succeed. In the final analysis, however, I have not found it productive to insist that clients choose a particular way of tackling problems that is against their preferences.

Case management

The following errors are often committed by inexpert rational-emotive counsellors in general case management.

Focusing too much on the therapeutic relationship in the early stages of counselling. While it is important for counsellors to develop a cooperative relationship with their clients, this can often be best achieved through a business-like focus on the clients' problems; the execution of a correct assessment of these problems; and an early start on helping clients to overcome these problems. I have found that problem-focused counselling is more successful at consolidating the therapeutic relationship than deliberate attempts to develop this relationship in the absence of task activities.

Switching from problem to problem in quick succession. It is important for rational-emotive counsellors to spend sufficient time on each of their clients' problems if clients are to benefit from counselling. Otherwise clients become confused and fail to understand both the cognitive underpinnings of their problems and how to overcome them. A particular error here occurs when counsellors switch frequently from ego to discomfort problems within a given session.

Failing to identify and work with clients' priorities in counselling sessions. When counsellors and clients have different priorities concerning what to discuss in sessions, it seems as if they are on parallel tracks and do not work together as a team. The result is that clients consider that their counsellors do not understand them and as such do not benefit from counselling as much as they would if they perceived their counsellors as empathic (Truax and Carkhuff, 1967).

Failing to work at a pace and using language appropriate to the learning abilities of clients. Rational-emotive counselling can perhaps be best viewed as a psychoeducational approach to counselling. As such it is important for counsellors to take into account their clients' learning abilities in executing interventions. Common errors here include working too fast, or too slowly, for clients and using too complicated, or too simple, language with the result that clients are insufficiently involved in the therapeutic process due to confusion or boredom.

Failing to ensure that clients understand rational concepts. As rational-emotive counselling is a psychoeducational approach to counselling, its practitioners should preferably make frequent checks that their clients understand rational concepts. It is important that counsellors do not take clients' verbal assurances, e.g., 'I understand', and non-verbal assurances, e.g., head-nods, mm-

mmhs, that they understand and agree with rational concepts at face value. This is particularly important when counsellors give didactic explanations of these concepts. Good questions to ask include: 'I want to make sure that I am making myself clear. Can you put into your own words what you think I said?'; 'What is your reaction to that point?'; 'Do you have any negative reactions about that?'. I have found it particularly valuable to recommend that counsellors ask clients about and deal with their reservations about rational concepts, otherwise their clients may 'resist' their counsellors' interventions without the latter understanding the source of the 'resistance'.

Failing to be sufficiently repetitive. Here counsellors believe falsely that if client change has occurred at one stage of counselling then lasting change has taken place. Thinking that once a topic has been discussed in a counselling session the client has thoroughly learned what needs to be learned, such counsellors fail to 'go over old ground' with their clients. In practice, dealing with issues repeatedly is almost always a feature of effective rational-emotive counselling since one-trial client learning hardly ever occurs.

Failing to determine the basis of client change. As has been noted in Chapter 3, client change may be inferentially-based, behaviourally-based or philo-sophically-based. RET counsellors consider that long-term change is rooted in changes in clients' beliefs (i.e., philosophical change). If counsellors do not establish the correct basis of client change they may miss opportunities of dealing with the philosophical roots of their clients' problems since clients may terminate counsel-ling, having made progress at the inferential or behavioural level of change.

Failures in the task domain of the therapeutic alliance. Bordin (1979) has argued that counsellors and clients each have tasks to carry out during the process of counselling and calls this the task domain of the therapeutic alliance. When obstacles to client progress occur due to problems in the task domain of the alliance the following are common counsellor errors:

a   Failing to help clients understand what their tasks are in counselling, or if they do understand these, failing to help them understand how executing them will help them achieve their goals.

b   Failing to identify and deal with clients' doubts about their abilities to execute their tasks.

c   Failing to help clients understand what their counsellors' tasks are and/or failing to help clients understand the link between their counsellors' tasks and their own tasks and goals.

d   Encouraging clients to carry out tasks that they cannot realistically execute, e.g., some clients are not intelligent enough to engage in the tasks of socratic disputing.

e   Failing to train clients in the appropriate use of their own therapeutic tasks, e.g., clients often need to be trained in the use of rational-emotive imagery if they are to benefit from this procedure.

f   Executing their own tasks in an unskilled manner.

g   Employing methods which are not potent enough to promote client change, e.g., disputing irrational beliefs without exposure is unlikely to help clients with phobias.

Failing to negotiate homework assignments adequately. In rational-emotive counselling, clients are encouraged to put into practice what they learn in counselling sessions through the execution of a variety of homework assignments. Inexpert counsellors often fail to suggest homework assignments and when they do suggest such tasks they make the following errors in negotiating assignments with their clients:

a   Failing to provide a persuasive rationale for the importance of homework assignments in rational-emotive counselling.

b   Assigning the tasks unilaterally instead of involving clients in the negotiation process. This often occurs when counsellors devote insufficient time to discussion about homework.

c   Suggesting assignments which are irrelevant with respect to clients' goals (Golden, 1983).

d   Suggesting assignments which do not relate to what has been discussed in the counselling session.

e   Negotiating tasks which are vague rather than specific. Clients are more likely to carry out a homework task when they know what to do, when to do it, and where to do it, and when they believe they are capable of doing it.

f   Failing to elicit commitment from clients that they will attempt homework assignments.

g   Failing to rehearse clients in homework assignments, e.g., in imagery or through role-play methods. Lazarus (1984) has argued that clients will be more likely to carry out homework assignments when they can picture themselves doing them in imagery.

h   Failing to identify and deal with potential obstacles that may prevent clients from carrying out their homework assignments.

i   Suggesting assignments which are too time-consuming for the client (Golden, 1983).

j   Suggesting assignments which are too threatening or anxiety provoking for clients at that stage of counselling (Golden, 1983) — see material on the 'challenging but not overwhelming' principle discussed earlier in this chapter.

Failing to check adequately clients' experiences in executing homework assignments. When clients agree to execute homework assignments it is important that counsellors discuss with them their experiences in carrying them out. This should ideally be done in the following session, although as noted in Chapter 9 it is not always possible to do this. Common counsellor errors in checking on homework assignments include:

a   Failing to ask clients for a report of their experiences in carrying out assignments.

b   Failing to ask clients for a report of what they learned, or did not learn, from their experiences in carrying out assignments.

c   Failing to reinforce clients' attempts at executing assignments.

d   Failing to correct clients' errors in written homework assignments when these have been completed.

e   Failing to ask for and assess clients' reasons for not attempting, or not completing, their homework assignments.

f   Failing to dispute irrational beliefs (in the domains of ego and/or discomfort disturbance) when these explain why clients did not attempt, or complete, assignments.

g   Failing to reiterate the rationale for assignments when it is clear that clients did not understand them, and thus did not attempt to complete them.

h   Failing to obtain clients' commitment to attempt the assignments again if appropriate.

Counsellors' irrational beliefs

Client progress can also be hindered because counsellors may bring their own disturbance to the therapeutic process. Ellis (1983 b) has outlined five major irrational beliefs that lead to therapeutic inefficiency:

'I *have* to be successful with all my clients practically all of the time'.

'I *must* be an outstanding counsellor, clearly better than other counsellors I know or hear about'.

'I *have* to be greatly respected and loved by all my clients'.

'Since I am doing my best and working so hard as a counsellor, my clients *should* be equally hard working and responsible, *should* listen to me carefully and *should* always push themselves to change'.

'Because I am a person in my own right, I *must* be able to enjoy myself during counselling sessions and to use these sessions to solve my personal problems as much as to help clients with their difficulties'.

In addition, counsellors often fail to dispute clients' irrational beliefs because they share the same beliefs. Thus one of my trainees recently did not dispute her client's belief 'I must not die at an early age and it would be awful if I did' because she too believed that it would be awful to die prematurely. Hauck (1966) has called this the 'neurotic agreement' in counselling and psychotherapy.

In such cases, it is recommended that RET counsellors apply RET principles and methods to search for and dispute their own self- and client-defeating beliefs which may (a) impede them from confronting their clients; (b) distract them and their clients from getting the therapeutic job done; (c) foster undue counsellor anxiety and anger; and (d) encourage inappropriate behaviour anathema to the practice of effective and ethical counselling.

Sources of Obstacles to Client Progress: Other Factors

In this section I discuss the following obstacles to client progress: client factors, relationship factors, and environmental and other external factors.

Client factors

In order to really benefit from RET counselling clients need to achieve three forms of insight, namely: (a) psychological disturbance is mainly determined by the absolutist beliefs that they hold about themselves, others, and the world; (b) even when people acquired and created their irrational beliefs in their early lives, they perpetuate their disturbance by reindoctrinating themselves in the present with these beliefs; (c) only if they consistently work and practise in the present and future to think, feel and act against these irrational beliefs are clients likely to surrender their irrationalities and make themselves significantly less disturbed.

Kempel (1973) has identified a number of client attitudes and feelings which predispose them to terminate counselling prematurely:

'I need to have a very close relationship with my counsellor'. Such clients may wish to terminate counselling because their RET counsellors generally avoid developing very close therapeutic relationships with them. As outlined in Chapter 5, such relationships are deemed to be counter-therapeutic in that they reinforce clients' approval needs.

'Change must be easy'. Such clients are loathe to put in the hard work that change involves and may leave RET counselling to seek a form of counselling that they perceive as less demanding.

'I want changes in A (activating events) not B (beliefs)'. Such clients seek changes in significant others or troublesome events but will neither do anything themselves to try to effect such changes nor work to change their irrational beliefs about these situations. When they realize that RET will not provide them with what they seek they usually terminate counselling.

'Shame about seeking help'. Such clients condemn themselves for being weak and not being able to solve their own problems. They are thus ambivalent about seeking help and may terminate counselling if their feelings of shame become acute.

Unless counsellors are sensitive to the existence of such client attitudes and feelings and can identify and deal with relevant irrational beliefs and misconceptions about counselling, clients will not stay in counselling long enough to achieve the three forms of insight outlined above.

Golden (1983) has noted four important client factors that impede client progress. First, some clients may have 'hidden agendas' that could interfere with rational-emotive counselling, e.g., a man who comes into counselling in order to stop his wife filing for a divorce, but who has no intention of seeking personal changes for himself. It is often difficult to identify such agendas, particularly early on in the counselling process and clients are, of course, 'motivated' to keep them hidden. However, if clients are not progressing it is important for counsellors to try and answer the question: 'What has this person to gain from not improving?' and to try and help clients to identify the irrational beliefs and inferential distortions that may underpin any hidden agendas that can be identified. However, it may happen that counsellors never become aware of the presence of such agendas that do in fact exist. This had better be accepted as one of the occupational hazards of all forms of counselling.

The second factor discussed by Golden is poor client motivation. This occurs 'when a client does not value the desired outcome of therapy enough to devote the necessary time and effort to change' (Golden, 1983, p. 35). In such cases rational-emotive counsellors would do well to renegotiate with such clients their goals for change.

Third, some clients demonstrate negative behavioural patterns such as counter-control which may take the form of negativism toward counselling or rebelliousness against the counsellor. In these instances I have found it helpful to show clients that they have a perfect right to act in such fashion and that the logical consequence of such behaviour is that they will not improve. I then enquire whether this is the outcome from counselling that they seek. It is important for counsellors to disengage themselves from any power-struggle with such clients, since the more counsellors try to 'win' such struggles, the more these clients will resist their efforts. Since these clients desperately seek to control situations, they can be calmly shown that they and not their counsellors are in control of whether they improve or not.

Finally, Golden (1983) notes that some clients do not profit from counselling because of neurological and other biological limitations. When counsellors suspect the existence of such factors, referrals to and liaison with other professionals are often indicated.

In a study by Ellis (1983 d) on the characteristics of clients who 'failed' in RET, the following findings emerged: (a) clients who did poorly in RET failed to do consistent *cognitive* self-disputation. They were characterized amongst other factors by extreme disturbance, by grandiosity, by lack of organization, and by plain refusal to do these cognitive assignments. (b) 'Failure' clients, who refused to accept responsibility for their irrational emotions and refused to forcefully and *emotively* change their beliefs and actions, were more clingy, more severely depressed and inactive, more often grandiose and more frequently stubbornly rebellious than clients who benefited from RET. (c) 'Failure' clients who did poorly in the *behavioural* aspects of RET showed 'abysmally low frustration tolerance, had serious behavioural addictions, led disorganized lives, refrained from doing their active homework assignments, were more frequently psychotic and generally refused to work at therapy' (Ellis, 1983 d, p. 165).

Thus clients' own extreme level of disturbance is a significant obstacle to their own progress. While a full discussion of what 'special' therapeutic methods and techniques to employ with such clients is outside the scope of this book (see Ellis, 1985 a), counsellors can adopt a number of strategies to enhance therapeutic effectiveness with these 'difficult' clients. Amongst other tactics, counsellors had better, first, be consistently and forcefully encouraging in their therapeutic interactions with these clients, showing them that they can do better if they try. Second, counsellors would be wise to keep vigorously showing these clients that they, the counsellors, do in fact unconditionally accept them with all their psychological difficulties and that they can indeed accept themselves in the same way. Third, counsellors can often be successful with such clients by consistently showing them that their refusal to work on their problems will generally lead to bad consequences and needless suffering. Fourth, counsellors should be flexible in experimenting with a wide range of therapeutic techniques (including some unusual ones!) in their persistent efforts to help their 'difficult' clients. Above all, rational-emotive counsellors had better be good representatives of their therapeutic system and accept themselves and tolerate the discomfort of working with 'difficult' clients while sticking to the therapeutic task.

Relationship factors

These can be first attributed to poor counsellor-client matching. Such mis-matching may occur for many reasons. Thus, clients 'may have a therapist who, according to their idiosyncratic tastes or preferences, is too young or too old, too liberal or too conservative, too active or too passive' (Ellis, 1983 e, p. 29). If these 'relationship match' obstacles persist, then it is preferable for that client to be trans-ferred to a counsellor with more suitable traits. Other relationship obstacles may occur because the counsellor and client may get on 'too well' and get distracted from the more mundane tasks of counselling. In such cases, the paradox is that if the client improves, the 'life' of the satisfactory relationship is threatened. As a result, collusion may occur between counsellor and client to avoid making counselling as effective an endeavour as it might otherwise be. This problem can be largely over-come if counsellors first help themselves and then their clients to overcome the philosophy of low frustration tolerance implicit in this collusive short-range hedonism.

In Chapter 5, I discussed how counsellors should preferably modify their thera-peutic style with different clients. In addition, clients may not benefit from counsel-ling when the interpersonal style of their counsellors does not maximize their opportunities for therapeutic learning. In other words the relationship 'milieu' may promote or inhibit client learning. For example, some clients are emotionally over-stimulated and hence the therapeutic task for counsellors is to create a learning environment which decreases their emotional tension to a level where they can adequately reflect on their experiences. With these clients counsellors are advised to make use of a lot of cognitive techniques and adopt an interpersonal style which aims to decrease affect. This style may either be formal or informal in character. These strategies are particularly appropriate with clients who have a 'hysterical' style of functioning. On the other hand, other clients require a more emotionally charged learning atmosphere. Such clients often use 'intellectualization' as a major defence and are used to denying feelings. With such clients counsellors should preferably endeavour to inject a productive level of affect into the therapeutic session and employ emotive techniques, self-disclosure and a good deal of humour. These 'challenging' strategies are best introduced gradually so as not to 'overwhelm' clients with an environment that they are not accustomed to utilizing. However, before deciding upon which interpersonal style to emphasize with clients counsellors should routinely gain information from them concerning how they best learn. Some clients learn best directly through experience while for others vicarious experiences seem to be more productive. I personally try to develop a learning profile for each of my clients and use this information to help me plan my therapeutic strategies and choose techniques designed to implement these strategies. Care needs to be taken however, that the counsellor does not use a mode of learning that may perpetuate the client's problems.

Environmental and other external factors

Golden has noted that the following environmental and other external factors can be obstacles to client progress in counselling:

> Deliberate sabotage from others (for example, threats of rejection or disapproval for being more assertive or successful).

> Inadvertent sabotage from others such as family members who become 'benevolent saboteurs'. An example is the individual who inadvertently reinforces a family member's agoraphobia by 'chauffeuring' the phobic person around, thus providing him or her with a 'secondary gain' for being phobic.

> Other 'secondary gains', such as those from disability and welfare benefits which provide clients with reinforcements for their 'disabilities'. (Golden, 1983, p. 35).

To which I would add: organizations, systems, and positions which provide limited opportunities for client growth, e.g., unfulfilling jobs, unemployment, prisons, totalitarian states.

In addition to helping clients to change their irrational beliefs about these obstacles, counsellors can use the following strategies to deal with them: When people who serve as willing or unwilling obstacles to client progress are members of the client's family they may be invited to attend for family or marital counselling; when such people cannot be legitimately invited to attend counselling sessions, clients may be specifically helped to deal with these difficult people — see Ellis' (1975) book, *How to live with a neurotic* — or encouraged to distance themselves from them as far as possible; clients may be encouraged to leave situations which inhibit their growth if these situations cannot be modified; and clients may be encouraged to give up the short-term benefits of secondary gains in order to achieve the long-term benefits to their mental health of doing without such 'gains'.

It should be remembered however that while environmental and other external factors can limit the client's opportunities for happiness they cannot directly cause their psychological problems, since it is clients' irrational beliefs about these situations which determine their emotional and behavioural responses to these factors.

Notes on Individualizing Rational-Emotive Counselling

One of the best ways of minimizing obstacles to client progress is to individualize the practice of rational-emotive counselling for each client. In this section I use Bordin's (1979) concept of the therapeutic alliance as an explanatory framework. Although I cover issues that I have already introduced, I believe that Bordin's ideas provide a fresh way of looking at these issues. Bordin argues that there are three components of the therapeutic alliances: bonds, goals and tasks. Bonds refer to the interpersonal connectedness between counsellors and clients. Goals refer to the objectives of both counsellors and clients and provide the 'raison d'etre' of counselling. Finally, tasks are best viewed as the means by which counsellors and clients attempt to actualize their goals.

It is in the nature of individual RET counselling that since counsellors are dealing with only one client, they can strive to tailor the practice of counselling with this client free from the concern that a particular style of interaction (and the use of an individually tailored treatment programme) may have an adverse affect on other clients e.g., in couples counselling, family counselling or group counselling. Thus, as I have shown both in Chapter 5 and in the present chapter the counsellor can modify his or her style of participation in individual counselling according to the personality structure of a given client in order to maximize that client's learning and to minimize the possibility that the client's problems are being unwittingly reinforced. This refers in particular to individualizing RET counselling in the bond domain of the therapeutic alliance (Bordin, 1979). Therapeutic bonds in RET counselling may change over time according to the amount of progress that the client makes and according to which bonds the client best responds.

In this latter regard, the counsellor can at the outset attempt to assess what might be a productive bond to form with a particular client, e.g., a formal or informal bond. Thus, the counsellor might ask the client, either on a biographical form or in person, what constitutes helpful and unhelpful counsellor behaviour in the client's mind. The counsellor might also ask the client about the latter's previous experiences of being helped, whether formally or informally, and during this exploration focus on what aspects of the other person's behaviour the client found most helpful and what aspects they found least helpful. It is important, however, to view such information critically because what a client has found helpful in the short term may not have been helpful in the long term. Thus, for example, counsellors can help clients feel better in the short term without helping them to get better in the long term (Ellis, 1972). Although the information that can be obtained from the client about possible helpful ways of intervening with that particular client may be useful, rational-emotive counsellors would be wise to answer by experimentation the question concerning which bond is most productive with this client at this particular time. Thus, the counsellor might try particular ways of interacting with different clients and observe how these clients respond to these different forms of therapist interaction.

Another way that RET practitioners can individualize counselling for their clients is to ensure that there is congruence between clients' goals and the goals of counselling. Ineffective RET counselling can often occur when clients wish to achieve one goal and their counsellors are working to help them to achieve a different goal. However, I advocate that counsellors do not uncritically accept their clients' goal statements as sacred. Indeed, a good RET counsellor sometimes spends some therapeutic time trying to talk a client out of goals that the client considers to be helpful but which the counsellor considers to be harmful to the long term welfare of the client. Good RET counselling therefore involves a fair measure of negotiation between counsellor and client concerning the client's goals. It is helpful if the counsellor does not dogmatically insist that a client gives up his or her unrealistic or harmful goals since such insistence may add to the client's problems.

Clients' goals can and often do change over time and counsellors had better be sensitive to the changing nature of their clients' aims and attempt to track changes in their goal statements. It is particularly helpful for RET counsellors to understand (and to help their clients understand) what underlies such changes in therapeutic goals. Remember that clients' initial goals are often coloured by the nature of their disturbance and that it is advantageous for counsellors to encourage them to postpone fixing on certain goals until they have achieved a fair measure of success in overcoming their emotional and/or behavioural disturbance. When this is done, RET counsellors are noted for helping their clients to pursue the latter's own individualized goals, since they believe that a particular client does not *have to* achieve satisfaction in any given way. Thus, clients are encouraged to actualize their potential in their own individualistic way, preferably after having achieved a large measure of freedom from emotional and behavioural disturbance. Thus, in general, RET counsellors encourage clients to first work on the goals of overcoming their emotional and/or behavioural disturbance before working to pursue individualistic goals that will bring them happiness.

The third aspect of the therapeutic alliance where rational-emotive counselling can be practised in an individualized way is in the task domain. Bordin (1979) has stressed that every therapeutic system favours particular counsellors' tasks *and* clients' tasks which then become embodied in the practice of that approach to counselling. RET counselling can be practised in an individualized way if the counsellor encourages the client to carry out tasks which are best suited to that particular client and which are likely to encourage that client to achieve his or her therapeutic goals. In this way the practice of RET can be seen as efficient as well as effective (Ellis, 1980 b).

Some clients seem to progress better by carrying out techniques which are more cognitive in nature, while other clients seem to benefit more from executing tasks which are more emotive in nature; yet a further group of clients do best by carrying out behavioural tasks. While a particular therapeutic technique draws upon all three modalities, it is also true that a particular technique may emphasize one modality over others. There are no firm guidelines for RET counsellors to use in determining, before the event, which therapeutic techniques are most appropriate for given clients. However, it may be helpful to explore with clients their past history of effecting productive changes while paying attention to their answers concerning which modalities they spontaneously used, or were encouraged to use. In other words, it may be helpful for RET counsellors to pay attention to a client's prior learning style and modify the practice of rational-emotive counselling accordingly. Once again, perhaps the best indication concerning which techniques clients will benefit from most is experimentation, which is the hallmark of individualizing rational-emotive counselling and the scientific method which rational-emotive theory supports. This involves trying out interventions, noting clients' reactions to these, getting clients' feedback on their reactions to these interventions and modifying future interventions accordingly.

11. The Distinctive Features of Rational-Emotive Counselling: A Review

Overview

In this final chapter, I review the distinctive features of rational-emotive counselling and contrast these with other approaches to cognitive-behavioural counselling. I conclude the chapter by outlining techniques that are generally avoided in rational-emotive counselling.

Introduction

The major goal of rational-emotive counselling is an ambitious one: *to encourage clients to make a profound philosophic change in the two main areas of ego disturbance and discomfort disturbance.* This involves helping clients, as far as is humanly possible, to give up their irrational beliefs and to replace these with rational beliefs as discussed in Chapter 3.

In rational-emotive counselling the major goals are to help clients pursue their long-range basic goals and purposes and to help them to do so as effectively as possible by fully accepting themselves and tolerating unchangeable uncomfortable life conditions. Rational-emotive practitioners further strive to help clients obtain the skills which they can use to prevent the development of future disturbance. In encouraging clients to achieve and maintain this profound philosophic change, rational-emotive counsellors implement the following strategies. They help their clients see that:

> Emotional and behavioural disturbances have cognitive antecedents and that these cognitions normally take the form of absolutist devout evaluations. RET counsellors train their clients to observe their own psychological disturbances and to trace these back to their ideological roots.

People have a distinct measure of self-determination and can thus *decide* to work at undisturbing themselves. Thus, clients are shown that they are not slaves to their biologically-based irrational thinking processes.

People can implement their choices and maximize their freedom by actively working at changing their irrational beliefs. This is best achieved by employing cognitive, emotive and behavioural methods — often in quite a forceful and vigorous manner (Ellis, 1979 d).

With the majority of clients, from the first session onward, RET counsellors are likely to use strategies designed to effect profound philosophic change. The counsellor begins the process with the hypothesis that this particular client may be able to achieve such change and thus begins to implement rational-emotive methods which he or she will abandon only after collecting sufficient data to reject this initial hypothesis. Rational-emotive practitioners regularly implement this viewpoint which is based on the notion that the client's response to counselling is the best indicator of his or her prognosis.

When it is clear that the client is not able to achieve philosophic change, whether on a particular issue or in general, the counsellor often uses other cognitive-behavioural methods to effect inferentially- and behaviourally-based change.

A good example of this change in strategy is one often reported by a counsellor of my acquaintance. He was working with a middle-aged married woman who reported feeling furious every time her ageing father would telephone her and enquire 'Noo, what's doing?'. She inferred that this was a gross invasion of her privacy and absolutistically insisted that he had no right to do so. The counsellor initially intervened with the usual rational-emotive strategy by attempting to dispute this client's dogmatic belief and tried to help her see that there was no law in the universe which stated that he *must* not do such a thing. Meeting initial resistance, the counsellor persisted with different variations of this theme — all to no avail. Changing tack, he began to implement a different strategy designed to help the client question her inference that her father was actually invading her privacy. Given her father's age, the counsellor inquired, was it not more likely that his question represented his usual manner of beginning telephone conversations rather than an intense desire to pry into her affairs? This inquiry proved successful in that the client's rage subsided because she began to re-interpret her father's motives. Interestingly enough, although he returned to disputing her irrational belief later, the counsellor never succeeded in helping this client to give up this irrational belief!

However, some clients are more amenable to re-evaluating their irrational beliefs *after* they have been helped to correct distorted inferences. We had better do research on this topic if we are to answer the question: 'Which strategy is most appropriate for which clients at which stage in counselling?'. Meanwhile, it is important to note that RET counsellors, if they follow this lead, are unique in that they are more likely to challenge their client's irrational beliefs and to dispute them much earlier in the therapeutic process than do other cognitive-behavioural counsellors. Further differences between rational-emotive counselling and other approaches to cognitive-behavioural counselling are listed below. While it should be noted that rational-emotive counsellors do use strategies derived from other cognitive-behavioural approaches, I want to reiterate that the focus in the previous chapters has been on strategies and techniques that are mainly associated with rational-emotive counselling.

Differences between rational-emotive counselling and other forms of cognitive-behavioural counselling

As opposed to other approaches to cognitive-behavioural counselling, rational-emotive counselling:

has a distinct philosophic emphasis which is one of its central features and which other forms of cognitive-behavioural counselling appear to omit. Thus, it stresses that humans appraise themselves, others and the world in terms of: (a) rational, preferential, flexible and tolerant philosophies and (b) irrational, musturbatory, rigid, intolerant and absolutist philosophies.

has an existential-humanistic outlook which is intrinsic to it and which is omitted by most other approaches to cognitive-behavioural counselling. Thus, it sees people 'as holistic, goal-directed individuals who have importance in the world just because they are human and alive; it uncon-ditionally focuses upon their experiences and values, including their self-actualizing potentialities' (Ellis, 1980 c, p. 327). It also shares the views of ethical humanism by encouraging people to emphasize human interest (self and social) over the interests of deities, material objects and lower animals.

favours striving for pervasive and long-lasting, philosophically-based, change, rather than symptomatic change.

attempts to help humans eliminate all self-ratings and views self-esteem as a self-defeating concept which encourages them to make conditional evaluations of self. Instead, it teaches people *un*conditional self-acceptance (Ellis, 1972).

considers psychological disturbance to reflect an attitude to taking life 'too' seriously and thus advocates the appropriate use of various humorous therapeutic methods (Ellis, 1977 a, 1977 b, 1981 c).

stresses the use of anti-musturbatory rather than antiempirical disputing methods. Since it considers that inferential distortions often stem from dogmatic musts, shoulds, etc., rational-emotive counselling favours going to the philosophic core of emotional disturbance and disputing the irrational beliefs at this core rather than merely disputing antiempirical inferences, which are more peripheral. Also, rational-emotive counselling favours the use of forceful logicoempirical disputing of irrational beliefs whenever possible rather than the employment of rationally-orientated, coping self-statements. When feasible, rational-emotive counselling teaches clients how to become their own scientists instead of parroting counsellor-inculcated rational beliefs.

employs, but only mildly encourages, the use of palliative cognitive methods that serve to distract people from their disturbed philosophies, e.g. relaxation methods. Rational-emotive counselling holds that such techniques may help clients in the short-term, but do not encourage them to identify, challenge and change in the long-term the devout philosophies that underpin their psychological problems. Indeed, these palliative methods may make it harder for people to engage in philosophic disputing since they may be less likely to do this when they are calm and relaxed than when they are motivated by their emotional distress. For these reasons, rational-emotive counselling also employs problem-solving and skill training methods, along with, but not instead of, teaching people to work at understanding and changing their irrational beliefs.

gives a more central explanatory role to the concept of discomfort anxiety in psychological disturbance than do other cognitive-behavioural approaches to counselling. Discomfort anxiety is defined as 'emotional hypertension that arises when people feel that their life or comfort is threatened; that they *must* not feel uncomfortable and *have to* feel at ease; and that it is awful or catastrophic (rather than merely inconvenient or disadvantageous) when they don't get what they supposedly must' (Ellis, 1980 c, p. 331). While other cognitive-behavioural approaches to counselling recognize specific instances of discomfort anxieties, e.g., 'fear of fear', (Mackay, 1984) they tend not to regard discomfort disturbance to be as centrally implicated in psychological problems as does rational-emotive counselling.

emphasizes, more than other approaches to cognitive-behavioural counselling, that humans frequently make themselves disturbed about their original disturbances. Thus, rational-emotive counsellors actively look for secondary symptoms of disturbances and encourage clients to work on overcoming these before addressing themselves to the primary disturbance.

has clearcut theories of disturbance and its treatment, but is eclectic or multimodal in its techniques. However, it favours some techniques, e.g., active disputing over others, such as cognitive distraction, and strives for profound or elegant philosophic change where feasible.

discriminates between 'rational' and 'irrational' negative emotions. Rational-emotive theory considers such negative emotions as sadness, annoyance, concern, regret, and disappointment as 'rational' affective responses to thwarted desires based on a non-devout philosophy of desire. Further it views them as healthy when they do not needlessly interfere with people's goals and purposes. However, it sees depression, anger, anxiety, guilt, shame/embarrassment, self-pity, and feelings of inadequacy usually as 'irrational' emotions based on absolutist demands about thwarted desires. Rational-emotive counselling considers these latter feelings as symptoms of disturbance because they very frequently, but not always, sabotage people from pursuing constructively their goals and purposes. Other approaches to cognitive-behavioural counselling do not make such fine discriminations between 'rational' and 'irrational' negative emotions.

advocates counsellors giving unconditional acceptance rather than giving warmth or approval to clients. Other cognitive-behavioural approaches to counselling tend not to make this distinction. Rational-emotive counselling holds that counsellor warmth and approval have their distinct dangers in that they may unwittingly encourage clients to strengthen their dire needs for love and approval. When RET counsellors unconditionally accept their clients they also serve as good role models, in that they also help clients to unconditionally accept themselves.

stresses the importance of the use of vigour and force in counteracting irrational philosophies and behaviours (Dryden, 1984 c; Ellis, 1979 d). Rational-emotive counselling is alone among cognitive-behavioural approaches to counselling in stressing that humans are, for the most part, biologically predisposed to originate and perpetuate their disturbances and often experience great difficulty in changing the ideological roots of these problems. Since it holds this view it urges both counsellors and clients to use considerable force and vigour in interrupting clients' irrationalities.

is more selective than most other cognitive-behavioural approaches to counselling in choosing behavioural change methods. Thus, it favours the use of penalization in encouraging resistant clients to change. Often these clients won't change to obtain positive reinforcements, but may be encouraged to change to avoid stiff penalties. Furthermore, rational-emotive practitioners have reservations concerning the use of social reinforcement in counselling. They consider that humans are too reinforceable and that they often do the right thing for the wrong reason. Thus, they may change to please their socially reinforcing counsellors, but in doing so they have not been encouraged to think and act for their own sake. RET counsellors aim to help clients become maximally non-conformist, non-dependent and individualistic and would thus use social reinforcement techniques sparingly. Finally, rational-emotive counselling favours the use of *in vivo* desensitization techniques since it argues that the former procedures best help clients to raise their level of frustration tolerance (Ellis, 1983 c).

While RET counsellors prefer to use these distinctive features of rational-emotive counselling wherever feasible they do not dogmatically insist that they be employed. When, on pragmatic grounds, they employ other cognitive-behavioural methods their therapeutic practice is frequently indistinguishable from that of other cognitive-behavioural counsellors.

Sources of other cognitive-behavioural methods

I have mentioned that rational-emotive counsellors use other cognitive-behavioural methods when rational-emotive methods are insufficient to help the client. Since this book focuses on the distinctive features of rational-emotive counselling, I have not discussed these other methods here. However, I recommend the following as resource material on these methods: disputing distorted inferences (Beck *et al.*, 1979; Beck and Emery, 1985); decision therapy (Greenwald, 1973; Wessler and Hankin-Wessler, 1986); self-instructional training (Meichenbaum, 1977, 1985); problem-solving therapy (D'Zurilla and Goldfried, 1971; Spivack, Platt and Shure, 1976); imagery methods (Lazarus, 1984); skills training (Trower *et al.*, 1978; Lange and Jakubowski, 1976). finally, a good general text on cognitive-behavioural counselling has been written by Cormier and Cormier (1985).

Techniques that are avoided in rational-emotive counselling

By now it will be clear that rational-emotive counselling is a multimodal form of counselling and advocates the employment of techniques in the cognitive, emotive and behavioural modalities. However, because the choice of therapeutic techniques is inspired by rational-emotive theory, the following available therapeutic techniques are avoided, or used sparingly in the practice of rational-emotive counselling (Ellis, 1979 c, 1983 c, 1984 b):

Techniques that help people become more dependent, e.g., undue counsellor warmth as a strong reinforcement and the creation and analysis of a transference neurosis.

Techniques that encourage people to become more gullible and suggestible, e.g., pollyannaish positive thinking.

Techniques that are long-winded and inefficient, e.g., psychoanalytic methods in general and free association in particular; encouraging clients to give lengthy descriptions of activating experiences at A.

Methods that help people feel better in the short-term rather than get better in the long-term (Ellis, 1972) e.g., some experiential techniques like fully expressing one's feelings in a dramatic, cathartic, and abreactive manner, i.e., some gestalt methods and primal techniques. The danger here is that such methods may encourage people to practise irrational philosophies underlying such emotions as anger.

Techniques that distract clients from working on their irrational philosophies, e.g., relaxation methods, Yoga, and other cognitive distraction methods. These methods may be employed, however, *along with* cognitive disputing designed to yield some philosophic change.

Methods that may unwittingly reinforce clients' philosophy of low frustration tolerance, e.g., gradual desensitization.

Techniques that include an anti-scientific philosophy, e.g., faith healing and mysticism.

Techniques that attempt to change activating events (A) before or without showing clients how to change their irrational beliefs (B) e.g., some strategic family systems techniques.

Techniques that have dubious validity, e.g., neurolinguistic programming.

Finally, to reiterate, RET counsellors do not avoid using the above methods in any absolute sense. They may on certain restricted occasions with certain clients utilize such techniques, particularly for pragmatic purposes. For example, if faith healing is the only method that will prevent some clients from harming themselves, then RET counsellors might either employ it themselves or, more probably, refer such clients to a faith healer (Ellis, 1985 a).

References

ADLER, A. (1927) *Understanding human nature*. New York: Garden City.

ADLER, A. (1964) *Social interest: A challenge to mankind*. New York: Capricorn.

ANCHIN, J. C., and KIESLER, D. J. (1982) *Handbook of interpersonal psychotherapy*. New York: Pergamon.

BANDURA, A. (1969) *Principles of behavior modification*. New York: Holt, Rinehart & Winston.

BANDURA, A. (1977) *Social learning theory*. Englewood Cliffs, NJ: Prentice-Hall.

BANDURA, A. (1986) *Social foundations of thought and action: A social cognitive theory*. Englewood Cliffs, NJ: Prentice-Hall.

BARD, J. A. (1973) Rational proselytizing. *Rational Living*, **12**(1), 2–6.

BECK, A. T. (1976) *Cognitive therapy and the emotional disorders*. New York: International Universities Press.

BECK, A. T., and EMERY, G. (1985) *Anxiety disorders and phobias: A cognitive perspective*. New York: Basic Books.

BECK, A. T., RUSH, A. J., SHAW, B. F., and EMERY, G. (1979) *Cognitive therapy of depression*. New York: Guilford.

BEUTLER, L. E. (1983) *Eclectic psychotherapy: A systematic approach*. New York: Pergamon.

BORDIN, E. S. (1979) The generalizability of the psychoanalytic concept of the working alliance. *Psychotherapy: Theory, Research and Practice*, **16**, 252–260.

BURNS, D. D. (1980) *Feeling good: The new mood therapy*. New York: Morrow.

CHESNEY, M. A., and ROSENMAN, R. H. (Eds.) (1985) *Anger and hostility in cardiovascular and behavioral disorders*. Washington: Hemisphere.

CLARK, D. M., SALKOVSKIS, P. M., and CHALKLEY, A. J. (1985) Respiratory control as a treatment for panic attacks. *Journal of Behavior Therapy and Experimental Psychiatry*, **16**, 23–30.

CORMIER, W. H., and CORMIER, L. S. (1985) *Interviewing strategies for helpers: Fundamental skills and cognitive-behavioral interventions*. (2nd ed). Monterey, CA: Brooks/Cole.

DIES, R. R. (1973) Group therapist self-disclosure: An evaluation by clients. *Journal of Counseling Psychology*, **20**, 344–348.

DIGIUSEPPE, R. (1984) Thinking what to feel. *British Journal of Cognitive Psychotherapy*, **2**(1), 27–33.

DRYDEN, W. (1982) *A guide for solving your emotional and behavioural problems by re-examining your self-defeating thoughts and attitudes*. London: Institute for RET (UK).

DRYDEN, W. (1983) Audiotape supervision by mail: A rational-emotive approach. *British Journal of Cognitive Psychotherapy*, **1**(1), 57–64.

DRYDEN, W. (1984 a) Rational-emotive therapy. In W. Dryden (Ed.), *Individual therapy in Britain*. London: Harper & Row.

DRYDEN, W. (1984 b) Therapeutic arenas. In W. Dryden (Ed.), *Individual therapy in Britain*. London: Harper & Row.

DRYDEN, W. (1984 c) *Rational-emotive therapy: Fundamentals and innovations*. Beckenham, Kent: Croom-Helm.

DRYDEN, W. (1985 a) Marital therapy: The rational-emotive approach. In W. Dryden (Ed.), *Marital therapy in Britain. Volume 1: Context and therapeutic approaches*. London: Harper & Row.

DRYDEN, W. (1985 b) Challenging but not overwhelming: A compromise in negotiating homework assignments. *British Journal of Cognitive Psychotherapy*, **3**(1), 77–80.

DRYDEN, W. (1986) Language and meaning in rational-emotive therapy. In W. Dryden and P. Trower (Eds.), *Rational-emotive therapy: Recent developments in theory and practice*. Bristol: Institute for RET (UK).

DRYDEN, W., and GOLDEN, W. L. (Eds.) (1986) *Cognitive-behavioural approaches to psychotherapy*. London: Harper & Row.

DUCK, S. (1986) *Human relationships: An introduction to social psychology*. London: Sage.

DUCKRO, P., BEAL, D., and GEORGE, C. (1979) Research on the effects of disconfirmed client role expectations in psychotherapy: A critical review. *Psychological Bulletin*, **86**, 260–275.

DUNLAP, K. (1932) *Habits: Their making and unmaking*. New York: Liveright.

D'ZURILLA, T. J., and GOLDFRIED, M. R. (1971) Problem-solving and behavior modification. *Journal of Abnormal Psychology*, **78**, 107–126.

EDELSTEIN, M. R. (1976) The ABC's of rational-emotive therapy: Pitfalls of going from D to E. *Rational Living*, **11**(1), 12–13.

ELLIS, A. (1958) Rational psychotherapy. *Journal of General Psychology*, **59**, 35–49.

ELLIS, A. (1962) *Reason and emotion in psychotherapy*. Secaucus, NJ: Lyle Stuart.

ELLIS, A. (1968) *Personality data form*. New York: Institute for RET.

ELLIS, A. (1972) Helping people get better: Rather than merely feel better. *Rational Living*, **7**(2), 2–9.

ELLIS, A. (1973) *Humanistic psychotherapy: The rational-emotive approach*. New York: McGraw-Hill.

ELLIS, A. (1975) *How to live with a neurotic: At home and at work*. (Rev. ed.) New York: Crown.

ELLIS, A. (1976) The biological basis of human irrationality. *Journal of Individual Psychology*, **32**, 145–168.

ELLIS, A. (1977 a) Fun as psychotherapy. *Rational Living*, **12**(1), 2–6.

ELLIS, A. (Speaker, cassette recording). (1977 b) *A garland of rational humorous songs*. New York: Institute for RET.

ELLIS, A. (1977 c) Intimacy in psychotherapy. *Rational Living*, **12**(2), 13–19.

ELLIS, A. (1978) Personality characteristics of rational-emotive therapists and other kinds of therapists. *Psychotherapy: Theory, Research and Practice*, **15**, 329–332.

ELLIS, A. (1979 a) The theory of rational-emotive therapy. In A. Ellis and J. M. Whiteley (Eds.), *Theoretical and empirical foundations of rational-emotive therapy*. Monterey, CA: Brooks/Cole.

ELLIS, A. (1979 b) Discomfort anxiety: A new cognitive behavioral construct. Part 1. *Rational Living*, **14**(2), 3–8.

ELLIS, A. (1979 c) The practice of rational-emotive therapy. In A. Ellis and J. M. Whiteley (Eds.), *Theoretical and empirical foundations of rational-emotive therapy*. Monterey, CA: Brooks/Cole.

ELLIS, A. (1979 d) The issue of force and energy in behavioral change. *Journal of Contemporary Psychotherapy*, **10**(2), 83–97.

ELLIS, A. (1980 a) Discomfort anxiety: A new cognitive behavioral construct. Part 2. *Rational Living*, **15**(1), 25–30.

ELLIS, A. (1980 b) The value of efficiency in psychotherapy. *Psychotherapy: Theory, Research and Practice*, **17**, 414–418.

ELLIS, A. (1980 c) Rational-emotive therapy and cognitive behavior therapy: Similarities and differences. *Cognitive Therapy and Research*, **4**, 325–340.

ELLIS, A. (1981 a) The place of Immanuel Kant in cognitive psychotherapy. *Rational Living*, **16**(2), 13–16.

ELLIS, A. (1981 b, Sept.) *New developments in rational-emotive therapy*. Address given at the First European Conference on the Cognitive-Behavioral Therapies, Lisbon, Portugal.

ELLIS, A. (1981 c) The use of rational humorous songs in psychotherapy. *Voices*, **16**(4), 29–36.

ELLIS, A. (1982 a) The treatment of alcohol and drug abuse: The rational-emotive approach. *Rational Living*, **17**(2), 13–16.

ELLIS, A. (1982 b) Intimacy in rational-emotive therapy. In M. Fisher and G. Striker (Eds.), *Intimacy*. New York: Plenum.

ELLIS, A. (1983 a) *The case against religiosity*. New York: Institute for RET.

ELLIS, A. (1983 b) How to deal with your most difficult client: You. *Journal of Rational-Emotive Therapy*, **1** (1), 3–8.

ELLIS, A. (1983 c) The philosophic implications and dangers of some popular behavior therapy techniques. In M. Rosenbaum, C. M. Franks and Y. Jaffe (Eds.), *Perspectives in behavior therapy in the eighties*. New York: Springer.

ELLIS, A. (1983 d) Failures in rational-emotive therapy. In E. B. Foa and P. M. G. Emmelkamp (Eds.), *Failures in behavior therapy*. New York: Wiley.

ELLIS, A. (1983 e) Rational-emotive therapy (RET) approaches to overcoming resistance. 1: Common forms of resistance. *British Journal of Cognitive Psychotherapy*, **1**(1), 28–38.

ELLIS, A. (1984 a) The essence of RET – 1984. *Journal of Rational-Emotive Therapy*, **2**(1), 19–25.

ELLIS, A. (1984 b) Rational-emotive therapy. In R. J. Corsini (Ed.), *Current psychotherapies*. (2nd ed.). Itasca, IL: Peacock.

ELLIS, A. (1984 c) *How to maintain and enhance your rational-emotive therapy gains*. New York: Institute for RET.

ELLIS, A. (1985 a) *Overcoming resistance: Rational-emotive therapy with difficult clients*. New York: Springer.

ELLIS, A. (1985 b) Expanding the ABCs of rational-emotive therapy. In M. J. Mahoney and A. Freeman (Eds.), *Cognition and psychotherapy*. New York: Plenum.

ELLIS, A. (1985 c) Jealousy: Its etiology and treatment. In D. C. Goldberg (Ed.), *Contemporary marriage: Special issues in couples therapy*. Homewood, IL: Dorsey.

ELLIS, A. (1985 d) Dilemmas in giving warmth or love to clients: An interview with

Windy Dryden. In W. Dryden, *Therapists' dilemmas*. London: Harper & Row.

ELLIS, A., and BECKER, I. (1982) *A guide to personal happiness*. No. Hollywood, CA: Wilshire.

ELLIS, A., and BERNARD, M. E. (1985) *Clinical applications of rational-emotive therapy*. New York: Plenum.

ELLIS, A., and DRYDEN, W. (1987) *The practice of rational-emotive therapy*. New York: Springer.

ELLIS, A., and HARPER, R. A. (1975) *A new guide to rational living*. No. Hollywood, CA: Wilshire.

ESCHENROEDER, C. (1979) Different therapeutic styles in rational-emotive therapy. *Rational Living*, **14**(1), 3–7.

FESTINGER, L. (1957) *A theory of cognitive dissonance*. Evanston, IL: Row, Peterson.

FRANSELLA, F. (1985) Resistance. *British Journal of Cognitive Psychotherapy*, **3**(1), 1–11.

FREUD, A. (1937) *The ego and the mechanisms of defense*. London: Hogarth.

FREEMAN, A. (1981) Dreams and imagery in cognitive therapy. In G. Emery, S. D. Hollon and R. C. Bedrosian (Eds.), *New directions in cognitive therapy*. New York: Guilford.

GARCIA, E. J. (1977) Working on the E in RET. In J. L. Wolfe and E. Brand (Eds.), *Twenty years of rational therapy*. New York: Institute for RET.

GOLDEN, W. L. (1983) Resistance in cognitive-behaviour therapy. *British Journal of Cognitive Psychotherapy*, **1**(2), 33–42.

GOLDFRIED, M., and DAVISON, G. (1976) *Clinical behavior therapy*. New York: Holt, Rinehart & Wilson.

GREENWALD, H. (1973) *Direct decision therapy*. San Diego: Edits.

GREGORY, R. L. (1966) *Eye and Brain*. London: Weidenfeld & Nicholson.

GRIEGER, R. M. (1985) The process of rational-emotive therapy. *Journal of Rational-Emotive Therapy*, **3**(2), 138–148.

GRIEGER, R. M., and BOYD, J. (1980) *Rational-emotive therapy: A skills-based approach*. New York: Van Nostrand Reinhold.

GUINAGH, B. (1976) Disputing clients' logical fallacies. *Rational Living*, **11**(2), 15–18.

GURMAN, A. S., and KNISKERN, D. P. (1978) Research in marital and family therapy. In S. L. Garfield and A. E. Bergin (Eds.), *Handbook of psychotherapy and behavior change*. (2nd ed.). New York: Wiley.

HAUCK, P. A. (1966) The neurotic agreement in psychotherapy. *Rational Living*, **1**(1), 31–34.

HAUCK, P. A. (1971) A RET theory of depression. *Rational Living*, **6**(2), 32–35.

HAUCK, P. A. (1972) *Reason in pastoral counseling*. Philadelphia: Westminster.

HEIDEGGER, M. (1949) *Existence and being*. Chicago: Henry Regnery.

HORNEY, K. (1950) *Neurosis and human growth*. New York: Norton.

JANIS, I. L. (1983) *Short-term counseling*. New Haven, CT: Yale University Press.

JONES, M. C (1924) A laboratory study of fear: The case of Peter. *Journal of Genetic Psychology*, **31**, 308–315.

JONES, R. A. (1977) *Self-fulfilling prophecies: Social, psychological, and physiological effects of expectancies*. Hillside, NJ: LEA.

KASSINOVE, H., and DIGIUSEPPE, R. (1975) Rational role reversal. *Rational Living*, **10**(1), 44–45.

KELLY, G. A. (1955) *The psychology of personal constructs*. New York: Norton.

KEMPEL, L. T. (1973) Identifying and confronting ways of prematurely terminating therapy. *Rational Living*, **8**(1), 6–9.

KNAUS, W., and WESSLER, R. L. (1976) Rational-emotive problem simulation. *Rational Living*, 11(2), 8–11.

KORZYBSKI, A. (1933) *Science and society*. San Francisco: ISGS.

KRANZLER, G. D. (1974) *You can change how you feel: A rational-emotive approach*. Eugene, OR: RETC Press.

LANGE, A. J., and JAKUBOWSKI, P. (1976) *Responsible assertive behavior: Cognitive-behavioral procedures for trainers*. Champaign, IL: Research Press.

LAZARUS, A. A. (1981) *The practice of multimodal therapy*. New York: McGraw-Hill.

LAZARUS, A. A. (1984) *In the mind's eye*. New York: Guilford.

LAZARUS, A. A. (in press). Eyes left! The cognitive modality reigns supreme. *Contemporary Psychology*.

MACASKILL, N. D., and MACASKILL, A. (1983) Preparing patients for psychotherapy. *British Journal of Clinical and social Psychiatry*, 2, 80–84.

MACKAY, D. (1984) Behavioural psychotherapy. In W. Dryden (Ed.), *Individual therapy in Britain*. London: Harper & Row.

MAHONEY, M. (1977) Personal science: A cognitive learning theory. In A. Ellis and R. Grieger (Eds.), *Handbook of rational-emotive therapy*. New York: Springer.

MAULTSBY, M. C., Jr. (1975) *Help yourself to happiness: Through rational self-counseling*. New York: Institute for RET.

MAULTSBY, M. C., Jr. (1984) *Rational behavior therapy*. Englewood Cliffs, NJ: Prentice-Hall.

MEICHENBAUM, D. (1977) *Cognitive-behavior modification*. New York: Plenum.

MEICHENBAUM, D. (1985) *Stress inoculation training*. New York: Pergamon.

MOORE, R. H. (1983) Inference as "A" in RET. *British Journal of Cognitive Psychotherapy*, 1(2), 17–23.

NEUMAN, F. (Leader). (1982) *An eight-week treatment group for phobics*. (Series of eight cassette recordings). White Plains, NY: F. Neuman.

NORCROSS, J. C., and PROCHASKA, J. O. (1982) A national survey of clinical psychologists: Characteristics and activities. *The Clinical Psychologist*, 35, 1–8.

PHADKE, K. M. (1982) Some innovations in RET theory and practice. *Rational Living*, 17(2), 25–30.

POPPER, K. R. (1959) *The logic of scientific discovery*. New York: Harper & Bros.

POPPER, K. R. (1963) *Conjectures and refutations*. New York: Harper & Bros.

POWELL, J. (1976) *Fully human, fully alive*. Niles, IL: Argus.

PROCHASKA, J. O., and NORCROSS, J. C. (1983) Contemporary psychotherapists: A national survey of characteristics, practices, orientations, and attitudes. *Psychotherapy: Theory, Research and Practice*, 20, 161–173.

PLATT, J. J., PROUT, M. F., and METZGER, D. (1986) Interpersonal cognitive problem-solving (ICPS). In W. Dryden and W. L. Golden (Eds.), *Cognitive-behavioural approaches to psychotherapy*. London: Harper & Row.

RAVID, R. (1969) Effect of group therapy on long-term individual therapy. *Dissertation Abstracts International*, 30, 2427B.

REICHENBACH, H. (1953) *The rise of scientific philosophy*. Berkeley, CA: University of California Press.

ROGERS, C. R. (1957) The necessary and sufficient conditions of therapeutic personality change. *Journal of Consulting Psychology*, 21, 95–103.

RUSSELL, B. (1930) *The conquest of happiness*. New York: New American Library.

RUSSELL, B. (1965) *The basic writings of Bertrand Russell*. New York: Simon & Schuster.

RUSSIANOFF, P. (1981) *Why do I think I am nothing without a man*. New York: Bantam.

SACCO, W. P. (1981) Cognitive therapy *in vivo*. In G. Emery, S. D. Hollon and R. C. Bedrosian (Eds.), *New directions in cognitive therapy*. New York: Guilford.

SHAHAN, L. (1981) *Living alone and liking it*. New York: Warner.

SICHEL, J., and ELLIS, A. (1984) *RET self-help form*. New York: Institute for RET.

SNYDER, C. R., and SMITH, T. W. (1982) Symptoms as self-handicapping strategies: The virtues of old wine in a new bottle. In G. Weary and H. L. Mirels (Eds.), *Integration of clinical and social psychology*. New York: Oxford University Press.

SPIVACK, G., PLATT, J. J., and SHURE, M. B. (1976) *The problem-solving approach to adjustment*. San Francisco: Jossey-Bass.

TEASDALE, J. D. (1985) Psychological treatments for depression: How do they work? *Behaviour Research and Therapy*, **23**, 157–165.

TILLICH, P. (1977) *The courage to be*. New York: Fountain.

TROWER, P., BRYANT, B., and ARGYLE, M. (1978) *Social skills and mental health*. London: Methuen.

TRUAX, C. B., and CARKHUFF, R. R. (1967) *Toward effective counseling and psychotherapy: Training and practice*. Chicago: Aldine.

WACHTEL, P. L. (1977) *Psychoanalysis and behavior therapy: Toward an integration*. New York: Basic Books.

WATSON, J. B., and RAYNER, R. (1920) Conditioned emotional reactions. *Journal of Experimental Psychology*, **3**, 1–14.

WERNER, E. E., and SMITH, R. S. (1982) *Vulnerable but invincible: A study of resilient children*. New York: McGraw-Hill.

16(1), 29–31.

WESSLER, R. A., and WESSLER, R. L. (1980) *The principles and practice of rational-emotive therapy*. San Francisco: Jossey-Bass.

WESSLER, R. L. (1984) Alternative conceptions of rational-emotive therapy: Toward a philosophically neutral psychotherapy. In M. A. Reda and M. J. Mahoney (Eds.), *Cognitive psychotherapies: Recent developments in theory, research and practice*. Cambridge, MA: Ballinger.

WESSLER, R. L., and ELLIS, A. (1980) Supervision in rational-emotive therapy. In A. K. Hess (Ed.), *Psychotherapy supervision*. New York: Wiley.

WESSLER, R. L., and ELLIS, A. (1983) Supervision in counseling: Rational-emotive therapy. *The Counseling Psychologist*, **11**, 43–49.

WESSLER, R. L., and HANKIN-WESSLER, S. W. R. (1986) Cognitive appraisal therapy (CAT). In W. Dryden and W. L. Golden (Eds.), *Cognitive-behavioural approaches to psychotherapy*. London: Harper & Row.

WEXLER, D. A., and BUTLER, J. M. (1976). Therapist modification of client expressiveness in client-centred therapy. *Journal of Consulting and Clinical Psychology*, **44**, 261–265.

YOUNG, H. S. (1974) *A rational counseling primer*. New York: Institute for RET.

YOUNG, H. S. (1977) Counseling strategies with working class adolescents. In J. L. Wolfe and E. Brand (Eds.), *Twenty years of rational therapy*. New York: Institute for RET.

YOUNG, H. S. (1984 a) Practising RET with lower-class clients. *British Journal of Cognitive Psychotherapy*, **2**(2), 33–59.

YOUNG, H. S. (1984 b) Teaching rational self-value concepts to tough customers. *British Journal of Cognitive Psychotherapy*, **2**(2), 77–97.

A comprehensive list of books and tapes on the application of rational-emotive ideas and further information on training courses in rational-emotive counselling can be obtained from either IRET (UK), 13 Wellington Crescent, Horfield, Bristol, BS7 8SZ, England or Institute for RET, 45 East 65th St, New York, NY 10021, USA.

Index